FEDERAL

FEDERAL

A Financial Thriller

by
Hotse Langeraar

"Behind the ostensible government sits enthroned an invisible government owing no allegiance and acknowledging no responsibility to the people."
—*Theodore Roosevelt.*

FEDERAL is a work of fiction. Certain incidents in FEDERAL are based on actual events, both past and present. Aside from well-known public figures referred to by name, all characters are a product of the author's imagination and are not construed as real. Any similarity to actual persons living or dead is entirely coincidental. Neither publisher nor author can be held liable for any third-party material referenced in FEDERAL.

The author, Hotse Langeraar, is a registered Representative with vFinance Investments, Inc, (VFIN), a member of FINRA and SIPC. The source of all material, including financially related topics and events discussed and/or depicted in FEDERAL, a fictional book written by Mr. Langeraar, should not be considered a solicitation to invest nor a reflection of any opinion given by VFIN, its directors, officers or employees.

10 9 8 7 6 5 4 3 2 1

Printed in the United States of America.
No part of this book may be reproduced, stored, or copied in any way without express written permission of the publisher.
Published by Templar CMI.
Lauderdale by the Sea, FL 33308
www.hotse.com
ISBN-13: 978-0615645513
ISBN-10: 0615645518
LCCN: 2012940786

FEDERAL could not have been completed without the undying support of my love and wife Caren, who spent innumerable hours reading and editing, trying to make sense of my often impossible syntaxes and objectively pointing out fissures in logic. Others who were instrumental in helping me were Chantal d'A. who initially showed me the way; my brother Wijnand and sister Elsbeth with ideas and criticism; Scott H. (aka Curly), Sean P. and Doug D. who took time and effort to read and suggest changes and additions; and Alan Rinzler as developmental editor guiding me in style and flow.

Fort Lauderdale, FL – September 2012

For Caren with a C

CHAPTER 1

Wednesday, February 17, 2010
Westlake Mall, Seattle, Washington

Perspiration and a lack of deodorant. Body odor reeks from the man behind me. It's too cold to be sweating, this guy is nervous. A nervous man with a gun. Not a good combination.

I've made a mistake. When walking to the side of the building with my Stetson wearing target leading the way, I had allowed him to turn to me where he could observe what was behind me, while all I could see was the wall behind him. So I never saw his partner make his way through the stalls and crowds until he was right behind me. I now have two firearms pointed at me and the advantage I thought was mine is gone.

Addressing the man at my back, the Stetson says, "I have him. Keep your eyes open. I'm sure he's not alone."

After the words are spoken I hear Anthony's voice, unseen but sounding as if he's right next to us.

"Dad, step away to your left," followed by, "And you, you're in my sights. Let him go."

"You're interfering with an Interpol-sanctioned extraction," the man in front of me replies immediately. "Continue and you will do so at your own risk. I was promised the thumb drive. Where is it?"

"And I was promised you'd be alone, so no drive," I hiss back and move left as instructed by my son.

Anthony appears from between racks of overcoats. Pointing his gun from the hip at my opponent, he approaches him from the rear, intending to defuse the situation and allow me time to get away.

What happens next is over in seconds, as without warning an arm forcibly comes around my neck, pulling me back in a chokehold and three muted puffs come from my attacker. I see Anthony stagger back and drop to his knees. His coat shows where he is hit, three clean holes evenly spaced from his sternum down to the middle of his abdomen in a perfect line, and in an emotional dissociative moment my mind flashes, 'Just like buttonholes...'

Then my training takes over and in one fluid motion I grab the hand on my throat, anchor it on my body and turn 180 degrees. Rotating with me, the pinned-down wrist locks and I feel it break. My opponent's face in view, I see his eyes widen in pain and surprise at my unexpected move. His smell is overpowering.

My other hand, in my pouch, has a firm grip on the .45 and with my thumb I pull back the hammer. Fully facing him, I fire four shots in rapid succession from my pocket into his body. Any sound from my gun is muffled by the suppressor and the cloth of my jacket. My target never made a noise as the rounds entered him.

Another shot rings out. This one clearly not suppressed, and so loud it shatters my eardrums. The explosion reverberates and resonates off the walls and ceiling and back into me. Shoppers look in our direction, wide-eyed with terror and alarm, screaming, ducking and running in all directions.

I let go of my attacker as he drops lifeless to the ground.

I check if I'm hurt but feel nothing and realize it's not me. Stetson stands frozen, but the hat is gone, eyes bulging and fixed into the distance, mouth open but no sound and his automatic drops to the ground. He falls forward, face first bouncing on the cement and I see the back of his head is missing. Bone and brain tissue are splattered as a red spray everywhere, the open gaping hole not bleeding, crushed strawberry-like filling speckled with white slowly dribbling out.

Then I see Anthony on the floor, the .45 with which he shot and saved my life, slowly slipping from his hand. The three buttonholes converging into one large, dark spot and growing.

"Dad? Dad... Dad..." I hear his voice when he was four and hurt his hand. I hear him calling me from camp when he was twelve and missing me, I hear him departing home for the Navy. And I hear my son saying good bye, leaving me.

CHAPTER 2

My name is Stephen Vinson and the series of events that ultimately led to the Westlake Mall incident where I watched my son get shot three times in the chest, began on Thursday, November 1, 2007.

A normal day as any other, without any noteworthy events. Even so, one decision I made that day was the cause of an unforeseeable chain of events, which cascaded to the tragic scene at the mall over two years later.

Late that Thursday afternoon I received a phone call from a colleague employed by the Wall Street trading house, Goldman Sachs. She explained about an imbalance in the allocation of a new stock issue she was underwriting, and she asked if I was interested in the IPO for Friday, November 30 settlement. I was familiar with the offering and liked this new company, so I agreed, and entered the order for my personal account in the interoffice order-entry system for twenty-five hundred shares at ten dollars each. Settlement would automatically be picked up by my assistants who would take care of the rest.

Unbeknownst to me, it was this decision that altered the course of my life. The change was ultimately so drastic that I would have thought it an impossibility. On November 30, 2007, during the settlement of the shares, an innocent error occurred. The mistake consisted of a minor mix-up and the consequent substitution of two stock certificates to be delivered to two different clients. Not uncommon and easy to correct. This time, however, with dire consequences.

That first day of November 2007, I left for the office as usual, long before daylight. Leaving the house, I always paused to listen to the wind in the trees, and absorb the sensation of the early, early mornings. It seemed the street possessed a surreal quality, everything dark, no cars, no traffic, no birds. Just the wind in the trees. It is that peace and silence of the early mornings how I choose to remember South Florida. All the other things that make tourists show up—the pretty women in their impossibly tiny bikinis, fast cars, mansions on the water with big yachts, the beautiful weather and deep blue ocean—all that stuff in the end is pushed aside, and what's left is the dark empty street with the wind through the palms.

At a quarter after three in the morning I would find the trading floor quiet, empty and brightly lit. Perhaps a few support staff would be around making sure computers were up and running, or preparing settlement instructions for a busy day. Entering the silent, open floor always gave me a similar dreamlike sensation as when I stepped out into the dark, quiet, early morning streets leaving my home. Rows of desks frozen in animated suspension by traders and sales-people, ready to pick up where they left off the day before. The emptiness of the moment did not fit the intrusive cacophony which would populate the space just hours later.

Trading floors are noisy and intrusively loud. A busy one, be it on any of the exchanges, or in the heart of the trading houses, is a place of extreme activity and interaction. Every sound, every person, every tool, every gadget, all the desks, chairs, phones, TV's, computers, printers, fax machines, and monitors, everything has only one function, which is to facilitate the trade, to make the deal happen, whatever the deal may be. And do it before the market moves away.

Good-sized floors can have hundreds to many thousands of traders, sales and staff packed in one giant room, at times the size of whole city blocks. Rows of desks, with monitors everywhere, hanging from ceilings or stacked on top of each other next to multiple phones, and keyboards and calculators and a mess of wires connecting everything and everybody. Paper and gadgets and toys and pens and food and drinks and people all over. To anybody from the outside looking in, it's chaos, a seemingly uncontrollable, noisy, threatening mess. All floors are essentially the same, whatever product or commodity changes hands. Salesmen on the phone convincing customers, traders announcing specifics over a PA system (the Hoot) while on the phone with outside firms, remote offices constantly chattering on speakers over open phone lines, people arguing and trying to get the best price, leaping up and about to deal with runners and secretaries and support staff, assistants questioning to make sense of contracts just written, printers running, faxes sending and receiving, phones ringing continuously and managers wanting to know who authorized what. And as business heats up, the decibels on the floor go up in tandem. A busy floor has a low grumbling hum that rises to a loud menacing pitch when markets are on the move. The tone can be intrusive, obnoxious and invasive.

My business was in bonds, in fixed-income. I traded in the debt issued by governments and companies. TCMI, the investment bank I worked for in 2007, was a big player in the international fixed-income arena. Our clients were exclusively financial institutions so we didn't deal with or sell to private individuals. Even though we were not a primary dealer, that select group of dealers that trades directly with the Federal Reserve, we were big enough to do business with many of the largest companies across the world and some of those were my clients. One thing should be made absolutely clear, the Federal Reserve is God as far as trading in bonds is concerned. But more about them later.

I was not the top, but certainly one of the top producers within TCMI. I had a proven track record for over twenty years and was consistent in my production. I was trustworthy to my clients, and no complaints had ever been lodged against me. I never had a trade back up on me, and I had earned the respect of my managers and colleagues. They left me alone to tend to my business as I saw fit. I was also the only guy on the floor fluent in five languages, with a working knowledge of a few more, and therefore very proficient in international markets.

I had clients in Portugal, Switzerland, the Netherlands, the United Kingdom, Germany, France, Belgium and Denmark. I had clients in Kuwait, the United Arab Emirates and Bahrain. I had clients in Panama, Columbia, Venezuela, Ecuador, Chile, and many all over the United States, from New York to California, from banks with less than 200mm ("mm" stands for million dollars in financial jargon) in assets, to state pension funds with portfolios in the many tens of billions of dollars. I was busy and I was good at it.

Before moving to the United States, I lived in South America and prior to that in Europe. Having lived all over, I was very much at home with the European geography and knew my way around. For business it mattered that when I spoke to someone in France, I could understand the nuances of acceptance and social integration, knowing if he or she was born in Morocco, or attended the impressive Polytech Paris. Having attended a public school in England, I knew the difference between a British public school and a boarding school. I'd been exposed to German aristocracy, some of whom sported self-inflicted facial scars feigning involvement in the noble sport of fencing. I had learned how to judge a wine on its legs and knew how to uncork a Champagne bottle with the swift move of the back of a "Sabre a Champagne."

I was sensitive to the subtle distinctions of schooling and family pedigree, the culture a certain trading house wished to portray, and the refined and ever-so-snobbish attitude of some of the premier AAA-rated companies. Europe, much more so than the United States, still adhered to a silent cultural divide where education, lineage, and ancestry mattered. It was never discussed, but always understood.

While still living in Europe, before South America and subsequently the United States, I had had a brush with Interpol. It was the result of having been implicated in the distribution of controlled substances in my late teens and early twenties. One of several transactions where I transported goods from either Paris or Amsterdam to London was compromised by a contact's need to cooperate with local law enforcement and save himself an extended stay under government supervision. As we were unwinding our business dealings, the duplicitous interest of my partner became apparent, and I had to expedite an unforeseen and hurried retreat. As if in a movie, I remember entering a public bathroom as a longhaired hippie, only to re-emerge as a somewhat arrogant, but well-dressed entrepreneur. I did get away at the time, albeit suffering a substantial financial setback in the process.

Ultimately, Interpol caught up with me in Southern France, and it was only through the intervention of my father and the contacts he had that I was able to maintain a blemish-free record. My father was an extraordinarily intelligent scientist with a brilliant career in the Navy. His expertise and innovations in mathematics and oceanography, plus the many chairs he successfully held in public office, even at the United Nations, made him a regular in the highest circles of society, including personal friendships with HRH Prince Bernhard of the House of Orange-Nassau of the Netherlands and Prince Rainier of the House of Grimaldi of Monaco. My father's contacts would be insignificant in this context were it not that it would unexpectedly become of consequence some thirty-five years later.

In any case, no one I currently dealt with in Europe or the United States knew of my checkered past, and being fluent in most of the European languages opened doors otherwise closed. The ability to formally meet and greet a client or counterparty in his own language with perfect pronunciation and etiquette leaves its mark, even though most business was transacted in English.

Only once did a notion of my past surface in my professional life years later, and it was I who brought it up. In the late 1990's I was one of four who had opened a new branch office in Ft. Lauderdale, Florida for a large Midwest dealer. We were told to expect a call from a publicity agent who was going to interview each of us for a news release about the new office.

I forgot all about this until about a month later, when a young guy, with a somewhat insecure voice, called and introduced himself as the interviewer from the press agency that was going to publish the release.

"What do you want to know?" I said.

"A little history, education, previous positions, any personal favorite anecdotes would be great," he said.

"OK….,I uh….." I began, but held back, not sure what to tell this young man, not sure which parts to filter out. Then after a few seconds I decided to have some fun and let him in on some of the finer details of my past, see what he would do with it.

"I grew up in Holland and dropped out of high school when I was sixteen. Got involved with dope and the usual juvenile trouble associated with such behavior. My parents sent me to England at seventeen in an attempt to have me finish my high school. Within a year, I ended in a mess with the law and was expelled from school and chased by Interpol. They later caught up with me in Southern France, where my parents lived at the time. I was prosecuted in absentia and had to stay out of the United Kingdom for ten years."

Since I didn't hear any protests from the publicity agent about the sordid details of my past, I took it as a cue to continue my monologue in a similar fashion.

"Then, at the age of twenty I spent a bit over three years in a therapeutic community, called Phoenix House for the treatment of drug addiction. At twenty-four I went back at night to finish high school, which is all the formal education I have. Then I moved to South America for a job as a runner on a trading floor in Bogota, Columbia. After that I moved to Quito and Guayaquil, Ecuador, where my son was born in 1980. I worked as a trader in industrial chemicals, which ultimately brought me to Houston, Texas in 1981. From chemicals I moved to trading refined products like gasoline, heating oil and jet fuel, and from there I ended up trading futures in energy, precious metals and currencies. In 1990 I switched to institutional bond sales, which I have been doing ever since and, uh… well… that's how I ended up here."

Silence. Then in a somewhat timid voice the agent asked, "What eh…, what about your private life, wife, children, all that."

Feeling in control and not caring any longer how my story came across, I shot back flippantly, "This wasn't private enough?" I laughed at my own humor, but apparently the wit didn't carry and there was no answer, so I continued.

"I married an American woman in Amsterdam and we had a son, Anthony. As I said, he was born in Guayaquil, Ecuador, but she and I divorced in Houston. I go to AA, and I have been clean and sober for many, many years. I like tattoos and have a full body suit in the Japanese Yakuza style. For the rest, I collect medieval books and illuminated manuscripts, and I'm fluent in five or six languages. And that's about it."

There must have been at least twenty seconds of dead air on the line after I finished. "Hey, you there?" I inquired, not hearing anything.

"... eh, ... yes, yes. Thank you very much," was all the interviewer finally said and hung up lacking any social graces.

My coworker whom I had been working next to for many years and who had been eavesdropping on the interview, looked up and asked, "What was that all about?"

"That was the press agent interviewing me for the news release," I informed him.

"You are shitting me," my colleague exclaimed while bursting out laughing. "Was that really for the press release?"

"It was," I sheepishly replied, and he couldn't stop laughing, knowing I had told the poor guy on the phone the absolute truth.

The press release was never issued, nor did any of us receive another call from the agency requesting more interviews.

There is a simple saying in my business, and it's the same with any of the different products and/or commodities I've worked in, which is "When you're done, you're done." What this means in all simplicity is "Your word is your word." When you say "You are done" to a client or a trader, you are confirming that the deal is done with the terms as agreed, and it might as well be written in stone. Even though this may be obvious, the reason is that when trading in high-dollar amount transactions, the deal is done the instant the words "You are done" are spoken, a moment later and the values will have changed due to a live market. Many multi-million dollars' worth of business transactions are executed long before any contract is ever produced. So by uttering these three simple words, numerous trades are initiated (for example, aside from the original trade, both buyer and seller may enter or exit hedge positions), and it is done on the trust that "When you're done, you're done," and you will not renege on it. Those who do break their word are blackballed in the business and might as well change professions because nobody will want to do business with them again. Too much is riding on it and the risks are too great if you can't trust somebody's word.

In all my years of trading there was only one event where I had to rescind my words and renege on my trade. The event was on an infamous day in the history of this nation. It was a Tuesday morning, and I was working two phones, one connected to a huge Swiss institution in Basel and the other with a trader on our desk in Minneapolis, who in turn was on-line with Lehman Brothers in New York, the broker/dealer firm that ceased to exist in 2008. The trade consisted of 48mm of a five-year final bond issued by a US bank. I had been working this trade for the previous ten minutes or so. Finally it came down to the nitty-gritty and I had both buyer and seller at levels where I would make an acceptable spread. From my trader I received Lehman's price firm for thirty seconds, and I offered my level to the Swiss. As they accepted, both the Swiss and I exchanged the magic "You are done" words. In the next second, as I was about to phrase the same to my desk, and they in turn to Lehman, the line with Lehman went dead. The time was 9:02:54 a.m. on September 11, 2001, when the second plane hit the South Tower, home of the Lehman office we were speaking with.

My trader communicated that his line with Lehman had gone dead and that we were not done. I had to tell my client the same, as the horror of that day developed in slow motion in front of our eyes, for the world to see.

I never learned if the Lehman trader made it out alive. When we ultimately regrouped and were able to reconstruct the transaction a week later, I remember asking if the deal was done with the same Lehman trader. The only answer I received was that a Lehman office in New Jersey had taken over. My question was never answered, nor did I ask again.

Generally, the activity on a floor is split between sales and trading. Sales deal with institutional clients, while traders (known as the "desk") transact with the dealer community, or the "street." When sales buys or sells to a client, it is the desk's job to ensure competitive pricing in order to make the transaction successful. This allows for sales to stay focused on customers' needs as the desk lets us know about market changes.

There were occasions, though, where I had no need of the desk's services. A great deal of my efforts were geared to creating a clientele that had interests in similar bonds. It allowed me the opportunity to cross the trade, which is to buy bonds from one of my accounts and sell them directly to another client of mine. This maximized my return because the desk would not be able to intervene and apply a "haircut." Throughout the industry, desks are infamous for this practice of haircutting, where they insert a profit margin for themselves while executing a salesperson's order.

Ten years earlier, when I worked for the capital markets division of another large international bank, an incident occurred that illustrates floor dynamics.

A client in Amsterdam asked me to bid 35mm of a specific bond, meaning they wanted to sell the issue. I approached the trader on the desk requesting a firm bid, which is a competitive price at which the bond can be traded. As I was waiting for the desk's answer, I made a few calls to other clients of mine, knowing they could have an interest in the issue.

When the trader on my desk, whose overwhelming feature was obesity and otherwise known as Big Bird, gave me his level, I took note it equaled another bid I had just received from a big London account. All things being equal, preference went to the desk, as it should be, working for the same company. I subtracted the profit margin from the number and communicated the resulting price to my Amsterdam client.

After some haggling back and forth, Amsterdam accepted my bid as the best he received from three different brokers and confirmed the trade by telling me I was done. Reciprocating and having just bought the 35mm bonds, I turned around, approached the desk and gave Big Bird a heads-up that the trade was done at the firm level he had quoted me.

A clean trade for all involved, as I had done many, many times before. Industry standard for settle date on this security was T plus three, or three working days from Trade date. The trade date of the transaction was on a Thursday, which meant that T plus three would cover the weekend and the settlement would fall on the following Tuesday.

Because Big Bird's price quote was given without special conditions, it was based on regular settle, or T plus three. However, experience had taught me that unexpressed assumptions have a way of screwing up agreements, for no other reason than that no effort is made to verbalize the obvious. So, I made sure to confirm T plus three, substantiating that all of us were on the same page. I then walked back to my desk to stamp and write the tickets.

"T plus three means Tuesday settle," came Big Bird's voice from behind me.

"T plus three is Tuesday. That is correct, reg settle," I agreed with Big Bird, ignoring the audible complaint in his voice without bothering to alter the stride back to my desk.

"My bid was for T plus one. I can't do that price for T plus three." A declaration of war.

I stopped in my tracks and turned around, not saying anything but eyeballing him.

"Best price for T plus three is six ticks lower," he rubbed it in while returning my stare without blushing.

Bonds are traded in intervals of $1/32^{nd}$ of a percent, or one tick. Lowering the bid by six ticks, meant a decrease of over sixty-five thousand dollars in the value of his bid.

This placed me in a very awkward position. I had just agreed to buy the 35mm bonds from my client and I couldn't go back to him on price. That meant business hara-kiri, as he could not trust my word. Big Fat Bird, of course, was fully aware of this and took advantage of the situation by forcing a haircut out of me. Did I mention we worked for the same company?

"T plus three is regular settle, and you should have specified your bid was only good for T plus one. You are done for 35mm, T plus three." My answer was loud and clear, so that those in the vicinity looked forward to the ensuing argument and show of force.

"You are not hearing me," came Big Bird's retort. "I will not do T plus three. Change your price or change your settle." Where I had raised my voice, Big Bird had lowered his in an effort to sound in control, not permitting resistance.

The finer point here is that changing my client's settlement to T plus one meant the price would not change, but he would be denied the benefit of earning two days interest (plus the weekend rate) on the 35mm, which was akin to lowering his price. Big Fucking Bird knew what he was doing, and I could see a smug little smile appear at the corner of his big, fat mouth, knowing he had me in checkmate.

Emphasizing *"not,"* in "So we are *not* done?" was my return chess move.

Emphasizing both *"you,"* and *"not"* in, "That is correct, *you* are *not* done," he confirmed, anticipating my decision to drop the price and my pants and subject myself to getting fucked.

I was pissed off, but I restrained from showing any emotion and returned to my desk, not saying a word. If the exchange had drawn the attention of those around me, we now had the attention of the entire floor, and an eerie silence hung in the air. Clearly a fight was brewing, and the crowds were salivating at the expected onslaught.

I was a managing director with seniority in the company. I had a solid, long, and proven track record. I was respected and did not antagonize anybody, nor play dirty. For Big Bird to pull this shit was uncalled for, and we both knew it. It was his attempt at a show of force, demanding respect from the rest of the floor. He just didn't know he was bullying the wrong guy.

The other thing Big Bird didn't know either was the bid I had received from my London account. With all eyes on me gauging what my response would be to this open gauntlet, I ignored the floor and picked up the phone.

Robin Myer had been a friend of mine for close to five years, and we had done substantial business over the years. He worked for TMI, a huge Japanese money center bank in London, and it was he who had given me the same bid as Big Bird had in the beginning. He was a reliable and strong counterparty of mine.

"Robin, Stephen here. Those 35mm you bid, that still alive?" I asked.

"Yep, it is. Gimme a sec," was Robin's answer. I could hear him pick up another phone and speak to one of his traders. After a brief pause he came back to me. "We like that name," he said, referring to the issuer of the bond. "If you can bring the size, I can improve my bid by two ticks." Things were looking up.

"That's T plus three?" I made sure.

"Of course, are we done?" was Robin's closing question.

"Just a second, stay there," I said, placing him on hold.

Big Bird had followed my conversation from across the floor and was ogling me intently, trying to figure out what I was up to. I was going to make him pay for what he'd done.

Muted phone in hand, I stood up and addressed Big Bird loudly, "I have eight ticks better than your throw away price, out of London. They're firm, for T plus three. Can you equal the bid?" I had to give my desk an opportunity to lift the bonds, as we worked for the same firm, in theory.

No answer from Big Bird. The smug look in his eyes from just moments ago had transformed into a blank stare, not understanding how the situation could have reversed on him so completely and totally in under a minute.

Another five seconds, and still no answer. Louder than before and now with a bite in my voice, I pressed the point. "I repeat, I have in hand a quarter point better, T plus three and I have to execute. Will you do the number?" I took pleasure in Big Bird's discomfort. This time it was he who was checkmated, and everybody knew it.

And this is where justification came my way. The head of the desk who had been observing the interaction, leaned over to Big Bird and quietly asked, "Can you do the number?"

Flushed and refusing to look at me, the self-induced humiliated Big Bird spoke the magic words, "Done, 35mm your price, T plus three."

I took Robin off hold, explained the desk took the trade, thanked him for his bid, and let him go. Victory was sweet and total.

Most of the morning on that first November day was spent organizing a business trip I was to take to Europe later in the month. In particular, I wanted to visit a large institution in Basel, and the Swiss National Bank in Zurich.

The Basel institution was an animal of a different kind. I remember calling it for the first time in early 1997, and I had very little information on it. The only thing I had found was a one-line entry in the *World Bank Directory* that noted the institution's initials and a city in Switzerland. No phone number, no address, and no information whatsoever. Other entries in this directory would list balance sheets, board members, locations of different offices, phone and fax numbers, SWIFT codes, correspondents around the world, specialties of the institution, and specific departments and their managers. But not this one, just a one-line entry, as if insignificant and unimportant, designed to be overlooked and discarded. I am not sure why it caught my attention, but it did.

Somebody once said "No amount of intelligence, talent or education will ever beat sheer tenacity." I like that saying. That's the approach I took with my business and about finding out what was behind that little one line entry in the *World Bank Directory*.

I found out that the city listing in the directory was wrong, whether by accident or on purpose to discourage curious minds. So I called and checked and dug and ultimately found the right address and phone number. Understand, even though the internet was up and running by 1997, it was far from where it is today, with the powerful search engines and systems that spit out information in seconds that would have taken days, if not weeks to unearth only ten years earlier. But I found out what I wanted, and in March of 1997 I made my first call to it and asked for the treasury department. That first call would be followed by many, and without knowing it then, I'd opened an invisible door into an international financial realm unknown to all, except for a few chosen elite. This institution was huge, and I'd seen it move markets just by its sheer volume of trade. And even though it may be known for whom they are in the financial world, I will only refer to it as the Swiss Institution. They exist and the traders were friends of mine.

Ultimately the person at the Swiss Institution whom I became closest to was Johan von Kreefeldt. There were many others I knew well, Dirk, Gitte, Yoshi, Ralph, and others. I made it my goal to learn who worked in their settlement department, and who ran the "middle office," which is the office deciding on the credit limits and the investment approvals. All in all, I made it my business to know their business and how they ran it. It was a common approach of mine with my clients. The more I knew about their way of operating, who was in charge of what and the kind of people they were, always made doing business easier. And it always paid off.

The first transaction came about two months after I had made my first call to them. It must have been the end of May 1997. I remember calling Johan at about nine thirty in the morning for me. Anticipating the 6 hour time difference, I didn't want to call after close of business in Basel. Johan answered, "Ah.., Stephen, wie getzt?"

"Johan, doing well here, how's Basel?" I replied. Not waiting for an answer I continued "I'll be brief, we are issuing our own 5 year paper in US currency on a 6 month Libor float. Any interest?" I knew they liked Libor paper and any positive spread they could get over the index was appealing to them. I only highlighted the bond, while withholding more detailed information, fishing for interest.

"What spread you offering?" Johan inquired hurriedly.

"6 month Libor plus five and a half," I quoted, sensing curiosity.

"What's the settle?" came the query for more information, a big sign of interest.

"T plus three DTC," I responded and shut up. DTC stood for Depository Trust Corporation. Basically that meant that the settlement, or clearing was done in the United States as opposed to the European settlement systems, either Euroclear or Cedel, now called Clearstream.

"Ok, give me a second and lemme check my limits on your name." I could hear paper rustling and a few muted words spoken on the other side of the phone. When limits on a name are checked, it is to verify how much can be invested in a specific name, in this case the bank I worked for.

Johan came back on the line and as a matter of fact said, "I can take 285mm at that level, can you do that size?"

Acting as if I get orders of this type all the time, I answered, "I'll check with the desk, can I have it firm?"

"Sehr gut, you have it firm for five minutes." Was Johan's reply.

"I'll be right back." I responded and hung up. Now I had been in business since 1978 trading a variety of products and commodities, from Liquid Caustic Soda and Poly-Ethylene to foreign currencies and precious metals, from BTX to Unleaded Gasoline and Heating Oil to Government Treasuries and Mortgage Backed derivatives. I had traded multi-million dollar full cargo sized quantities of many products and was used to dealing with 5mm to over 50mm orders routinely in the bond business. 285mm was a sweet order.

Having it firm for five minutes meant that I had five minutes to get back to him within which I could confirm the order. After the five minutes the order expired. So I called Mary at the Treasury desk of our bank who issued our paper and told her she was done for 285mm on their 5 year listed offer.

"We're not writing 5 year paper, so nothing done," was her abrupt answer.

"Mary, you're listing 5 year at five and a half over on your run. If you're not writing any, then why list it?" I said, checking an impulse of impatience and anxiety. 'Fuck this' I remember thinking, 'I won't lose this order.'

"Yes, we listed at five and a half to discourage buyers. We have no need for 5 year paper, so we listed it very expensive." Mary's voice sounded irritated.

"Well, it didn't work and you have an order for 285mm and I expect it filled for T plus three." My tone of voice was aggravated and I tried hard not to come across panicky—it didn't look good and the order was falling apart right in front of me. Opening a new account is difficult enough as it is, one of this size is next to impossible and not being able to fill a first order is a disaster. We went back and forth like this for a few more expensive moments until I realized I was not getting anywhere and decided to call in bigger guns.

A good sales manager is one who is on the salesmen's side as opposed to management's. He acts as an in-between and smoothes ruffled feathers and bruised egos and gets trades done which died due to personality conflicts between traders and sales—or he would be on your ass if your production and work ethics were low—not a problem I ever dealt with. His payout was based on an override of the sales floor's production, so he understood who were important to him.

I ignored knocking, or even checking if he was busy and barged into my sales manager's office, which was right off the floor. Large windows all around so he had an unobstructed view of his domain, I shut the door to approximate a sense of privacy while I had about three precious minutes left—two and a half after I explained the situation. Jeff was a salesman's manager. He understood it was our effort which made him his money and I have seen him fight superiors in order for us to work undisturbed by internal bureaucracy. That day proved no exception.

"Who's the client?" he inquired. After hearing the name and realizing it would be a new account, he just looked at me for a second and then called Treasury on the speaker phone.

Mary immediately answered on the offense without any courtesies, expecting the call, "Jeff, we are not writing five year paper, no matter what."

"Hold on Mary, stay on the line, don't go anywhere." Jeff replied ignoring the attack, placed her on hold and called the big boss, the President of the bank, by-passing all kinds of VP's and egos and hierarchical structures and conferenced him in, taking another grueling thirty seconds or so.

"Treasury is listing five year paper at five and a half over. I have a sales floor pitching this all over and we caught an order for 285mm and Treasury does not want to write." Jeff came right to the point.

After a moment's pause, "Client's name and who's the floor?" came the question over the speaker and Jeff mentioned the Swiss Institution and my name. I was sure I was running out of time during the ensuing quiet.

"Will they take partials, 95 a week three times?" this time directed to me.

"No," I lied, "it's AON (all or none) and we have about one minute left firm."

Another break and he ordered, "Mary, write the paper," after which he hung up.

By now three traders had slipped into the office, one of them the head of the desk, attracted by the obvious activity and sensing a trade in the make. I ploughed passed them, ran to my desk and called Johan, "You're done on 285mm at five and a half over six month Libor, DTC T plus three, ticket on Bloomberg asap. Thank you for the business." I confirmed.

FEDERAL

With a quick, "Done, danke shön," Johan thanked me and hung up already busy doing a next transaction on another phone.

The ultimate show of respect on any trading floor isn't applause, or handshakes, or backslaps, or people congratulating you. No, it's when it turns quiet, when the floor realizes a big deal was done. All stop in their tracks to find out how it was done and how big the ticket was. Well, it turned quiet when the desk announced a new international account took 285mm proprietary paper. They used it as a sales pitch tolling the virtues of continued prospecting and like I said, it was quiet.

There is a saying in my line of business, 'You're as good as your last trade' and I felt pretty good that moment. One of those moments which stands out and everybody works for, but only few have the blessing to experience.

Johan became a very good friend whom I visited often, and likewise, he visited me. He stayed at my home various times and saw my son grow up and become a man. And I became close with his family outside of the professional arena and was grateful for his friendship.

Through Johan I was able to learn some of the finer points of the Swiss Institution. One of the more intriguing aspects was its board of directors. I was surprised to find that the chairman of the board of this institution was none other than Alan Greenspan, the same Alan Greenspan who was the chair of the Federal Reserve.

Now why would the chairman of the Federal Reserve be chairman of this huge Swiss financial institution? Who were these guys, and what was their link to the Federal Reserve?

I remember a discussion I had with Johan about this aspect and asked him, "Why is Greenspan on the board?"

"It's not just Greenspan," Johan answered. "All the G7 finance ministers are on the board. This is their safe haven. They come here to get away from the cameras, the news hounds and to be frank, away from the controls and restrictions placed upon them in their own countries. I guess you noticed the security when you enter our offices and the two hermetically sealed doors that can not open at the same time?"

I answered affirmatively looking back to the first time I visited Johan and his team. The circular office building that housed the Swiss Institution was walking distance between the train station and the Hilton, which is in the center of Basel. According to an old law, no structure in the city can be taller than the local cathedral. This directive applied to this building as well.

I was met with extraordinary security measures, unusually so for an otherwise nondescript financial institution. But then again, I was to find out there was nothing ordinary about this organization. In the main entrance, my first encounter was with an armed guard who was not at all like the ones we see doing detail outside banks or riding in armored cars moving money around. No, this guy was serious, with a bullet proof vest, Heckler & Koch MP5 sub-machine gun on his right shoulder, two Glock side arms with extra clips on the belt, and commando boots with a large knife fitted on the outside of the left calf.

He wore a black uniform with a single small insignia on the right shoulder representing the Swiss colors, a red shield with a white cross in the middle and no other insignia or signs of affiliation, and no name badge, no number, nothing.

He was not alone. Two others similarly dressed and armed stood at a desk and never said a word to me. The desk was part of a massive bullet-proof glass separation splitting the entrance into an initial receiving hall with the guards and a single passageway through the glass partition leading into a second lobby. This did not resemble any bank or institution I had ever entered.

Johan had prepared me for this reception so I wasn't surprised when they asked for my passport. Handing it over, I was asked to state my name, employer, country of origin, and whom I had come to visit. All this was double checked on the computer while my attaché case was inspected thoroughly. After receiving the OK, neither my case nor passport were handed back to me and I was instructed to enter through a two inch thick glass door that slid open silently and allowed me to enter a small glass portal. My belongings would meet up with me again on the other side, I was told. Once in the portal, the glass door behind me swished closed and for a few seconds I was wrapped in absolute silence. No sound could enter these glass walls. I could see out, and I watched as the guard slid my effects through another smaller airlock, which was part of the desk and connected on the other side of the glass partition. The door on the other side of the airlock opened with similar quiet ease, and I was able to enter the main lobby of the Institution.

No armed guards on that side. Instead, I was met by a well-dressed gentleman with impeccable manners, who approached me in perfect English and informed me that my passport would be handed back to me upon departure, and while wishing me a pleasant visit, he instructed me to take a seat. My case was already waiting for me on the low table in front of a row of very comfortable dark-brown leather arm chairs. Light was sparse in the semicircular receiving room. Three doors on the opposite wall, one through which the gentleman receiving me left, and I was alone.

Johan appeared a few minutes later. He was medium height, with grayish short hair, not overweight, but could stand to lose a few pounds—a pleasant face with smiling eyes that conveyed trust and at the same time a level gaze putting you on notice that you were dealing with a sharp and agile mind. After a friendly hello and customary pleasantries, he looked at me smilingly and asked me a peculiar question.

"Do you know where you are?"

I just looked at him with raised eyebrows. But he insisted, "No really, do you know where you are?"

I answered by naming the Institution's name to which Johan replied affirmatively and pointedly inquired again, "Correct, but where is it located?"

"Basel, Switzerland?" I guessed sheepishly, feeling I was being set up.

"That is indeed the location geographically where the building is. But here in the building, after you entered through those glass sliding doors, you are no longer in Basel. You are no longer in Switzerland, nor even Europe or the European Union. That's why they requested your passport. Because you are no longer in any country. This is international territory, outside of international borders—in a way this is no-man's land. It is the only place like it in the world. Impressive, huhè?" Johan smiled, knowing he conveyed a piece of information with profoundly deeper implications than the words alone indicated.

I was dumbfounded and in a strange way intimidated learning this. A feeling that was reinforced when, on a later occasion, I found out all of the traders on the trading desk were required to carry diplomatic passports—as I stated earlier, this was no ordinary financial institution.

So, that first Thursday in November I prepared for my trip, did some business and at some point in the afternoon received the call from Goldman Sachs that proved to be the precursor to life changes I had no idea could occur. Certainly not to me, I thought.

CHAPTER 3

As I told the interviewer for the never released press release, my son Anthony was born in Guayaquil, Ecuador and he and I lived together until he entered the US Navy at the age of nineteen. When he left, the house turned strangely quiet and empty and it was hard getting used to home without him.

The armed services have an acute and effective approach of tailoring instructions and special courses to new recruit's affinities and natural capabilities. Anthony's intellect and drive allowed him to excel in the demanding trainings he had chosen. He seemed to thrive in situations that challenged him to his core, and I believe my pride matched his when he successfully passed the grueling Navy SEAL training and received his Trident.

He was stationed first in Korea, but he became progressively more vague about where he was sent and what he was doing. At times he'd disappear for weeks without notice, and I had learned not to ask. When on leave we'd talk about the conflicts and politics of US interests around the world, but the subject would trail off and the topic end up changing. It was clear there were things not to be discussed about his activities and what he was engaged in. Also, I had noticed an alteration in his demeanor. He always had a certain carefree attitude with a boisterous streak as a kid, but after a few years in the service, he was less quick with opinions and preferred to observe rather than get involved. He had matured.

The proof of this change came unexpectedly during one of his visits home, when we were out together at a local sushi bar. Toward the end of our meal, an unkempt looking man walked in and positioned himself at the counter about six feet away from us. In his late thirties he appeared physically strong, but messy, with a general "I don't give a fuck" attitude. Violence, or at least the threat thereof, was written all over him. A hard, unshaven weathered face, untended long hair combed slick back, dirty slacks and an open shirt exposing prison tats added to the image.

As the guy was hassling the owner's teenage son behind the counter, the rest of the patrons became aware of a potential problem in the making. At that point, Anthony stood up and placed himself next to the man's right side, hips touching but not making eye contact. All he did was ask the kid, "You all right?" without a trace of hurry or constraint.

"Stay the fuck out of it," came the crude reply from the bully.

Ignoring him, Anthony again quietly addressed the nervous teen behind the counter. "Just tell me, what's going on?"

Voice shaking ever so slightly and with fear in his eyes he replied, "This man insists we owe him money, but we don't."

Then, without warning the man's left arm shot out intending a surprise attack. As if expecting the move, Anthony effortlessly turned his upper body, deflected the blow with his right forearm and with his left reached over his opponent's throat and forced him into a deadly backward embrace that would break his neck if he let the poor guy slump.

The whole event was over before it even started. The motion was carried out so swiftly, with such ease and deadly force, that is was obvious Anthony had received more than just extensive training, he had become an expert.

And as was custom on the trading floor, respect was shown in identical fashion, as the restaurant turned completely quiet observing this sudden skillful feat of defense and attack in one single move. The only sound was Anthony's low voice, asking, "You want to pursue this any further?" while still holding him up with the neck lock. The response was a single movement of the man's head. I don't think he could actually speak with his throat in the embrace.

Then, almost gently, Anthony released his grip, helped the guy stand up, and walked him out the door. Full of pride I looked at my son as he sat down, and he returned my gaze with just the slightest hint of a smile.

That night we ate free.

The woman in my life in 2007 was Nicole. We had been together for a bit over three years. We saw each other three, or four times a week, and occasionally she'd stay over. Our relationship had been rocky to an extent, having ended twice previously. But we would drift back, attracted by the safety of a shared history and the ease of familiarity with each other. Our mutual regard had changed though, from one where Nicole could see a possible future with me, to one where just being together for the moment was enough. At least, enough for me. I knew this was not what she was looking for, but I liked my life alone and really didn't want anybody else living with me. So if that meant life without Nicole, then so be it.

"Hi baby, what you doing? Care to get some dinner tonight?" I called her from the car at about three thirty that afternoon. I had left work early, as I usually stayed to catch West Coast clients in the late afternoon. But that day I was tired and looking forward to being with Nicole and spending the night with her.

Nicole had been able to construct her life in an impressive manner. She was an independent woman, and her job and professional life reflected that quality. She majored in art history, and even though her passion was art, specifically early medieval European religious art, her business was working as an independent consultant advising multinational corporations and individuals on housing and living arrangements in major cities in Europe.

How she became involved in that I never really knew, but I was always impressed with the network she had been able to set up in numerous Northwestern European nations. She provided corporations with detailed outlooks for housing, be it rental or purchase in the major capitals and in many smaller cities as well. It was her business was to know pricing for housing, what areas in town were attractive, where the expats lived, where the golf courses were, how to attain gym memberships, where the international schools were, and lots of other mundane but important details I would never think of. She had a network that was impressive, and it seemed to work seamlessly.

Anticipating her dinner preference, I suggested Café Martorano, a local Italian restaurant where the food was consistently good.

"Yes, pick me up at about six thirty or so, or shall I come by your place?" she offered.

"See you at my home," I said and then asked, "By the way, I'm off to Europe at some point this month. You have any trips lined up?"

"I have to go to Rouen and Antwerp and maybe Slough in England. Would be nice if we could do something together." I could hear excitement in her voice. We travelled well together and we both enjoyed the fact we each had our own business. I liked flying into Amsterdam, or Paris, or anywhere with her, both going our own ways and then meeting up somewhere else again. Sometimes we would only have a few hours, spent either in a hotel or a restaurant or at an airport on our way through to somewhere else. Or at other times we were able to take a few days and rent a car and disappear for a long weekend.

"I have to be in Zurich, Basel, Koln, and Amsterdam. I was thinking we could take a week and have a few days for ourselves. We'll get a car and see the middle of France. Or whatever. We can just hang around and do nothing for a change," I offered. The thought of taking some time and not running from hotel to hotel, not having to prepare for meetings, or checking markets and dealing with clients or the office... all that sounded just fine with me.

"Yes, sounds like a plan. See you in a bit, honey," Nicole said as she hung up.

My home was in a quiet residential neighborhood, and even though it was located close to the beach, tourists usually didn't pass through. It allowed for a peaceful community with a tough police force, resulting in low crime and a safe feeling all around. Being close to Miami, only forty miles north or so, this was a very desirable quality. And Nicole was close by. Whereas I preferred my single-family home, she owned a spacious condo in a high-rise on the beach perhaps two miles from me with an unbelievable view of the ocean from the thirty second floor.

She walked in that evening, using the key I had given her only a few months prior. I actually dreaded giving her that thing, fearing superstitiously it would be the kiss of death. But so far, things had worked out well. She made no overtures of needing to move in. She never dropped hints that the relationship should move into the next phase. Either she was pleased as it was, or she was a very smart woman.

Short dark-grey silk skirt, a wide black belt, and a grey-toned silk shirt, buttoned up just above the swell of her breasts. She showed enough to pique the interest without a hint of sleaze. Not too tall, her two-inch heels made her lips reach mine with just the slightest stretch of her neck. Dark hair with a touch of red made her blue eyes stand out. The Eastern European lift of her cheekbones and her focused gaze could make men look away if she wished it so. Being the object of her interest made me feel proud and special. It made it all the better knowing she felt the same when with me.

The food at Café Martorano was great, as usual. After dinner, the evening being cool and quiet, we took the car and slowly cruised the beach. Moon on the water, quiet ocean, beaches wrapped in darkness so as not to disturb the season's last hatchling turtles finding the water, we parked the car and sat at an outside café for the night's last espresso.

Later that night she surprised me as she so often did, with her strange mixture of vulnerability, sexual aggression, and a desire that seemed so tailored to me, to my personality. At times it would take me aback and make me hide, as if too much of my person would be exposed, but then her touch and lips would change my mind, and kissing her she would melt in my mouth.

CHAPTER 4

The name, Federal Reserve (remember God?), implies this institution to be a federal institution and that it somehow retains reserves (i.e. huge amounts of money in some inviolable form, like gold bars buried in underground vaults). This is far from the truth. The Federal Reserve is as federal as Federal Express, and there are no reserves other than the cotton/linen fabric on which they print pretty pictures and symbols and numbers, and then call it a dollar.

Unknown to most, the Federal Reserve is a private company. It is not a US government agency. It is not government controlled nor sponsored, and it is not part of the US Treasury Department. It is a private company. A private company with a monopoly over the issuance and control of the US money supply. It sets the monetary policy for this nation and much of the world. Additionally, and unlike any other company in the United States, domestic or foreign, private or public, the Federal Reserve is not subject to paying taxes, and it can not be audited.

If you ask any politician about this, they will tell you that the Federal Reserve is "semi-private," based on the fact that the board of governors is appointed by the White House, but all that is theater. Just ask them how many shares of the Federal Reserve our government owns and the answer will probably be, "I don't know." The truth is the US government owns zero shares of the Federal Reserve. And according to the 1913 Federal Reserve Act itself, no Senator or representative of Congress can be a member of the Federal Reserve Board, nor an officer of a Federal Reserve bank.

They will also tell you that the Federal Reserve is subject to audits, and there is some truth to this. The GAO, the Government Accounting Office, actually does audit the Federal Reserve, but only on very basic issues and on an extremely limited basis. The audit is so generic that in 2009, Congressman Ron Paul initiated House Resolution 1207, asking for a full general audit of the Federal Reserve in order to gain insight into the business practices of this secretive and powerful organization. Although he received plenty of verbal support for his resolution, it never became reality.

The Federal Reserve is too powerful and has too much control over our government, as will become apparent.

The obvious questions to ask are, "How is this possible? How could this have happened, and how could we have given a private institution that much power?" The answer takes us back in history, back to the early 1900's. Conceptualized in 1910 on Jekyll Island, enacted in 1913 by Congress, a group of very influential bankers convinced a young New Jersey governor named Woodrow Wilson to back their plan for the institution of a central bank. It was to be created separate and outside the control of the US government, while being authorized by Congress. In return for backing this plan, these bankers promised Mr. Wilson unlimited financial support in his bid for the presidency of the United States, thereby basically guaranteeing him the election.

Woodrow Wilson was elected president, and on December 22, 1913, when most of Congress was away for the holidays, the Federal Reserve Act of 1913 was passed in the dark of night and signed into law by president Wilson.

The relationship between the United States government and the Federal Reserve is symbiotic in nature. Congress needs money to operate and to fund its programs, and the Federal Reserve prints the money. When Congress needs funds, it issues promissory notes (i.e. Treasury bills, notes and bonds) to the Federal Reserve. The Federal Reserve sells these through a network of primary dealers to the public at large and passes the proceeds on to Congress. The national debt which is created as a result is (supposedly) paid back by the citizenry of the United States through the levy of taxes and collected by the IRS. But because our monetary system is not backed (collateralized) by gold, or any other hard asset, the Federal Reserve can print[1] unlimited amounts of funds and Congress has taken full advantage of this, resulting in burgeoning liabilities that are becoming impossible to repay. And as in any monopoly, the product produced by the Federal Reserve, the US dollar, is inferior, evidenced by the fact it has lost 98% of its value since the 1913 Federal Reserve's inception.

---

[1] Ben Bernanke November, 21 2002: "The U.S. government has a technology, called a printing press - or today, its electronic equivalent - that allows it to produce as many U.S. dollars as it wishes at essentially no cost."

FEDERAL

A closer look at the US dollar itself clarifies the immense power of the Federal Reserve. One would assume the currency of a nation to be an obligation of that same country. But such is not the case in the United States. Nowhere on a dollar bill does it say "US currency," or "US Note." Nor does it say "US Treasury Note," which is what it really should be. No, it states first of all "FEDERAL RESERVE NOTE" clarifying it as an obligation of the Federal Reserve. Secondly, printed under these words it explains that these notes are specifically issued for use of "THE UNITED STATES OF AMERICA."

It might as well say, "Made in China," or "Made in Japan," because it is no more than a Federal Reserve note, the promissory note of a private company which can not be audited and does not pay taxes. Meanwhile, most people are under the impression the dollar is an obligation of the US government. It plainly is not.

But this Federal Reserve phenomena can not be fully appreciated without considering the men behind it and their histories. The common denominator through all their business acumen was the ability to create financial monopolies and the uncanny gift of orchestrating panics and crises to their advantage, many times at the cost of the welfare of whole populations. The relationship between those who control the financial monopolies and the weapons and arms manufacturers, today known as the military/industrial complex, became apparent immediately. To note, shortly after its inception in 1914 the Federal Reserve System was to 'loan' $25 billion dollars to the Allies in Europe to finance WWI. This loan, this money belonging to the American public was never repaid, even though large amounts of interest payments were earned by various bankers associated with forming the Federal Reserve.

Separation from England came to the United States in 1775 and even though an independent sovereignty had been created in 1776, the London bankers were not willing to forgo this profitable 'colony' and the potential it promised. The intent to retain financial control became evident when President Alexander Hamilton succumbed to extensive pressure from European bankers to institute a Central Bank modeled after the Bank of England. This resulted in the formation of the First Bank of the United States in 1791. This initial attempt at the creation of a privately owned Central Bank died in 1811, when Congress was narrowly defeated and unable to renew the bank's charter causing the First Bank of the United States to close.

Not taking no for an answer, the subsequent attempt for a private Central Bank came five years later when in 1816 The Second Bank of the United States opened.

President Andrew Jackson understood the destructive force it imposed on the nation and when Congress proposed to renew the charter in 1831, Jackson vetoed the Bill. He then proceeded to withdraw all government funds from the Bank and deposited these in state banks, which resulted in prosperity throughout the country. The new economic expansion allowed the government to pay off the entire national debt while creating a surplus of $50 million dollars.

The Second Bank of the United States' charter expired in 1836 and the bank was ultimately closed in 1841.

Jackson's successful action against the continuance of the Second Bank of the United States did not go unpunished. But it was not him at whom the wrath was directed. The majority investor in the Second Bank of the United States was James de Rothschild of Paris. The Rothschild's answer to the expiration of their American experiment was the sudden refusal by the Bank of England (controlled by the House of Rothschild) to deal in any securities connected to the former colony. This immediate suspension of liquidity caused what became known as the Panic of 1837 and anybody owning any United States stocks or bonds was ruined, as any semblance of credit evaporated.

A perfect crisis to be taken advantage of by those with ample funds through their connections with the Bank of England. The Rothschilds, Browns, the Morgans and Peabodys were able to secure these same United States securities for mere pennies on the dollar from the desperate masses trying to raise funds at any cost. And thus the stage was set for similar scenarios to play out untold times in the future.

An important lesson in control and manipulation, it was not lost on the financiers that in order to gain a firm and lasting grip on any privately owned Central Bank in the US, the Presidency had to be dominated and mastered. A process which they refined during the ensuing century, resulting in the third endeavor at a privately owned Central Bank, The Federal Reserve System.

The Bank of England has its roots dating back to 1649 when the Bank of Amsterdam financed Oliver Cromwell's ascent to power in the British Isles. Later, in 1689, these same bankers promoted King William of Orange from the Netherlands to take control of the British throne. Doing so, the King promptly rewarded his financiers by requiring the State to borrow £1,250,000 pounds sterling and commissioned them with the Royal Charter for the Bank of England. A national debt had been established. The repayment of this debt, including interest, was secured through the institution of taxation of the population.[2]

Control over the Bank of England by the House of Rothschild traces back to the Napoleonic Wars. In a classic portrayal of things to come, both Napoleon and his opponents were financed by the Rothschilds and their agents, assuring victory regardless of outcome, establishing debt on both sides. The Rothschilds had advance knowledge of the outcome of the Waterloo Battle, and caused panic selling by manipulating the London Exchange into thinking Napoleon was winning the conflict. Then, during the height of the crash, Rothschild started anonymously and quietly buying any and all securities they could get their hands on. The profit was so large that the saying at the time was that even though the Allies had won Waterloo, it was Rothschild who won the war. It was these profits which gave Rothschild the financial strength to gain control of the Bank of England by monopolizing the bank's shares and bonds—a control which subsequently never left the House of Rothschild and to this day exists.

The 1857 Panic was caused by the manipulation and subsequent collapse of the grain market and the bankruptcy of Ohio Life and Trust. Over 900 additional American companies failed in the aftermath. The only firm who prospered during this time of national hardship was the firm of George Peabody and Co. (the roots of the House of Morgan), who had access to a £5,000,000 pounds sterling loan by the Bank of England, fully controlled by the Rothschilds. The rest of the story is obvious, being the only firm with access to cash and credit, the Peabody/Morgan consortium was able to buy at just pennies on the dollar, securities which were resold later at maximum value when sanity prevailed over the markets again. A familiar story.

The Rothschild/Morgan relationship dates back to this Panic of 1857. Rothschild's banking activities had caused a considerable negative

---

[2] Note the similarity between the creation of both the Federal Reserve and the IRS in 1913. The IRS was strictly set up to act as the collection agency for the Federal Reserve, anticipating the national debt – to note, the US didn't have a national debt in 1913 when the Federal Reserve originated.

sentiment against the name. So Morgan acted in the USA covertly on behalf of Rothschild. It explains the easy and generous cashflow issued to the Peabody/Morgan firm by the Bank of England.

In 1891 a new secret alliance was formed in London by Cecil Rhodes, his banker Rothschild, Lord Curzon, Lord Rosebery and another Rothschild, collectively known as the Round-Table Group. The American counterpart of this alliance was the Morgan Group and it became known as The British-American Secret Society. This association, together with the already existing agreements between Morgan and other financiers in London headed by Lazard Brothers, became the cornerstone of the affiliation between the Houses of Morgan, Rothschild, Drexel, Warburg and Grenfell in both Europe and the USA. After WWI the Round Table Group changed its name to the Council of Foreign Relations in the US and to the Royal Institute of International Affairs in the UK, both still thriving to date.

The US Presidential election of 1912 was initially divided between the popular incumbent, Republican William H. Taft and the more unknown and socially awkward Democrat Woodward Wilson. Both Parties promoted some type of financial reform bill, the Republicans pushed the Aldrich Plan and the Democrats the Federal Reserve Act.

As is the case in many elections, the incumbent was by far the favorite. Until Theodore Roosevelt entered the arena. With seemingly unlimited financial and media support, he caused a divide in his own Republican party causing Woodrow Wilson to become victorious.

As for the financiers backing the candidates, they imagined a Democratic President ascending to power with a Democratic Congress who would aid in the structuring of a Federal Reserve Act. From the beginning it had been doubtful Taft would have been able to deliver the unpopular Aldrich Plan, subject to strong public disapproval, it being dubbed a 'Wall Street Plan.' The formation of a Central Bank under a Democratic Presidency and Congress seemed far more probable and profitable. Hence, Roosevelt was brought in to successfully create the political mechanism to upset Taft and assure a Democratic victory.

On Monday December 22, 1913 the bill passed the House by 282 – 60 and the Senate by 43 – 23 and the Federal Reserve Act became a reality. The Act provided for the printing of Federal Reserve Notes. Notes issued without gold or bullion backing and deriving its value solely from the fact the government says it is so, otherwise known as 'fiat'[3] money. Prior to passing the Bill, the objection had been raised that it would create a never ending expansion of Federal Reserve Notes in circulation, with the obvious danger of inflation. It was exactly this unlimited power over the economy the bankers backing the Bill were after and had succeeded in obtaining. Congress, who through the Constitution is the only institution empowered to coin money, passed this privilege to a private company owned by banks whose owners were and still are private individuals in the United States and Europe. Their allegiance is not to the United States of America, but to their own empires and fortunes.

---

[3] FIAT – Latin for 'Let It Be Done'

CHAPTER 5

Good assistants are worth their weight in gold, and I had two of them in Sharon Webb and Kevin Marconi. Both were Series 7 licensed, which meant they could speak with my clients and not only discuss settlements, but talk pricing and offers and take orders. They shared a Bloomberg—one of the (indispensable) perks and expenses coming out of my pocket—and knew my accounts, how to reach them, and what they bought. They knew my business inside out and it was my job to keep them happy, so they would not walk out and shop my business and detailed client information elsewhere.

While they were bound by contracts, non-compete clauses and privileged information constraints, they were my Achilles' heel and I was well aware of it. So I kept them happy. And on top of their company salaries they received an override on each settled trade and a generous Christmas bonus which came directly from me. A camaraderie and trust had developed over the years we'd worked together, and I felt comfortable leaving on trips, knowing they would be there taking care of business and putting out fires, if necessary.

One of the tasks they performed was confirming all the relevant trade information to all parties concerned. Each financial instrument, each security without exception, is identified by a number. Very much resembling a social security number for individuals, securities issued in the United States and Canada are identified by a unique nine-digit alphanumeric number known as a cusip number. When a new issue is being structured and before it's free to trade, a temporary cusip is assigned until the final number is allocated. This new and final cusip number has to be entered manually into the system, so there is always the risk of entry errors. Rare as they may be, they can be costly and time consuming to correct. This was my assistants' responsibility, to be sure all current data was in place so settlements would not be delayed. The new stock issue I purchased from my colleague at Goldman Sachs carried such a temporary cusip and my assistants were aware of this and knew how to handle it.

FEDERAL

Before Nicole and I departed on our trip to Europe, I had asked my neighbor and friend Carol to take care of my black retriever, Sparky, for the time I was gone, which was an arrangement that had been in place for some time.

We had decided to leave Friday, November 23, 2007, the day after Thanksgiving and booked our flights into Paris and planned to take a day or so together. From there I'd continue to Zurich and Basel, and Nicole would already be close to her first appointment in Rouen. Depending on how it all worked out, perhaps we would meet up again at some point later in the week.

That Friday we had a car pick us up in the early afternoon from my home for a quiet forty-mile or so ride to Miami Airport, where our Air France flight left at five-thirty five in the afternoon, for arrival in Paris at eight o'clock the next morning. After checking in and the usual security spectacle of taking off shoes and jackets, opening bags, and taking out computers, we landed in the first-class lounge with over an hour to spare till boarding. As a matter of custom, I logged into the Bloomberg system on my laptop and confirmed with Sharon the clearing of a few bonds that should have been done that day.

The trip was smooth and easy, the food on the plane great, and the ride comfortable. We arrived in Paris in the morning, and the car we had arranged to pick us up was present as we exited the arrival gate at about nine o'clock.

November in Paris, like anywhere in Northwestern Europe, can be glorious or miserable. This time it was the latter, drizzly rain with a cold northern wind and temperatures bordering on freezing. Daylight arrived late at this latitude and the drive to the hotel was in a dark morning grey making the otherwise inviting city seem forlorn, cold, and inhospitable. The George V Hotel though, was a different story. Warm and tempting with staff eager to help, it was a pleasure to be tended to and without any effort to be escorted to the suite we had reserved.

Time with Nicole away from home, away from work, with nothing else to do other than just hang out and decide where to have dinner, was a treat. I knew Paris well and that evening we took a cab to the Quartier Latin and walked around the ancient narrow streets. We ended up eating couscous in a small Moroccan café with only a few other patrons present. Desert was a large coffee only the French know how to make—impossible to see the cup's bottom, it's always strong and delicious.

Nicole had finished a half bottle of Muscadet and had become ever so pliable on my arm as we walked around after dinner. Even though the weather was cold and wet, I liked the old cities of Europe best this way, the streets quiet, cobblestones glistening in the rain. When we reached the Place de Saint-Michel, we hailed a cab, returning to the warmth and safety of the suite which was ours for the next two nights. Loving her that night was languid and passionate, like ocean swells building and cresting, only to build again and again. I did love loving her.

Monday I woke up early and took a flight to Zurich. Nicole took the train to Rouen, which was only an hour or so away from Paris and we agreed to meet up in Amsterdam at the end of the week.

I arrived in time for lunch in Basel, where I met with Johan as planned and paid my respects to a few of the others in the offices of the Swiss Institution. Basel is an ancient city with a medieval town center, which remarkably has remained untouched over the centuries by wars and therefore was preserved as very few others are. The city is strategically located on the Rhine River, and one can imagine the calculated power it commanded in times past. Its geographic dominance enabled it to control the traffic up and down this river, this artery for all goods flowing in and out of Northwestern Europe for as long as man has populated the region.

Basel has the unusual feature that it is located on the corner of three countries, France, Germany, and Switzerland. However, as the old, beautiful, ornately decorated and pristinely preserved town hall is located in Switzerland, the city is and has always been Swiss.

Johan and I were pleased to see each other again, and we decided to have lunch at a small restaurant in the heart of downtown. The place was located in an old home, narrow, crooked and leaning against its neighbors. Over time the steep stairs and floors had settled unevenly, and creaked with each step under our feet. Only twelve tables spread over three floors were reserved for dining, with the kitchen located in the basement. We were seated on the second floor, just big enough for four tables, one of which was unoccupied.

As all of downtown, the building was ancient, dating back to the thirteenth century. The windows were subdivided into small rectangular partitions filled with equally old glass of varying tints. Originally without color, slowly over the centuries, due to minute variances in chemical composition, each panel's hue had changed so that one differed from the other. Distinctly thinner at the top, uneven in width and set in place with the thicker side at the bottom, every piece of glass displayed the medieval manner of production where molten glass was blown, flattened and then spun into a disk, resulting in a thicker outer edge, before being cut into panes. It distorted the world outside.

I had begun to understand the power of the Swiss Institution and how closely it was related to the Federal Reserve. I was impressed at how much of the Fed's activity was executed and controlled by the Swiss Institution, away from the United States, in no-man's land, away from prying eyes and wondering minds and questioning politicians. What the Fed could not do at home, in the United States, it could facilitate through the Swiss Institution, and as such it could deny any participation or knowledge of certain financial activities.

Nobody could or would question the activity of the Swiss Institution—extending credit to the Iranians and Israelis alike, funding Hamas and Hezbollah, helping the poppy-derivatives export out of Central Asian nations like Afghanistan and Pakistan, supplying arms factories for Hugo Chavez and helping him at the same time transfer vast portions of his nation's wealth into his private offshore accounts. Through their Hong Kong office, the Swiss Institution coordinated the complicated transactions typical of the North Koreans buying and selling arms. There were many more sinister and disturbing details this Institution was involved in with the Federal Reserve, some I would learn about much sooner than I would have ever suspected. Having Johan as a friend had proved invaluable, personally and business alike. The information he had shared with me over the years, had given me untold insights I would not have obtained anywhere else.

After we'd caught up about our personal lives, I changed the subject.

"With the Federal Reserve easing late last month, where do you believe its target is for the funds rate?" I asked.

"The Fed is not telling anybody what is worrying them," Johan said. "They never have and they never will. Better to leave us guessing then give us the ability to predict. But the truth is, they're worried and see trouble on the horizon. From where I sit we are seeing a lot of setting up and positioning, which is foreshadowing much lower rates, and you know what that means."

I agreed, acknowledging that lower rates means a slowing economy.

"The Fed has been shifting huge amounts of funds away from the United States, moving into the euro, yen, gold, and other safe havens. All the positions we set up for them are defensive in nature, anticipating trouble with the dollar, but more so anticipating deeper systemic rifts, as if they are preparing for a 1930's scenario or worse," he said.

His voice had lowered, and his body language told me what I already knew. This was off the record, not to be discussed with others. I had known and done business with him and the Institution for over ten years, but there was no mistaking it. I was an outsider, just a broker from another counterparty. Our friendship, however, had made us understand each other's ideas and convictions, and many times we discussed the more in-depth implications of the Federal Reserve's actions and the behind the scenes role the Swiss Institution played in the Federal Reserve's market activity.

We ordered our meal, and we resumed our discussion on the Federal Reserve.

"The fact is they're anticipating the one event they have no defense against, and have been trying to avoid it more aggressively over time. Do you remember how inflation just disappeared in the mid 1990's?" He stopped to allow the waiter to pour his wine and my Perrier. "Inflation disappearing from the consumer products arena was not in the Federal Reserve's interest. Their main focus was to keep everybody borrowing and control the issuance of money so that all believed they were getting ahead, while in reality nobody can ever get even."

"God forbid the consumer stops spending." I interjected.

Smiling deviously, Johan referred to the basic tenets of the Federal Reserve's preservation of inflation so that the need to print ever more money never diminishes. He appreciated the simple logic of the system and the beauty of such a clean plan executed on such a gigantic scale.

There was something specific I wished to talk about and I lowered my voice to bring up the subject. "I believe the big crashes, the big socio-economic events are foreseen, anticipated, and managed long before they actually occur. Perhaps the minutia, the timing and ultimate severity, may be unpredictable to an extent, but the overall set-up, the choreography of the stage if you like, the placing of the ingredients and key factors are not only foreseen, they are carefully arranged and integrated into the system over long periods so that they may seem to benefit current events or economic situation, but ultimately only advantage those who instituted them in the first place. It takes an unencumbered view of the bigger picture in order to appreciate this."

"I agree with you, but I would like to know how you envision this," was all Johan said and then remained quiet to let me continue.

"Contrary to popular belief, I think the crash of the housing and mortgage markets is secondary to the real events to occur. Take the Great Depression for example, and the resulting Banking Crisis, or the 1929 Banking Crisis and the resulting Great Depression, whichever you feel came first. It doesn't matter. At the time, the Federal Reserve didn't approve of an independent banking system outside of the Federal Reserve System. The result of the Great Depression was the destruction of thousands upon thousands of banks whose assets were bought for literally pennies on the dollar. The new banking system that survived was 100% Federal Reserve controlled. Who suffered? The people. Who gained? Those who controlled and supported the Federal Reserve. To believe it is any different today is naïve and short sighted."

Johan sat back, and said, "You are correct. The general consensus of the cause behind the Great Depression was to blame over-leveraged and out-of-control speculation of the roaring 20's. That certainly was part of it, but all that speculation was the result of systems put in place that promoted and encouraged the behavior. I agree with your thinking in that the Great Depression was orchestrated, just as today's events are." He waited a moment and then asked, "What are your views of what was put in place to cause the current economic troubles?" His voice was inquisitive and persistent at the same time, and I had the distinct feeling that I was somehow being tested and that it was important to answer his inquiry correctly.

It took me a few moments to gather my thoughts. I had never verbalized them before, even though the topic had been an issue of much interest and study for me. I knew I was not about to tell Johan anything new, but I wanted to let him know what I observed and perhaps he would reciprocate and share some of his knowledge with me. "There was a combined effort where the ultimate goals were disguised so that a grass roots movement would do the ground work and unknowingly aid in the final goal of a bank and real estate meltdown."

"Interesting. I like that statement, go on," Johan prompted me.

"There were two forces at work. First, legislative by the passing of laws and the creation of an infrastructure that relaxed the extension of credit and eased regulations under which lesser affluent groups could obtain financing to purchase homes. Second, the activation of community organizers who strong-armed financial institutions into extending credit to these lower-income groups and minorities who otherwise would have been considered bad credit risks. This enabled them to qualify for mortgages and financial services that they had no business acquiring." I drank my Perrier while the waiter approached our table. Neither of us spoke as lunch was served.

"The whole disaster was ironic, and it still is," I said. "The idea was sold as a benefit for minorities and lower incomes to become homeowners. But the truth is, it was never meant to assist them. Quite the opposite, it destroyed them. It took their money and invested it in homes at the highest stage of the housing bubble when values were already inflated to the max. They never had a chance, and the one and only result that could happen to them was to lose their homes and the few dollars they had to start with."

I had Johan's attention and continued, "I find it amusing to see how all those community organizers fought so hard and took to the streets but never understood how badly they were being used. It was pathetic. The experiment never went wrong. It was never meant to succeed."

Taking the wine glass in his hand and looking through the burgundy liquid, Johan said, "You are absolutely correct. The real losers are the same people they were professing to help. First, make them spend their savings on a down payment on a home, then crash the housing market. Not only is their money gone, so are their homes. Classic transfer of wealth at the expense of the most vulnerable in society."

"I think, Johan, the price these lower-income groups paid was no more than collateral damage, an unintended by-product of a much larger, decades-old scheme that purposely drove up real estate values to the breaking point." Again Johan looked at me, intrigued with the idea that I was on to something. "And you just said the magic words, 'transfer of wealth.' That is what this is all about. Where the community organizers were convinced they were fighting for the underdog, all they did in reality was play into the hands of those who really benefitted from this redistribution: Congress and the financial networks financing them."

Johan brought me back to the subject. "I'm curious about what you said earlier. How do you see the legislative force being structured?"

"In short, it started with Carter creating the CRA. The basic idea was to have banks commit to extend credit to businesses and residences in their local communities, specifically minorities and those less affluent, who had previously been denied access to these services."

"I know what CRA is," Johan informed me tersely.

"I know you do, but you asked, and I have to start there. Sorry if I am stating the obvious, but I am trying to make a point. These population groups were denied financial services because they posed an adverse credit risk. But this argument was turned around and regurgitated as if they were victims of discrimination. And 'discrimination' is the magic word. The argument was clever, albeit wrong, and it did the job. Under the guise of giving minorities access to financial services, CRA created a population group to contribute to the housing frenzy and add to consumer spending if and when the baby boomers slowed down."

"You have a way with words. I bet it got you in trouble at times." Johan smiled as he made the remark.

Ignoring the jab, I went on. "Then every four years or so since the CRA's inception, changes were made to the act, making it more stringent and penalizing those financial institutions that did not adhere to it. In 1991, a rating scale was introduced based on the financial institution's compliance with the act, and the information was made public."

"And we know that really fueled the fires of the community organizers," Johan remarked.

"It was designed to put pressure on the banks and give the organizers ammunition to take the fight to the streets," I agreed. "And they did. The community organizers recruited mobs that would descend on a local bank, which according to them was not active enough in the community. Then they would picket the entrance so that customers would stay away or have trouble entering and exiting. They'd take over the lobby with about a hundred people or so, and each would go to a teller and ask to change a one-dollar bill into one hundred pennies, then go back in line and request the one hundred pennies be changed back into a dollar bill. Basically rendering the branch incapable of doing business and forcing them to comply with the CRA guidelines."

"Which meant forcing them to make adverse and risky credit decisions," Johan said.

"You are correct," I affirmed. "It is interesting to note how credit requirements became less-stringent, and how rules became more and more relaxed until we had the phenomena of NINJA loans, the No Income No Job Application loans."

We ate our lunch, and I thought about our discussion. I wanted to let Johan know how I saw the progression over time, and in return I wanted him to let me in on what he knew. For the moment, I just had to lay out my ideas and see where it went. It usually worked that way between the two if us. He let me talk and then it would be his turn and he would choose what to share with me.

"Congress understood all along that if it pushed financial institutions to make adverse credit decisions, that these same companies would need a venue to sell the bad loans they had been forced to make. Without this outlet it would never have worked, and I am referring to Fannie Mae and Freddie Mac. They were purposely manipulated over decades in order to promote more mortgage activity."

Fannie Mae and Freddie Mac were to dominate the mortgage industry by buying most of the home and commercial loans issued in the United States, thereby fueling the ability to promote and produce more and more loans. As banks were forced to lower their credit standards, both Fannie Mae and Freddie Mac simultaneously expanded and eased their requirements year after year, creating a seamless conduit through which they could absorb the same bad loans from the banking and mortgage community.

"This is the perfect way to socialize losses and privatize gains," Johan interjected. "That has always been the progressives' motto, and here you see it in action."

Johan had been eating steadily and was about to finish, but I had hardly taken a bite.

"Then, in 1999, Congress repeals the Glass Steagall Act, which was the 1933 law enacted to prevent another market crash. It paved the way for banks to get even more involved in investment activities, the one thing the act had sought to prevent."

"What does that have to do with the CRA?" Johan asked.

"It permitted banks to buy loans and mortgages and structure them into collateralized debt and loan obligations, CDO's and CLO's, and sell these instruments directly to the public through their own dealer companies. Previously, the Glass Steagall Act prohibited banks to deal directly in these products. The repeal added liquidity and allowed for even more questionable debt to be originated and moved."

Johan drank his wine as I finished my lunch and then simply said, "Agreed."

"But that wasn't all," I said between bites. "It couldn't have happened without a coordinated effort from everybody involved, beginning with the buyer of the loan to the end investor of the CLO."

The table was cleared. Johan ordered coffee, and I a double espresso. I continued, "The appraisers were part of it and so were the rating agencies. Without the right appraisal the loan could not be made, and with the right rating, CLO's and CDO's could be structured in such a way that it made nuclear waste look like gold. The Rating Agency Reform Act of 2006 basically insisted on more competition in rating agencies. So here you have a situation where you could shop for better ratings and play the agencies against each other. As I said, legislative action to promote more spending, regardless of the quality or the consequences."

The check came, and as I paid Johan asked, "You mentioned that the housing bust and the resulting minorities' transfer of wealth was not the real intent. If not that, then what was?"

We descended the steep stairs and stepped outside. The streets were wet, shiny and empty since it had rained while we were in the restaurant, though, none was falling at the moment. As we walked, I answered, "Remember when 'mark to market' rules were introduced in 1993?"

I was referring to a set of rules that forced banks to divide their investments into special portfolios where the value of their trading investments had to be "marked to market," which meant adjusted to the current market value of similar investments. In the event the market value was either higher or lower, the difference had to be either added or subtracted from the working capital of the bank. All was well when the market value was higher, but when it was lower the bank had to assume a loss, when in reality none was taken, and thus they have less capital to work with. The bank was forced to adjust its working capital to compensate for a lower market value of the investment portfolio.

However, when market values went low enough and the application of mark to market rules threatened to severely diminish the working capital, the institution ran the risk of loss of book value. Then counter-parties became wary, which created a lack of liquidity and ultimately insolvency.

"Sure I do," Johan replied. "Greenspan's answer to the S&L crisis."

"That was how it was sold," I contradicted Johan. "As a promise to protect and save the public's money, they instituted the mark to market rules. But in reality they installed a time bomb, and they knew it. They knew it because mark to market accounting rules were responsible for the failure of the financial system during the Great Depression. Not until 1938, when FDR abolished the rule, was the economy capable of mending and recovery. But not before over nine thousand banks failed during the 1930's, destroying the banking world."

A slow drizzle had started as we were walking back to the office. Not enough to have to duck for cover, but still sufficient to decide to take the tram, which was frequent and well organized.

Once we were inside the electric car I went on. "You see, I believe it was agreed upon long before they introduced these rules. All they were waiting for was the right opportunity, and the early 1990's gave them exactly that."

Johan looked at me and with a somewhat amusing smile asked "And whom do you suppose *'they'* are? You sound like one of those conspiracy junkies who see a deeper truth in anything they can't easily explain."

The sarcasm didn't escape me, and even though the jest was in good humor, I could feel my temper rise. Not taking the bait, I countered, "Derision and ridicule are the usual response when a subject is approached that attacks an established institution or idea. The facts, though, are clear. Let me put them in order." I had to remember whom I was speaking to. Johan was an integral and significant figure at the Swiss Institution, but more importantly, he was my client. No matter how passionate I felt about this subject, it was not worth pissing him off and threaten a friendship and his business.

Toning down my attitude a few notches, I said, "They, and I will get to whom I think *'they'* are in a minute, realized three or four decades ago that the baby boomers would at some point slow down their spending spree. Knowing this, specific legislation was put in place, which we discussed. Simultaneously, a popular ground-swell was organized, conveying the opinion that certain benefits should be seen as rights. When Congress transmits this message long enough, people will start to believe in it. I am not discussing whether privileges should be rights, or vice versa. All I am saying is it's been happening as a means to guarantee votes for those in Congress promoting it. The result of these movements, the one in Congress and the other in the streets, was the creation of an endless and constantly increasing stream of loans and mortgages whose quality deteriorated as the amount increased. Over time, this grew to massive amounts of bad debt disguised as triple-A paper."

The tram stopped, allowing passengers to exit and enter, and we shuffled around as the car filled up. The drizzle had transformed itself into a steady rain, and the shelter of the public transport was a popular idea.

"Go on," Johan prompted me.

"This continuous flow of substandard mortgage paper could not have been created without the help of the Fed and the very sloppy and accommodative oversight of both Fannie Mae and Freddie Mac. I just don't believe it was a coincidence that after the 1993 mark to market rules the Fed embarked on a very low interest rate scenario, flooding the market with cheap money. Thus, fueling the housing market into a feeding frenzy, while at the same time Congress facilitated liquidity by allowing Fannie Mae and Freddie Mac to continue to lower their underwriting standards and to gorge themselves on subprime loans."

Johan laughed at my choice of words and remarked, "I see where you are going. It makes sense and I think you are correct. There are fingerprints of involvement all over the course of events."

"It is just too convenient not to have been planned," I said and looked directly at Johan, emphasizing my point. "They began by planting the idea that lower income families should have the same access to funds and services that higher incomes enjoy. Then they make it sound as if the denial was based on race or ethnic background, not because it was a bad credit risk. Then they have community organizers intimidate those institutions that don't want to play along, and this created the subprime markets. Finally, they allow it to grow and flourish, they create legislation paving the way and promoting liquidity, and they take away marketing stumbling blocks, as in Glass-Steagall. But not before the time bomb is installed, disguised as a safety measure for the public, the 1993 mark to market rules."

Johan raised his eyebrows, surprised at the remark. Without waiting for the question, I answered, "I'll tell you why it's a time bomb. Once institutions' and banks' portfolios are filled with repackaged and overleveraged debt instruments based on this low-grade loan paper, it's only a matter of time for it to explode. Perhaps the final timing may not be predictable, but that it will happen eventually is in my mind a certainty. You can't deny that all the ingredients have been carefully put in place so that when the market turns, when the consumers stop spending and the housing market stops, then all this inventory will be exposed for what it really is, very expensive and very high-risk paper backed by hugely inflated real estate. Portfolio values will be destroyed, and in turn the mark to market rule will destroy the companies. Just as it did in the 1930's. There will be no going back. Right now, as we speak ratings are being reversed from triple A one day to junk the next. Hedge funds are imploding, and Fannie Mae and Freddie Mac stocks are in a free fall. Healthy institutions one day become takeover targets the next, on the edge of bankruptcy, and they will be bought at pennies on the dollar. And that was the real intent of the whole system. To create a scenario where perfectly good companies can be brought down to their knees and taken over at a fraction of the cost. Just as in the Great Depression, the reigning financial system and the government that it supports will be the ones to gain more power."

The tram stopped at Aeschenplatz where we exited and crossed the street. It was around two thirty in the afternoon and I knew Johan still had to finish his day, and I needed to get back to the hotel to make some calls and get in touch with the office.

Before we parted I said, "You asked me who 'they' are. 'They' are those who benefit from the scenario I just painted. 'They' are the ones who created the Federal Reserve, the power behind the United Nations and the IMF, and everyone in Congress who initiated the necessary legislation and depend on the system to stay intact, the new elite. The only way 'they' get away with it, is by promising the non-elite that 'they' will receive handouts and tokens, hence the entitlement wave the United States is engulfed by. Without it, 'they' could never make it work."

No remark whatsoever came from Johan after I stopped speaking.

He just smiled.

"I have to go, my friend," Johan said. "Tonight, come to my home and we'll have dinner." He shook my hand, and as he was about to turn, he volunteered, "One more thing, like it or not, being part of the Wall Street machine, you and I are 'they' as well."

CHAPTER 6

The house was new. Johan and his wife Varna had moved in just three months earlier and he was proud to show me around. As required by Swiss law, it contained a bomb shelter. It was equipped with air, water filtration, six months of rations, a chemical toilet, and everything needed to sustain a nuclear attack. On a hill, overlooking Basel, I knew a single-dwelling home at this location was not an inexpensive find and I was pleased to see them comfortable.

Varna cooked as she had done on previous occasions when I passed by and the uncomplicated, relaxed atmosphere felt as if at home.

At about ten thirty or so, Johan invited me into his office, offering me a cigar. He dipped his in the brandy he had poured in a large snifter, not offering me any, knowing I did not drink.

Enjoying the smoke, we were quiet for some time. No need for words, just two friends relaxing. I had the feeling he wanted to continue the earlier discussion, but I did not push and just sat in silence.

His office portrayed his achievements, pictures with heads of state, an autographed one with Greenspan, another with both the Clintons. A framed degree from the London School of Economics next to another from Cambridge. Books lined the shelves in various languages, covering subjects from religion to cash-flow analysis and error compensation in statistics. Plenty of tombstone plaques commemorating new bond issues brought to market in which Johan had been involved. Two flat-screen TV's on the wall and a quad-monitor computer on his desk with the indispensable Bloomberg system always active.

"I like your analysis and your insight is astute. I have been aware of the same for some time, but wanted to find out how you interpreted the situation. I commend you, not many see a pattern so well disguised over such a long time," Johan said, breaking the quiet. "Even so, the public in general will not believe it to be true. They just will not believe the lengths to which power will go to get what it wants. Mostly they just want their TV, their beer, to get laid, have a job, and a sense of security and be left alone for the rest."

Another long pause, while he looked at me as if to consider what to say next. Then, apparently making up his mind, he said, "As you shared your thoughts and vision, let me share a few with you. Some I know you don't know." Johan smoked his cigar, tasting the smoke and sipped his brandy. Sometimes we get a gift unwittingly and without asking. This was one of those times.

"Sell Bear Stearns and Lehman. We already have," he quietly stated. "Your new president will be a surprise. For America and for the world." That was all he said, but it was his eyes that conveyed the message that what he shared was significant.

That was information I had not expected and I had no other response than a single "What?" and again Johan took his time.

"Contrary to what most think, the voting process is, and always has been swayed and controlled by the long-term financial interests behind every nation. Ask yourself who rules the money and you find who rules the nation. Very rarely do they not get who they want as their front person, and if and when these persons do not perform what is expected of them, they are removed. Just look at your country's history and the veil of mystery associated with JFK. That was classic Northwoods, but that truth isn't fit for public knowledge." Johan continued looking at me thoughtfully, as if weighing in his mind what else he wanted to confide in me.

"What was that about the president? What do you know? Whom are you referring to?" I asked truly surprised, "And how is Northwoods relevant?"

"Follow the money. Always follow the flow of money," Johan offered, refusing a more direct response. "From where I sit, I can see the flow and most often the current speaks clearer than words ever will. There is no mistaking the loyalty of money. It only knows one owner. Its origin and destination clarify the owner's interests."

He waited as if searching for the right words. Then he said, "As for Northwoods, the idea is to blame others for self-inflicted acts of terrorism. There exists a near perverse relationship between the military/industrial complex and the Federal Reserve. JFK did two things which proved to be bad for his health. First, he wanted to end the Vietnam war thereby severely limiting military spending and expansion. Second, in June of 1963 he signed executive order 11110. In this order, he returned the power to coin money back to your Treasury Department and away from the Federal Reserve. Six months later he was publicly executed. The order never went into effect and the war continued. Coincidence? You decide."

46

Barely able to grasp the significance of his words, I pushed on trying to get as much information as I could. "And what's going to happen to Bear and Lehman?"

But all he said was, "I won't say anything else," and then a few moments later, he added, "You are correct, though, in your assessments. There will be a financial upset of unforeseen size and scope, and the Federal Reserve will step in, and it will appear as if they have provided a solution." His gaze and smile silently conveyed the fact he knew more, much more, but chose not to reveal it.

I never did get a more succinct answer from him that evening, but he continued to speak, and even though I thought he had changed the topic, he actually offered more information couched inside his sentences. As long as I had known him, he had fascinated me by his simple, but always profound perspective and impressive ability to effortlessly reduce complex scenarios to straightforward ideas and concepts. That evening was no exception.

"You know the Federal Reserve rules the money in the United States. You know as well what our position is here in Europe. We are a direct extension of them." Johan answered his own question without waiting or expecting any input from me. "There are other banks that act as we do, but we're in Switzerland, the banking capital of the world, and in Switzerland we are in no-man's land. So we can do things that otherwise would not be easily explained or justified. And when I see unusual financial interests developing among the Federal Reserve, United Nations, IMF and various Middle Eastern families that were not there before, then I know something is formulating and I keep my eyes open and follow the money."

We sat in his office and for some moments neither of us spoke. I did not want to distract his train of thought, so I said nothing and let him speak at his tempo.

Nearly absentmindedly, as if absorbed in other thoughts while studying his brandy snifter, he continued.

"Money has the peculiar ability to outline infrastructure to those who move it—you'd be amazed how much bankers know about their customers, just from seeing their funds move." Johan paused again, this time keeping his cigar alive, letting the smoke drift around him.

"Following the flow of funds, I see new alliances, arrangements and compositions of agreements and partnerships. I see the Federal Reserve with the United Nations setting up systems and agreements in the Middle East and Africa, as if they are contemplating major monetary shifts of currency preferences. Remember, the euro currency could not have been set up without the European Union having been established first as its basis. So, if and when there is a consideration of a new world currency other than the United States dollar, a governing body has to be set up first. And a governing body can only be set up if and when the political tide and players are ready to do so. The Federal Reserve is looking outside the United States to the Middle East and Africa. The tie between the Federal Reserve and the United Nations is umbilical in nature, if not recognized as such by many. The obvious next move is somebody who can make that shift from the United States to the Middle East and Africa. All I do is put two and two together and take it to its natural result."

He took a break and then said, "Let me ask you a question." And once more without waiting for my input he continued. "In a war or a military conflict, how can you predict the winner? Or better, how can you place your bets so that you will always be on the winner's side, no matter the outcome?"

A question from nowhere, seemingly not connected to the discussion at hand, but obviously associated somehow. "I don't know. How?" I answered.

"Bet both sides and you will always pick a winner," came the answer. "What is lost financing the side that loses will be recovered many, many times over by those you financed to win." Johan gave me that same smile, evidently pleased with the simple, brilliant logic of the scheme.

"This is not new," he continued. "I did not come up with this. It's been done for many centuries by men and women with immense power and wealth so that they can get more of the same."

Johan took time to sip the cognac. The smell of the alcohol was strong and mixed with the smoke it had a near irresistible effect on me. It had been decades since I had my last drink. Abstinence for me is essential. I don't know how to have one drink and I can't imagine having just one. I would want the whole bottle and then top it off with some whiter-than-the-driven-snow marching powder, so I could drink even more and not get drunk and not get wired and get more to drink and more powder, making sure the mixture was such that I could do it for days on end. And I would get some reefer and perhaps some other goodies and more booze and then some rocks and... and I would never stop again. So I don't drink.

Having refilled the snifter with the amber glowing spirit, Johan elaborated. "The Napoleonic wars were financed on both sides by the Rothschilds. They financed both sides of the First World War. They financed

England, Russia and Italy in the Second World War, including Hitler. But Hitler had no interest aligning his banking system with an international banking cartel. He wanted a central bank owned by the German state funded by gold. That is why the first thing he did when invading another nation was to plunder that country's gold from its central bank and transport it to Berlin. Not wanting to work with the international banking cartels is the real reason why Germany was finally destroyed by the Allied forces in 1945. They knew about the Holocaust for years, but that was not reason enough."

"How is this pertinent today?" I asked, fearing the answer. "Is this going on in the conflicts we are involved in right now?"

"Suffice it to say that there is no reason for the behavior of power to change if and when the outcome has been successful. Your internal domestic strife, the archaic one nobody dares mention, the one between white and black, has similarly been funded on both sides by the same group, this time by your own Congress. While fueling anger and resentment from black to white and at the same time creating guilt and fear from white to black, untold financial opportunities arise by keeping the races at each other's throats. And it's not just white and black. It includes Latinos, Asians, Native Americans and on and on. Somebody has an interest in prolonging these conflicts. It is the perfect breeding ground to buy votes. If not, it would have been resolved long ago. And again, somebody will be put in place as your president who will continue stoking the conflict. Because as long as the conflict is alive, the cry for entitlements will continue and it is the promise of entitlements that buys the votes."

I interjected, "Good point. Imagine Congress having to deal with a united and cohesive society without racial conflicts. They would not be getting away with half the stuff they pull. There is great advantage in promoting a racial divide. Just look at all the government programs in place that deal with the same inequality they work to maintain."

Johan smiled and said, "Now look outside your domestic realm. Ask yourself whom you are fighting and I will tell you their funding, however obscure and shadowy, will trace back through large international organizations and foundations to those who have interests in the Federal Reserve." Johan had stopped smiling and resumed. "There is a shift coming in loyalties—faithful friends of the past will be neglected and new alliances will be courted. Again, it is the flow of funds that leaks the truth. They want to court the more traditional Muslim nations and through them gain access to the continent of Africa. Those in control of the money have set their eyes on their next targets and their time is at hand."

"To what end? What is there to gain?" I asked.

"It is during any type of redistribution of wealth that those who control the money will gain. They gain more money, more power, more influence, more control. So by financing both sides of a conflict and by reinvigorating it, by fueling it, or just by starting one, a redistribution of wealth is originated and those who started it will win. This applies equally to your domestic issues as well as to the international ones." Johan looked at me, realizing the incendiary information he had parted with. Knowing him, he would not just give opinions, these were facts.

I marveled at the Machiavellian type of brilliance the argument portrayed. It made absolute sense and the logic worked. The ruthlessness and calculated absence of compassion, though, was another matter. It would take time for me to understand what type of ambition would, or could manipulate the markets with such indifference for suffering. But then again, history is filled with the stories of many such men and women, some revered, others despised, depending on who won and how history was written for us to read and ponder.

Johan stood up and we joined Varna in the living room for another hour or so. When I left his home in the early hours of the morning, my mind was spinning with information, full of questions unanswered.

The next day I went to Zurich to meet with the Swiss National Bank and inched my way closer to becoming one of their counterparties. After Zurich came Koln, then Bonn, and the end of the week was spent in the Netherlands, in Amsterdam and the Hague, where I did business with a few banks and large pension funds. I had wanted to take a day in the United Arab Emirates and visit two large clients in Abu Dhabi, but I opted for spending a day with Nicole in Amsterdam, then drive to Paris to catch the Sunday morning flight back home together.

We had Friday evening and Saturday to ourselves and we spent it at our leisure—dinner in Amsterdam, then lunch on Saturday in the old and stately Hotel des Indes in the Hague—we saw Vermeer's *'Girl with a Pearl Earring'* in the small Maurits House Museum close to the hotel and quietly walked the ancient streets where the thirteenth-century government's Knight's Hall still stands.

FEDERAL

At some point that Friday morning, about five thousand miles away, the new issue shares I had purchased a few weeks earlier for my own account received its final cusip designation and through the help of my assistants it was delivered and I became legal owner of record. A trivial event, which unforeseen to all would have enormous consequences for me and a few others I was still to meet.

CHAPTER 7

The rest of 2007 was uneventful other than that I was busy. Year-end has always been a time when companies close their books, dress up portfolios and most of my competition takes off. So I stayed at my desk during December and attended to my client's needs and wishes. Many were the times when I was able to transact with a new client, or one whose loyalties were not always with me, just because I was available and ready to do business, and my competition was out on vacation. December usually was one of my better months.

It was just before Christmas when something unusual occurred. My personal investments were held at the financial firm I worked for, and monthly portfolio statements were sent at the end of the third week. Upon receiving the December statement, I made a cursory check to verify the new stock issue I had bought was there and had settled in November. It was identified as a rather odd entry in the equity, or stock side of my personal portfolio. Most of my investments were in bonds, or fixed income. Experience had taught me long ago that I was terrible at picking stocks and did better if I just kept with what I knew best, bonds. At times I would stray and this was one of those occasions when I had trusted the Goldman trader selling me the issue.

Normally, an entry in my statement would name the company, amount of shares, purchase and market price, if available. But this entry read as follows:
FRB.NY—2,500; fr:A-sr—price: n/a—street—#8765ZUS$—Book-Entry; NY/
Goldman #Fed-Res; fao Citi 003301; TCMI ffao:ktp 65-4885R215
I recognized these as delivery instructions identifying the money trail, cusip and designated account recipient. The fact the Fed-Res was mentioned just meant the flow of funds was Federal funds, through Citi, ultimately into TCMI and my account, or so I thought. Even so, it did not make sense and I decided to take it up with one of my assistants as soon as possible. The date was Friday, December 21, 2007, and the earliest I would be able to do so was the middle of the following week due to the long holiday weekend.

FEDERAL

Christmas came and went and so did New Years. The first trading day of the year, January 2, 2008, started off with an ominous 220.86 drop of the Dow, a menacing message. The public likes to follow the Dow to get an indication of how the economy fares, but the Dow is probably the least informative indicator of all as the industrials are comprised of only thirty stocks, constantly altered to keep the index strong. Nonetheless, that first day of trading in 2008 justly predicted worse times to come.

When economic times become uncertain and stock markets drop, the tendency of the public at large is to move its funds onto safer grounds, a so-called 'flight to safety' and rightfully so. The obvious safer grounds are always to be found in bonds, in fixed income. And the beginning of 2008 was no exception to this rule.

As the economic world became shakier, the effect of flight to safety became more apparent when large amounts of funds started to move from equities into fixed income. The Dow dropped from a high of 13,279 in early January to a low of 11,634 within the course of three weeks, warning the world of troubled financial times ahead. Meanwhile, the bond market was on fire and those working in it were busy, very busy.

January, February and March were a blur. The ten year Treasury Note dropped about sixty basis points in yield, which meant that the price went through the roof and that was good news to those investing in bonds.

At the same time, banks were going out of business, companies were laying off people, housing prices were collapsing, and the Dow continued its downward spiral. And as we were doing trades and making sure that the deals we had done were put to bed correctly, I lost track of that odd entry in my portfolio. I do remember telling my assistant, Kevin, about it and asking him to check on it. And he may have and he may not. It does not matter anymore. The fact is, we were all too busy, and I forgot about it altogether.

But my memory of the odd entry was jarred back to life when I received a letter addressed to me at my work around the middle of March 2008. The envelope came delivered by special courier. Kevin received it while I was on the phone. He signed for it, only after submitting a business card and identification to the courier demonstrating that he was acting as my personal assistant.

A formal envelope, creamy white in color. Engraved in large, red, bold letters, the front read, "PRIVATE and CONFIDENTIAL" next to my name and address. The sender's information at the top left only displayed a round emblem with a one-line address "Washington, DC 20551," under it. No company name, no person's name, just the one line. The weight somehow felt wrong in my hand and as I turned it over I understood why. The verso was sealed using vermillion wax, embossed with what appeared to be the same emblem as on the cover. I turned the envelope again to identify the design and to my surprise it read, "Federal Reserve System."

Kevin looked at me as I inspected the delivery and I realized he was waiting to see me open it. Obviously he too had read who the sender was and was hanging around to learn more. He had a way of hovering, which on several occasions had prompted me to say, "Why don't you ask what you want, instead of hanging around hoping I will guess what it is you are looking for?" But to no avail, and that day was no exception. Overweight, but not fat, not too tall, but not small in stature either, I assumed his plain physical characteristics mimicked his personality and he was not one to assert himself. I could feel him loom in my vicinity trying to gain a glimpse of what was in the envelope.

"Thank you Kevin, I got it," I said and turned my back to him. This was none of his business and I did not need spectators watching over my shoulder as I opened my mail. Brushing my own curiosity aside, I placed the object nonchalantly on my desk, picked up the phone, and called a client while Kevin retreated back to his area with his tail between his legs. When I was positive no one was looking, I picked up the envelope, broke the seal and took out the letter.

FEDERAL RESERVE SYSTEM
21 Constitution Ave NW
Washington, DC 20551

March 13, 2008

Mr. Stephen Vinson
Managing Director
Templar Capital Markets, Inc.
6600 N. Andrews
Ft Lauderdale, FL 33040

Dear Mr. Vinson:

As an established shareholder with privileges, your presence is requested at the Steering Committee hearings in preparation of the full assembly to be held June, 2008 in Chantilly, Virginia. The Committee will meet at the offices of Warburg Private Bank, Parkring 12, Zurich, Switzerland commencing May 14, 2008, at 10:00 hrs. local time. Attendance is favored through May 18, 2008, 12:00 hrs.

Presentation of this letter and at least one form of international ID verifying your identity will be required upon entering the facility. Your personal entry code for this sole event is set at:

32-B405BC2

A full program disclosure is being forwarded to you under separate cover by the hosting Institution, including your private biometric password generator. Upon receipt of the generator, follow the instructions carefully so as to personalize the item to your sole identity.

In case you require further assistance, please do not hesitate contacting me

At Your Service:

Virginia Gottirgio / 1st Assistant - European Steering Committee
Tel: 202-452-3000 -- Fax: 202-452-3819

I was surprised as to how this formal invitation ended up on my desk and after reading the correspondence a few times, I still couldn't imagine why it was addressed to me. Only after I realized I'd been equally at a loss about the unusual entry in my portfolio did I surmise a connection between the two and decided to ask Kevin. Walking over to his desk, which was only fifteen feet or so from mine, I asked, "Kevin, remember the equity entry in my portfolio, that new issue I bought back in November? Did you ever get an answer on that thing?"

Kevin looked up and cocked his head sideways in an expression of wonder while trying to recall. It took him a few moments, and his response was, "I'm sorry, Stephen. I didn't tell you, but I asked settlement if a mistake was made, and they answered that there wasn't. There is no outstanding DK or an unsatisfied delivery attempt. So I assumed all was well, and it slipped my mind to let you know. I'm sorry."

I understood his answer. The assumption was that all contracts were satisfied and that we received and paid what we agreed on. So no reason to look any deeper into the issue.

But that didn't answer my question as to what was actually delivered into my account or why I had received this letter. I needed to satisfy my curiosity and get to the bottom of this.

"OK, do me a favor please," I instructed Kevin. "First, check on that issue again and this time find out *exactly* what was tendered. Secondly, retrace the delivery back to who issued the cusip and what occurred during settlement that caused an alteration."

My voice must have sounded somewhat annoyed, judging from Kevin's reaction—he nodded and replied, "I'm on it" and was busy immediately, apparently feeling my irritation that an issue I had brought up previously had not been taken care of to my satisfaction. It's not that I needed to be catered to at every whim, but where money is concerned I had learned that not confirming unresolved matters can cost vast amounts of funds. I had hammered this into my two assistants. So the assumption that all was well was just not good enough, and he knew it. The bottom line, though, was that the fault was mine. I had not verified with Kevin, and I had assumed it was taken care of. It was not a big issue, or at least it didn't seem to be and I was sure he'd find out what the facts were soon enough.

Soon enough came that same day at about two-thirty in the afternoon. Less than four hours after I had had my discussion with him, Kevin asked to talk to me privately in one of the conference rooms lining the trading floor.

Entering the glass room without bothering to take a seat in one of the eight leather chairs around the table, he came to the point at once.

"Do you know what was delivered into your personal account?" he asked hurriedly, eyes wide open with a mixed expression of disbelief and excitement.

"That's what I asked you to find out twice now," I said with a barely disguised hint of exasperation. "What is it?"

Ignoring my tone and demeanor, he continued speaking, obviously wound up.

"When I ran the cusip it made no sense at first. Bloomberg lists it as a non-traded security of a private company. Clearly that was wrong, so I called settlement and asked them to reconfirm the cusip, which they did and it matched, but they could not confirm the issue itself because, again, it was an unregistered, private security. I then asked them who issued the final cusip and was told it came directly from Goldman."

That made sense as Goldman Sachs was the underwriter of the issue from whom I had purchased the shares.

"So I called Goldman and asked them to verbally state the issue to me, what was actually delivered into the account," Kevin went on, "And the answer was 'Federal Reserve System class-A senior twenty-five hundred shares." Here he stopped so as to gauge my reaction, but I had none. I just looked at him knowing this was an impossibility.

Reacting to my stare, he reiterated, just louder, "I am not shitting you, they said, 'Federal Reserve Bank New York class-A senior twenty-five hundred shares' and I asked them if they were sure and they said they were and I said 'OK, thank you' and hung up and then I came to see you." The whole sentence was voiced in one breath as if it were one very big uninterrupted word. His voice excited, he knew the ramifications of the information he relayed.

I sat down in one of the chairs and Kevin followed suit. This made no sense. But I now knew one thing for certain, the letter and the stock information were connected. Another thing we both knew was that nobody, and I mean NOBODY can own Federal Reserve stock. But here it was, in my portfolio, confirmed by settlement through my assistant and then through a letter from the Federal Reserve itself. So I decided to minimize public knowledge. I asked him offhandedly if he had told Sharon, my other assistant, or anybody else for that matter.

"I just hung up with them and spoke to nobody," he said. "I went to you immediately."

Sharon had been eyeing the activity between Kevin and me and was standing behind her desk, looking at us through the glass walls. Understandably curious about what was going on and feeling entitled to be in on the activity as one of my assistants, she moved to join us in the conference room.

"Kevin, don't discuss this with anyone. Leave it just between you and me until further notice. And that means not discussing it with Sharon either."

She knocked and without waiting for an answer pried open the heavy plate-glass door.

"Stephen, Nicole called and so did Anthony. Anything I can help with?" was her innocent enough attempt at getting in on the action.

"OK, thank you—and no, all is under control. Thank you." I said, dismissing her and her offer. She waited just a second or two before she closed the door and returned to her desk. I could see puzzlement and disappointment on her face, and I knew she would quiz him extensively, wanting to know what was up.

Sharon is an attractive woman, mid-thirties, aggressive and smart. Kevin, even though a few years older, was no match for her persistence if and when she put on the charm. They had worked together many years and knew about each other's professional activities so that each could take over at any point on any issue. Not being let in on something must not have felt good, and I understood, but that's where it was for the moment and I didn't want to indulge her feelings just now. So I warned him in no uncertain terms that this issue was between us and that the only time Sharon would know about any of it was when I decided she needed to know. I stressed the point, making sure he understood I was serious, and I believe he did after hearing my tone of urgency.

Getting back to my desk, I called Nicole and reconfirmed a dinner we had agreed to go to over the weekend. Then I called Anthony.

My son's activities precluded him from staying in touch on a regular basis. His responsibilities were not clear to me, nor were they supposed to be. Nor did I ask. The previous time he called me must have been about six weeks earlier from Singapore. He had mentioned trying to reach me from East Timor at some point. So it was a pleasure hearing from him—even more so as he left me a number and it confirmed his general location as originating in East Timor.

I dialed 011-670-741-9951 and listened to the ring from the other side of the world after a long, crackling connecting silence.

"Dad, that you?" came the voice on the other side.

"Anthony, good hearing your voice, Son. How are you?" I knew better than to ask what was going on, or where he was, or anything relating to the details of his situation. He would tell me only what was necessary.

"Hey, Dad, it's all good here, nothing we can't handle. The reason I called is because I will be in Germany for some training around the middle of May. Not sure exactly about the final location but we'll probably end up somewhere in the south, probably Pfullendorf. It's a combined NATO/United Nations deal and they want us there for about three weeks. I thought if you're in the area we can meet and catch up a bit. What you think?"

I could hear people speak and laugh in the background, some in English, some in Portuguese, others unintelligibly, and the sound of bottles clanking. Sounded as if he was having some down-time and I was touched he thought of me and reached out. It was unusual for him to know that far in advance where he would be, but I guess with NATO it's all set up and arranged long before.

"I have to be in Switzerland mid-May, and I can easily drive anywhere and meet up," I said. As if needing an excuse, I decided on the spot to accept the letter's invitation.

"You gonna see Johan?" Anthony asked. Over the years my son had learned to appreciate the knowledge my friend possessed, and he had not been shy asking about the finer details of the Swiss Institution and its place in international finance. Not always receiving the answers he wanted, Anthony respected him, and Johan enjoyed the young man's interest. "Give him my regards if you do."

"I will." Then as the background noise swelled to a crescendo I asked, "What's going on behind you?"

I could hear Anthony laugh and say a few quick words to those with him that I didn't understand, other than to recognize it was Portuguese, and the noise subsided. "We're staying in this shit-hole in Baucau, and the only decent spot is this bar close to the beach. But it's the Wild West over here. No laws and all outlaws, guns everywhere, and too much booze and dope. I'm glad I am not alone." He laughed again. "OK Pops, hold on to this number—it's my cell phone and I'll keep this one for a bit, I think. We'll be in touch before May I'm sure—I love you." And with that, the line went dead even before I could respond with my expression of love for him.

I had to use Google Earth to find Baucau, and it indeed was in East Timor. I knew enough about the situation there to know it was volatile to say the least—a newly created independent nation, separated after twenty-five years of Indonesian rule in 1999, with its share of problems of corruption, political infighting, war-lords and a basically lawless societal rule of order controlled by force and intimidation. The capital, Dili, crawled with special-ops mercenaries from the world over, openly armed to the teeth. What I didn't know was that the United States had an interest in the area, but then again, why not? Where there is strife and unrest, there is something to be gained, especially if and when you support and finance both sides, I was told. Anthony had sounded unconcerned, while I had to suppress the uncomfortable feeling my son was in danger, or at least in a dangerous environment. Looking down from space on the small colonial village somewhat eased my fears, as if Google Earth personalized and untangled the mishmash of homes and huts and dirt roads and made it seem safer.

Chapter 8

I took no further action that Friday afternoon in March 2008 when I found out I had become an owner of the impossible-to-obtain Federal Reserve System stock. After my talk with Kevin I went home, making sure the information was to remain between us and nobody else. Nor did I want him to speak with clearing and request the correct security to be delivered, which would have been the appropriate thing to do in order to resolve the delivery error. The fact was nobody had made a claim since the November 30 settle, and I was not about to.

I spoke briefly with Sharon, putting her at ease that my talk with Kevin was personal and had no bearing on her work. Thus sufficiently assured that I had covered my bases, I went home early that afternoon prior to market close, which was uncharacteristic for me.

That weekend I spent doing mostly research—trying to find out how a private citizen could become part owner of the Federal Reserve, and how the ownership and structure of the Federal Reserve operates. Having been delivered Federal Reserve stock registered under my name meant that I had become a part owner of this institution—a small owner percentage wise, but an owner nonetheless. And apparently owners of the specific stock I was delivered were invited into meetings the nature of which I had absolutely no clue. But that would change soon enough.

I had been under the impression that private individuals could not become shareholders of the Federal Reserve System by statute, but I learned I was wrong. The system is governed by a seven-member board of governors, operating out of Washington, D.C., appointed by the president of the United States. This board is advised by the Federal Advisory Council, which consists of twelve advisors, each one representing one of twelve districts formed by twelve privately owned Federal Reserve banks situated throughout the United States. It divides the country into twelve districts. It is the Federal Reserve Bank of New York, though, which is the all-powerful and ruling bank. The Federal Open Market Committee, whose main task is, among others, the setting of monetary policy and interest rates, consists of the seven-member board of governors plus a rotation of five (of twelve) Federal Reserve bank presidents.

I also learned that any private bank in the nation calling itself a national bank, about thirty-five hundred in total, is considered a member bank. These member banks are required to invest in and buy shares of the Federal Reserve bank located in their district, up to 3% of their (the member banks) asset size on which they earn a fixed 6% dividend, as established in the Federal Reserve Act of 1913.

And then I found in the Act itself how it was possible to gain possession of this stock. Although there is no public mechanism for the exchange of private ownership of the shares, an arcane provision in the Act allows for personal possession of up to twenty-five thousand dollars per individual. Such ownership would then be entered in the books as public stock. This proviso never had been called upon or exercised, according to the Federal Reserve itself—not until November 2007, when they were unintentionally issued to me.

But that information didn't explain how I was delivered Federal Reserve stock instead of the new issue I had bought. I realized, though, the few occasions in the clearing process where errors occurred were those when humans were involved in entering information into the system. Specifically, where it concerns the manual cusip entry or designated account information. So something must have occurred at one of these spots that had caused the wrong product to be delivered into my account. Evidently a transaction involving shares of the Federal Reserve was occurring at the same moment as my transaction, in the same trading house, on the same settlement desk and more than likely by the same settlement clerk, trying to finalize multiple transactions on a Friday afternoon. I've seen huge errors occur as a result of a hectic end-of-day rush to get everything in the system before the Federal Reserve window closes. If it is too late, the funds will not flow, and settlement will be delayed until after the weekend.

I realized I was at the receiving end of such a rush error and I knew compliance should have been informed about it and the resulting letter, but I was too fascinated with the situation, I rationalized, and decided to take the weekend to think it over. The promised "background material" and what that "background" entailed intrigued me to no end. Clearly, I was willing to take the risk in order to find out what was on its way to me.

Another week passed, and I had done nothing about the shares that had somehow found their way into my portfolio. And as happens so often when decision making is delayed, the situation made its mind up for me.

FEDERAL

About eight or nine days after the discovery of my new ownership, another courier showed up at the office asking for me. This time I made myself available and walked up to the front desk, just outside the trading floor. A well-groomed man dressed in a dark suit and tie, no uniform but a corporate look, met me in the reception area. He offered no name, nor any formal greeting, no handshake, and he wasted no time.

"Mr. Stephen Vinson, I assume?" was his question. Upon my affirmative response he requested, "Can I please verify your identity?"

"Who is asking?" I wanted to know, already suspecting the answer.

"I am a private courier employed to distribute confidential and time-sensitive material." No smiles, just those words as if they would be enough. And they were.

After a satisfactory perusal of my driver's license, he opened his attaché case on the lounge table and pulled out a clipboard which subsequently he offered, "Sign next to your name please."

"What is it exactly I am signing?" I inquired.

"I am to deliver paperwork for your eyes only which can not be released without your formal acceptance." No smiles.

I looked the guy over and knew he was delivering the anticipated background material. Nothing about the man in front of me betrayed him as being a courier, or working for any company. Sunglasses in his hand, he looked fit and in shape with short blond hair, a dark suit, light-grey shirt with a dark-blue tie, and shoes that didn't fit the attire—flat black without laces, fit for running, certainly not for office. An odd and in some way alarming combination.

"And where is this paperwork originating from?" I inquired again, trying for a more elaborate reply.

"You have been requested to attend a meeting, as you must be aware of by now. This is the information you will need for the occasion."

The sentence was spoken as if rehearsed, without emotion, smile, or any social grace. With that he produced a non-descript one inch thick manila folder from the same case and handed it over to me. An eerie guy.

"Is there anything else I may be of assistance with?" was his final question, and upon my denial he closed the briefcase and walked out of the office. No goodbye, no handshake, no fuck you, no nothing.

"That was weird," giggled the secretary from behind the desk. All she witnessed all day long were people entering or leaving. Nobody hung around, aside from the odd male flirting with her pretty face and sexy body. So the exchange between us certainly was a diversion for her and she was right, the whole event was weird—the lack of etiquette, the few words spoken, no handshakes, no greetings, and no goodbyes.

"Yes it was, did he say anything when he came in?" I asked her.

"All he said was your name and asked if you were in, that's all—he creeped me out." She giggled again, seeing some humor in the event somehow, then she resumed answering and transferring phone calls.

Walking over to my desk I inspected the folder. No distinguishing marks on the outside, no name nor return address. In it was a binder, appearing to be some type of strong, rigid, light-grey impregnated linen. It was secured with three cotton strands, each looped through reinforced holes in the overlapping flap and tied to another three exposed buttons at the base. Each strand in turn was fortified to the exterior by a similar vermillion seal wax as was used on the letter, hot dripped, joining the thread and material, pressed down with an implement leaving a now-familiar visible seal in the wax. My name appeared at the top left engraved in dark burgundy as if woven into the cloth. Very impressive and very expensive little package.

Sitting down, I took care to return the package to its manila folder, placing it amongst the typical mess of my trading desk—phones, keyboards, gadgets, papers, yellow pads, notes, pens and pencils, pictures, three coffee cups (one of them empty), and the uneaten remnants of lunch. I was not about to open it right there on the floor, for everybody to see. At the same time, my curiosity as to the contents knew no bounds. So I stood up, straightened up my desk to an extent, talked to Sharon and Kevin for a moment informing them I could be reached at home, picked up the parcel, and left the office.

Once at home I still didn't give in to my curiosity. First I took Sparky for a long walk on the beach and then fed him. He always attracts lots of attention. Sometime earlier I had gone through the effort of locating a nice bright-red hair dye at the local Walgreen. Using the ingredients in the package, I prepared the bleach and took Sparky in the shower and proceeded to bleach his tail, until the black was transformed into a light grey. Next I applied the red dye to the plumy retriever's tail and let it set. The whole thing took close to an hour and a half and not once did Sparky protest, laying down between my knees, trusting what I did to him was OK. When it was all done, he looked magnificent. A pitch-black retriever with a bright-red tail and I believe he was actually proud of it. People would stop us and ask what kind of dog he was, and I would answer, "A red tail retriever, very rare," and walk on as if it were perfectly normal, with Sparky donning his red plume in the air as if to say, "I look pretty good."

I made myself a double espresso and sat down in my home office with the promised background material looking at me. The presentation was so impressive I hardly wanted to destroy it, so I carefully cracked the wax seals, undid the three ties, and opened the flap inspecting the inside. Two files, each wrapped in a double layer of dark-grey paper, elegantly tied by a red and blue silk ribbon. One of the files contained writing, the second a thin rectangular box that caught my attention first.

Untying the ribbon, then unwrapping the grey paper, I was confronted with an unmarked white box about a quarter-inch thick, hinged on one side. Once opened, it revealed a letter and a clean white surface with two simple cutouts, one of which held a thin credit-card-sized silver implement and the other a dark brown leather etui, or small ornamental case. The letter had the simple word "Instructions" printed on it.

I have always been a sucker for gadgets and this obviously was the biometric password generator referred to in the letter. I was impressed. Taking it from its snug compartment, it felt solid in my hand, and its visual simplicity betrayed its complexity. A round push button in the middle, two rows of buttons numbered zero through nine and the letters A through F below, a biometric device for reading fingerprints at the bottom, and a rectangular LCD screen on top.

The letter stated I was to hold down the power button for five seconds, initializing the device, and scroll past a few statements in the LCD until the final one read, "initiate," then place my finger of choice on the biometric touch-pad and follow the directions. After having repeated the placement three times the screen confirmed, "recorded." Next, I was to enter a six-digit alphanumeric password of my choice into the keypad and repeat this step twice, followed again by the "recorded" message.

The letter explained that upon entering the facility in Zurich, I was to use this generator at the premises. When requested, I would have to feed the six-figure alphanumeric code I just recorded into my generator. Once it was accepted, I would need to place my finger on the fingerprint pad. That done, I was to enter the code I received in the letter into my machine, which would then furnish a final cipher that would grant me access. The instructions explained this code would work on location only, so I was warned against trying it out, as that would require reinitiating a new unique-password sequence. Talk about security, this one was intense and thorough.

Sipping my double espresso, I turned my attention next to the remaining wrapped documents and placed them on my desk. The sheet count was a disappointing three, and I suddenly realized that I had turned a corner. I could not go back. Before receipt of this material I still had the option to call the number at the bottom of the letter and inform them of the error, or tell settlement about it and have it corrected. But I had allowed the situation to take over and let it decide for me. I knew what I was doing though. I very well knew what decision I was making by not deciding. After all I had read about the Federal Reserve, and after my discussions with Johan, this opportunity, this occurrence was just too intriguing to pass up.

So here it was, right in front of me, a small pile of information I was sure was not meant for public scrutiny, but it had my name all over it.

The cover page outlined an itinerary for the meeting in Zurich. It introduced a private contact person, named Gustav, and his direct phone number. Assigned specifically to me, he could arrange for lodging, take note of specific dietary needs, make any reservations I would want, and be available to cater to any requests I might have.

The pages briefly described the topics to be discussed on each day of the conference. The outline was synoptic and didn't give any further indication on the depth of the information or its dissemination.

The first day was informal, with a luncheon and cocktails later in the afternoon followed by an introduction meeting early in the evening. The second and third days were to deal with financial markets and the upcoming United States elections. A specific point was made to expect outside speakers from Fannie Mae and Freddie Mac, a guy from the Service Employees International Union and others. Topics ranged from the subprime housing markets, to rating agencies, to special exposures in the derivative markets and some specific companies were to be discussed. Bear Stearns, AIG and Lehman Brothers were mentioned by name and it occurred to me that not six months earlier Johan had told me to sell two of these. By that time, Bear Stearns had already folded in spectacular fashion and I wondered what was to happen to Lehman and AIG.

Reading on, I learned that we could expect a surprise speaker, name withheld, representing the Federal Reserve. He would discuss current and future international financial trends, tied in with the presidential elections. And a Middle Eastern visitor was announced, again name withheld, who would illustrate the ease of movement of assets through the system. What system they referred to was unknown to me, but I figured I would find out at the meeting itself.

The fourth day would be spent discussing actual conflict areas in the world. Cited were Iran/Israel, Egypt, Libya/NATO, Sudan and Yemen Al Qaeda concentration, the Haqqani Network and other hotspots. Emphasis would be on financing and allocation of resources, which at that moment made no sense to me, but would become clear soon enough.

The last day, Sunday, was set up as an informal day with a final luncheon and opportunity for some casual time to spend with friends and associates.

Succinct as the information proved to be, the subjects were intriguing, but any details of content had been omitted and the lack of more in-depth, or incendiary information which I had secretly hoped for, disappointed me somewhat. Nonetheless, I knew the material had not been intended for my eyes and I felt as if I had been spying into someone's private journal. The feeling had kept me from sleeping. So, the next morning, long before daybreak, I took Sparky for a walk in the dark and while sitting on the beach, with only the wind and the waves washing over the sand, I sensed the previous night's reading, sparse as it was, to be the precursor to an absolute and total change of my life. The feeling was unsettling and disturbing. Somehow this would come back to bite me. How I didn't know, but I could not shake the premonition.

Even so, I changed nothing, never discussed the mix-up with compliance or settlement and kept everything quiet. Nor did I inform anybody I was to attend the Zurich meeting. Not Nicole, no colleagues, no sales manager, no assistants, nobody. I was free to travel for business as I saw fit, so no questions would be posed if I were to leave on a trip.

Once the meeting was over, I would probably know what to do next. And then, in one of those rare, lucid forward-looking flashes, it occurred to me that to put some cash aside would not be a bad idea, just in case. In case for what I was not sure, but the idea sounded good and made sense.

The next weeks passed slowly. Kevin didn't bring the issue up again, for which I was grateful. Business was good, but I felt absent and was preoccupied. Under normal circumstances the activity of the markets and the subsequent actions of my clients would have been highly welcomed and taken advantage of. But I suffered from a sense of loss over not being able to discuss with anyone what was going on. I had been tempted to discuss the issue with Johan, but decided against it, he being too close to the source.

Nicole noticed my lack of attention, and after having tried unsuccessfully to pry information from me, she made herself scarce while feeling rejected and I made no efforts to alter her sentiments. Anthony called once more and confirmed the dates he would be at Pfullendorf as Wednesday, May 6 through Monday, May 28 and we agreed I would firm up with him later as to when we would visit. The only one giving me a sense of fulfillment and distraction was Sparky, whose prime directive was none other than be with me.

Years prior I had set up a trust in Luxemburg with a local attorney as the trustee, without disclosing myself as the settlor which made my ownership hard to identify. My attorney set up a second trust with himself and the first trust as the owners, giving the first trust 100% voting power. Subsequently a third trust was formed, controlled 100% by the second, thus fully disguising any ownership identities. This third trust in turn formed a legal corporation in Brussels, Belgium, specializing in the buying and selling of antique books and illuminated manuscripts.

As I have been a long-time collector of such antiques, I would deal with the European auction houses through this corporation, who would then invoice me in the United States and a "legal" flow of funds would be established. The beauty was that no product needed be shipped. An invoice from the "art dealer" would be enough to move funds overseas, which would then be transferred to subsequent accounts so that tracing it would be practically impossible. My precaution in moving the money proved well worth it, as I found out later.

I arranged to leave for Amsterdam on Saturday, May 10, 2008, and I planned to spend a day or so there. Instead of renting a car I decided on taking the train from Amsterdam to Basel on Monday, then visit Johan on Tuesday and continue the same day to Zurich to spend the night there in preparation of the meeting on May 14. Not having a clue of what to expect in Zurich, I felt a mixture of excitement and anxiety in anticipation each time thought passed my mind. A feeling that became pronouncedly more acute as the date drew closer.

Leaving the usual instructions with my assistants and arranging Sparky's care with my neighbor, Carol, I left for Amsterdam, arriving the following morning at about eight o'clock at Schiphol Airport. I took a cab and checked in at the Marriott on the Stadhouderskade in the center of the city. Feeling refreshed after showering and a two-hour nap, I went for a walk into the city.

FEDERAL

As the final destination of my trip drew closer, I was at odds on how to deal with my emotions. Doubt had crept in plenty of times, usually in the early morning hours when I would wake, wondering why I had let the situation evolve to this point. I could easily have refused the package after receiving the letter. After all, I was a registered securities dealer and I knew the absence of corrective action on my side could very well threaten my livelihood and place my registration and business in jeopardy. Even so, my curiosity was piqued to the max, and the suspense of being on the inside of one of the most secretive societies in the world knew no equal. What caused my discomfort was the jarring sensation that I was in way over my head and was involved in something much bigger and more powerful than I could ever imagine. It was with these pervasive feelings occupying me that I went looking for lunch. I was in no mood for company.

The Café Americain was just across the bridge from the Marriott. Springtime, when it is sunny and not windy, is when Amsterdam is at its best. It draws out the crowds after having been cloistered indoors during the winter months. The terrace in front of the Café was packed with them. Continuing my stroll I found another spot on the Leidse Plein, next to the Opera Hall, where I landed at an empty table. Amsterdam is not a boring city, nor is its population. Sitting at my table, I was thoroughly involved in the spectacle of those passing by. It took the worry off my mind and helped put me at ease.

After lunch, I called Nicole, telling her I arrived in one piece and that all was well. Prior to leaving I had taken the time to apologize for my non-communication and shutting her out. I couldn't tell her what was going on, though, as I didn't want her to know. Plausible deniability was the best defense in case questions were ever raised. In the event Nicole was asked how I became involved in this Federal Reserve thing, she would know nothing.

The rest of the day was spent roaming the old streets, taking in the beautiful architecture, and doing some light shopping. Returning to the hotel at about six o'clock, I ordered room service, watched a movie, and packed my bags preparing for the next stage of my trip up the Rhine on my way to Basel and beyond.

I had probably done the train ride from Amsterdam to Basel and back a minimum of ten times, and even though the ride was close to eleven hours, it never bored me. Following the Rhine River upstream, the fluvial highway since the dawn of man in Europe, the views were astounding. History unfolds itself at each turn. Ancient strongholds—some in ruins, others gloriously maintained and transformed into expensive retreats and hotels, or still dynastically inhabited going back many, many centuries—flock the banks. Imposing structures quietly guard the river from strategic high points, observing traffic and the passage of goods coming and going. The magnificence and majestic splendor was awe-inspiring. The strength and imposing supremacy these bastions depict still intimidates and commands respect. It was a good background against which to contemplate my journey and what was to come.

The Basel Hilton was within walking distance from the train station. Leaving the Bahnhof through the Switzerland exit, I walked the few blocks and booked myself into the hotel.

My visit with Johan the following day was pleasant, without any deep discussion about the Federal Reserve or world affairs or any such earth-shattering topics. Lunch was with two other traders I knew well, and the four of us had a nice time just taking it easy. When bidding my farewell to Johan, he wished me luck with what he assumed was my reason for visiting Zurich, my dealings with the Swiss National Bank. It had become a good client many years prior, not the least because of Johan's intervention in my favor.

I thought it a coincidence when he informed me, while parting ways, that he had to be in Zurich as well in the following days, but I didn't ponder the issue for long.

Later that afternoon I eased into the Sheraton Neues Schloss Zurich Hotel on the Stockerstrasse. I liked the place, unassuming from the outside with great comfort and service on the inside. The location was perfect, being only four blocks from the Parkring address where the conference was to be held. I spent the rest of the afternoon and early evening browsing the waterfront, letting my mind drift as I gazed over the lake in an effort to find a semblance of peace. Returning to the hotel, I ate a light snack in my room and turned on the TV. Morning would come soon enough.

CHAPTER 9

Wednesday, May 14, 2008

I left the hotel at twenty minutes to ten in the morning and walked the few blocks to the Parkring address. Not sure what was expected of me, I took the password generator, my passport with the letter and the folder in a small attaché case. The mild and sunny weather made the walk pleasant and gave it a peaceful quality.

I had called Nicole again the previous evening and indicated that I would be attending an important meeting the next day. Somehow a feeling of being lost had overwhelmed me and even though I was used to traveling alone and moving from hotel to hotel, it never had the effect on me as it had that evening. It was unsettling and I wanted to hear Nicole's voice and be reassured by the familiarity of her presence in my life. So we spoke and talked about our life together and what we would do when I returned home. But much as I needed emotional comfort, I knew the source of the imbalance was within me and could not be filled from without. I left the call feeling empty and insecure.

The building was not what I expected. Three-story granite and red brick with a turret on one corner, resembling a large and expensive patrician's home from the nineteenth century. There was a well-manicured garden and lawn surrounding the structure, a small parking strip in front at street level, and a well-manicured driveway leading onto the grounds.

I noted the absence of activity and only a few cars in front, and it didn't seem to be the correct address until I saw the armed guards. Similar in attire and armament as those I encountered when entering the Swiss Institution, the guards wore Heckler and Koch MP5 submachine guns, two Glock side arms each, and the same black uniforms with only the Swiss colors on the right shoulder. Two just outside the gate and two inside.

Approaching the entrance, I was addressed by one. He said, "Passport, bitte schön," which once produced was checked against an electronic list on a handheld device. "Herr Stephen Vinson, wilkommen. Please proceed to the main entrance for further identification." And I was free to enter the compound. The apparent quiet of the building and its surroundings was deceptive at best. Walking up the driveway, I noticed many more armed personnel in similar uniforms all over the grounds. Hidden from the street, a fleet of at least ten stretch limos was parked on the left of the building and as I was walking, two more limos passed slowly by me.

At the main entrance another three guards coordinated the final security measures. Producing the letter for verification, I was asked to initiate the password generator. I turned the device on and the little screen read "Pers Passw" which returned a "Place Finger" message after I successfully entered my six-digit code. Having read my fingerprint, the screen flashed, "ID Valid" for a few seconds followed by "Enter Code." Here I typed the code specified in the letter, being careful not to screw it up.

I was no longer alone. Aside from the three guards, the limos had produced three attendees wanting to enter the building as well. One of them was similarly busy entering his information and the other two were patiently waiting, speaking to each other in muted tones. The final message on my little bio-generator screen was a ten-digit alphanumeric hexadecimal code, which was checked against another handheld device, into which the guard had also entered the same code from my letter. The final passwords being identical, my letter was returned. One of the armed guards opened the doors, and I was allowed in, just like that.

Entering a foyer with paneled walls and double glass doors, I was met by a well-dressed gentleman who was obviously waiting for me and aware of my identity.

"Mr. Vinson, it is an honor having you as our guest. My name is Gustav and I will be at your service. I understand this is your first meeting. I am correct?"

Well dressed in a charcoal tuxedo, white shirt, and silk bow-tie, Gustav extended his hand, welcoming me. A small earpiece was visible by the curled wire extending from behind his lower ear, disappearing into his suit at the neck. I confirmed this was my first meeting and after exchanging some pleasantries about traveling to the location, he said, "Identification tags are not issued, but if you wish you can attach this button to your lapel that will give access to your name and credentials if you desire them to be known. Of course there is no obligation at all to wear this."

He handed me a laminated ID card that resembled a United States driver's license and a gold button with a bright-blue enameled top the size of a United States quarter. Within the blue enamel a number and letter were visible inlaid in gold: 7R. The back of the button had a sharp pin with fastener so that it would stay put once attached. The whole thing was quite beautiful and subtly elegant.

"If you do choose to wear the pin, your personal identification information will be available to those wanting to know. Likewise, if you wish to inquire about somebody's identity, and they are wearing the button, all you have to do is supply me with the number and I will furnish the information. The information supplied will match what appears on your card."

Here Gustav pointed at the ID card. I noted it contained my stats: full name, company and location, telephone numbers (including cell phone), and a current picture. It occurred to me that I had not supplied anybody with my cell phone or a current picture.

Gustav continued while I was still examining the card. "It is appreciated not to directly address those wearing the button until you have been supplied with their credentials. The assigned number on your button is yours and will not vary at other meetings in the future. We don't issue attendee lists, and we have found this process to be discreet and effective."

Taking the pin, I put it in my suit jacket's side pocket, not being sure if I wanted to wear it as of yet, if at all, but appreciating the relative anonymity it offered. I held on to my ID card, being somewhat intrigued with how they obtained my picture, which didn't come from my driver's license or passport, I was sure. But the simplicity and efficiency of the system overruled my wonderings, and I couldn't stop but admire the typical practicality of Germanic inventiveness.

"One more thing, regard the pin as an invitation to be approached by those you don't know as of yet and vice versa. Conversely, by not wearing it, you are indicating your desire not to be engaged."

"Thank you, Gustav," I said. "What is the decorum from here on?"

"First of all, Herr Vinson, I am here to be of assistance only to you. If and when you need me and can not find me, please feel free to ask any of the staff for me. I will never be far or unavailable. I would appreciate it, though, if you could confine your requests and questions to my person only, as we all have designated attendees to care for." He paused for a second as if apologetic about what he was going to say. "One last formality, if I may. There are no cell phones, PDAs, laptops, or recording devices of any kind allowed inside the building, including cameras. So when you enter, be so kind as to release any of these items to me for safekeeping. All entrances are supplied with detection devices that will pick up anything electronic you may be carrying, just in case you forget to deliver them to my attention."

He smiled as he gave me this information. A very nice way of telling me I should not try sneaking something in. So I surrendered my cell phone and was assured it would be there waiting for me whenever I needed it.

"Now allow me to show you around so you are comfortable with the surroundings."

For the next ten minutes or so Gustav guided me throughout the building and explained the meeting schedules. Entering the building from the foyer where we had met, we came into the main room, or hall, which was a better description. Large as the hall was, four French doors opened to even more additional space on the left and to another four on the right. Three matching palatial Persian carpets, each measuring at least forty-five by thirty feet dominated the floor. Recognizing the design as Iranian Moud with silk and kork wool, I marveled at the impossible cost of securing not just one of these masterpieces, but three matching specimens next to each other.

The hall was so large that it didn't seem crowded, despite the number of people in it. Four separate areas were set up with couches and leather chairs, enough to seat a small army but arranged so that a sense of intimacy was approximated and the largeness of the space minimized. The floor was made of mahogany and other hardwood with inlaid designs. The walls between the doors were interspersed with antique tables, above which hung paintings by some of the great masters. Indirect light lit up the ceiling from recessed panels, while standing floor lamps and Tiffany reading lights on the side tables illuminated the sitting areas. Not too bright, it gave the huge area a certain sense of comfort and informality, while retaining it's obvious splendor and the understatement of immense wealth. There were two open bars at either side of the entrance through which I had just entered, and at the far end were another set of two French doors opening to immaculately manicured grounds beyond. Taking advantage of the pleasant weather, the doors were open, giving a relaxed and informal feel to the event.

Perhaps a total of forty-five people were present, and an additional number of men dressed identically to Gustav, whom I assumed were staff.

Of those present, I recognized some from news events, money managers, a few senators, and officials of the Treasury Department. Others I knew to be high-ranking politicians of various countries, but most were unknown to me and paid me no attention as I walked through the area guided by Gustav to the French doors at the far right. They opened to a large staircase with double elevators adjacent. The downstairs area we were leaving served as an informal place to relax, meet, and/or speak with other attendees. The second and third floors were set up as six large conference rooms, four on the second and two on the third floor. Again, the exterior of the building belied the actual size inside. The third floor was to be used for larger gatherings, where the two rooms could be joined to form one large space with two conference tables seating thirty each and a small podium with a wooden lectern in front of a large plasma screen.

The lectern stood out, as much as an implement like that really can. But it caught my eye, constructed of black ebony, the elegant lines inlaid with strips of red capuli alternating with spotted chonta striped the full length of the neck, folding into a reading surface easily large enough to accommodate a laptop. Delicate lines which somehow had been manipulated into a strong, but slim object of beauty and functionality.

Having completed the tour, Gustav left me to my own devices, but not before being assured I was comfortable and needed no further assistance. I retreated to one of the bars next to the entrance, and even though I don't drink, the relative safety of placing myself at the corner against the wall and ordering a double espresso and a Perrier somewhat eased my nerves. Not that I was out of control, but I certainly was not in my comfort zone. I knew my presence was the result of an error, and I was not about to make myself stand out.

It definitely was an interesting view. I believe only a small number of those present were American, the majority being European, and a few were in traditional Arab garb. The gender mix was about three-quarter male, and the racial mix was skewed from Caucasian in the majority to about one third with darker complexions. Aside from two Japanese gentlemen, no other Asians were present. The atmosphere was relaxed and easy, with evidently many already familiar with each other. I decided to wear my gold and blue enamel pin and see what would happen.

As I was fastening it on my lapel, a female voice surprised me. "Mind if I join you in your corner?"

Thick, luxurious auburn hair framed a pleasant mid-forties face. About five feet seven inches, she had distinct Eurasian features, but unmistakably was of European stock, and quality stock from the looks of it. Well attired in a bit-too-conservative business suit, with jacket and vest over a pale-green silk shirt and matching skirt reaching down to just slightly above the knees. Modestly betraying affluence while still maintaining a conservative approach. The fact she was also in very good shape couldn't be hidden by any outfit, and not flaunting it made it so much more attractive.

Shaking her offered hand, I stood up, while gesturing her to the seat next to mine. "My name is Margaretha Matzuka, and you are?" As I introduced myself she handed her business card which identified her as a senior officer of the Deutsche Bundesbank from Berlin, the German central bank. She spoke with a smile. "I know I should have inquired after your information before coming up to you, but it is so cumbersome and unnecessary and really meant to protect the image and ego of some of the self-appointed aristocracy walking around. Besides, you were just about to wear your pin."

"It's a pleasure, and I appreciate the informal approach. This is my first meeting, and I am not sure what not to do." I answered as I presented her my business card in return.

"Your first meeting!" she said and smiled, dimpling her cheeks and squinting her nearly black eyes. With her pale skin, full lips, and confident demeanor, she was attractive. Perfect teeth I noticed, contrary to so many Europeans who just don't seem to find that part of personal appearance important, and as a result present a bike rack when opening their mouths. "You are in for a treat. Aside from the contacts you will make, the information will be worth it. Just wait." She ordered a gin martini, specifying it to be dry and dirty. While studying my business card, she said, "TCMI? I don't recognize this name. What is the connection to our group?"

Having anticipated the question I was ready to answer, but fumbled around in attempting to explain my ownership, not knowing how much to say or not. "I represent a small corporate ownership in the Federal Reserve," was what I came up with.

This seemed to suffice, or at least the subject was dropped. Not knowing if I had just made a fool of myself, I pressed on moving away from the topic, wanting to know the rest of the day's schedule.

"Today will be quiet, a presentation later welcoming everybody and explaining the meetings over the next days. It's all perfectly boring for now. But a few friends and I are having lunch at the Kunsthaus just across the river. You should join us if you wish. Give you a chance to get to know some of the others outside the meeting atmosphere."

Her English would be best explained as the Queen's English with a hint of a German accent. Probably Ivy League educated and very much at ease, she was a pleasure to speak with. I accepted her invitation, and we continued discussing our businesses, mostly hers though. I learned she was participating in the meetings as a representative of the German central bank and was instrumental in the long-term policy settings for her bank's relationships with other central banks, specifically in the Middle and Far East. She decided the strategic credit arrangements and loan covenants in politically sensitive areas. Born in Germany, her unusual striking looks the result of hybrid vigor, with her father Japanese and mother German; she was captivating in her speech and manner.

As we were speaking, two gentlemen approached the bar. One was stocky with bristly, short grey hair, wearing a loosely fitting dark suit buttoned to disguise a protruding belly, and not much taller than Margaretha. The second was a slim, elegant, close to six feet tall, very slightly balding man impeccably dressed in what must have been a midnight-blue Brioni, carrying a slim black attaché case in his left hand. I guessed both their ages at mid-fifties. They waited a few feet away from Margaretha to be introduced.

"My lunch dates are here," she said, looking at me as she turned to meet them. "Yuri, Jean-François, meet Stephen from Florida. I have asked him to join us for lunch. Are we ready?" Dismissing the possibility of any objections to my invitation she moved out of the way, giving me a chance to introduce myself.

Yuri Sergeyevich Bazan, or just Yuri, was the stocky one, with a heavy Eastern European accent. Jean-François de Beauvais was obviously French, though his English was just short of accent free, the result of an Oxford and subsequent Harvard education, I later discovered. Aside from the physical opposites, the contrast between the two was nearly comical. Where Yuri lacked in refinement, Jean-François certainly had too much. Yuri's laced brown shoes could use a polish, and Jean-François' were sleek black crocodile Ferragamos. Yuri's choice of suit was ill at best and bad fitting, and as I said, Jean-François' was a perfectly tailored Brioni, and where Yuri's hair could use some tending, the French's coiffure was flawless. It was only Yuri who reciprocated with his business card after accepting mine, while Jean-François never bothered to give me his. But both greetings were comfortable and seemed genuine enough, so I dismissed the card thing.

Margaretha had her own "Gustav" whom she addressed briefly, as I became familiar with the two lunch companions. Then she clutched both Yuri's and Jean-François' arms and led the way back through the foyer to the covered entrance outside as I followed. One of the limos I had observed earlier parked at the side of the building drove up, and the other Gustav opened the doors for us to enter. The ride was easy and uneventful and mostly spent with small talk between Margaretha and Jean-François in French. Being fluent in the language I tried to listen in on the conversation, but was unsuccessful due to traffic noise. So I looked outside at Zurich passing by.

The Kunsthaus is Zurich's, and for that matter Europe's preeminent museum for modern art, even though the many collections hold significant pieces stemming from the Middle Ages and the Renaissance. The place is known for its concentration on Swiss art and the Zürcher Kunstgesellschaft, the Friends of the Museum, is known as the largest and oldest art society in Europe. Although built in 1910 in a neo-classical style on the Heim-Platz, the structure still looks modern and is in immaculate condition. On the right, the lower wing is dedicated to a restaurant where the terrace is a popular place to sit, weather permitting. And even though weather did permit, the table Margaretha had reserved was inside giving a great view of the plaza through the full windowed walls.

I discovered Yuri liked to drink and smoke, and even though Margaretha had no aversion to alcohol, Yuri took it to a whole different level. Before our appetizers arrived, he had downed three good-sized tumblers of Chivas and was ordering his fourth when Jean-François spoke to me directly for the first time.

"So how has this come to be your first meeting? Did your company send a new representative, or is this a new alliance?"

Of course I was the only one aware of the error through which my presence was justified and none could know I was an imposter, or so I thought. So I collected myself and explained.

"I represent TCMI. I'm a bond trader specializing in international fixed income," I said and left it at that. It was enough, or so it seemed and was not brought up again.

I learned that Yuri worked for the Belarus Central Bank in Minsk and Jean-François was a representative of the United Nations—what he actually did at that international organization was not disclosed, and all that was offered was that he had offices in New York and Genève.

Yuri's business was in line with Margaretha's in that Yuri was instrumental in policy development with other nations, especially those belonging to the Commonwealth of Independent States (CIS). Headquartered in Minsk, it was a loosely formed alliance of former Soviet satellite states that became independent after the USSR dissolution. His activities were even more interesting, considering the CIS initiated the Eurasian Economic Community (EAEC), which basically is an economic pact among the CIS, Russia, Kazakhstan, Kyrgyzstan, and Uzbekistan, allowing for freedom of movement and trade. It occurred to me that the EAEC was a perfect corridor, or conduit, to permit the undetected movement of assets (not just human), funds, and products between Europe and the Middle East. Considering the United States was at war in Afghanistan and Iraq, basically neighboring nations to those of the EAEC, I couldn't help but wonder how Yuri's knowledge would emerge in this meeting organized by the Federal Reserve.

Lunch was amicable, and the food was impeccable. Jean-François took it upon himself to order the wine, intimating that he was the connoisseur, and more than likely he was. I stayed with my Perrier and watched the alcohol take its effect on the others. Mostly, they became louder and more animated. Two bottles later of what smelled to be quality Burgundy red, I had finished my salad Niçoise, and the conversation changed to Bear Stearns. Being the rookie I had kept my mouth largely shut, and with the subject moving into familiar territory, I was curious what this group had to say about the situation. I had witnessed the implosion of the famed broker/dealer up close just a month earlier.

Bear Stearns, the New York investment banking house that was started in 1923 and ultimately became the seventh-largest securities firm in the United States, ended up the victim of its own investments in thinly traded securities whose decline in value proved unstoppable (the net effect of mark to market rules). On March 17, 2008, JP Morgan/Chase offered to buy the firm for a mere two dollars per share, which ultimately was raised to ten dollars per share. On its own, this was a remarkable story, but a curious thing took place during the final downward slide of the share price of this doomed institution. I would not have thought about it again, were it not for a single and simple remark Jean-François made that afternoon at the lunch table.

"I guess we were correct insisting on the issuance of the low priced Bear Stearns puts," was all the Frenchman said, and it made my heart skip a beat, much like when you have a sudden clarifying, enlightening realization, because I knew a few things about the last trading days of BSC, the ticker symbol for Bear Stearns. Having been an options trader myself, I was aware of some very irregular option trades that had taken place during the previous month with ticker symbol BSC.

There are two kinds of options, calls and puts. The buyer of these instruments acquires the right to either buy (call option) or sell (put option) a certain security at a predetermined price (the strike price) on or before a predetermined date (expiration date). Although the idea behind these financial instruments seems simple enough, they are highly sophisticated and complicated structures whose pricing is subject not only to the price of the underlying security, but to the time left to expiration, the volatility or speed with which the price of the underlying security moves, interest rates and many other factors whose risks are expressed as delta, gamma, theta, vega and rho, and that's where it gets complicated.

The basic concept is that on or about March 10, 2008, a telephone call was placed (identity of the caller unknown to date) to OPRA, the Options Price Reporting Authority, with the request to list Bear Stearns (BSC) put option contracts (the right to sell) at an ostensibly low and not relative value to where the stock itself was trading. OPRA, for unknown reasons complied with this irrational request, which made no financial sense unless the caller was aware of nonpublic information. The result of these listings and the subsequent huge investment made by unidentified investor(s) caused surprise and disbelief in the general dealer community observing this activity. Such was the magnitude of the investment that the CEO of a well-respected Wall Street dealer firm was heard saying the investment only made sense if the investor knew something nobody else knew.

A week later, on March 17, 2008, this investment netted a profit of more than $149 million. Apparently somebody had known something, but he, she or they were never identified and an investigation into insider trading quietly faded into nothing.

Therefore, Jean-François' casual statement of, "I guess we were correct insisting on the issuance of the low puts on Bear Stearns," during lunch at the Kunsthaus caught my attention, to say the least.

"What was the issue with the puts on Bear Stearns?" I asked nonchalantly feigning ignorance.

The question was posed to the Frenchman, but it was Margaretha who answered. "Remember what I said earlier that the information we obtain at the meetings would be worth it? You will hear and learn details that you will not gain knowledge of anywhere else. This is why we meet, to be informed and to direct our combined strength into maximizing what is best for the group." After a slight pause she went on. "We often pool resources in order to remain anonymous and realize a stronger position."

Jean-François interjected, "We were instrumental in the decision to suspend Carlyle Capital from trading in Amsterdam in early March 2008. We knew Bear Stearns had too much exposure to Carlyle, and Bear's demise was of interest to us. So, Carlyle's trading suspension created a liquidity issue for Bear. We then invited Morgan to make a deal with the Federal Reserve at extremely low levels for Bear's immediate takeover. As the whole tactic was ours to start with, the put strategy made sense and paid off well." The delivery of information was matter of fact, as if it were business as usual.

I, on the other hand, couldn't believe what I was hearing. The manipulation and use of insider information on this scale was unbelievable. I had a hard time getting my head around the magnitude of the operation. My curiosity overcame my previous intention to be silent and discreet.

"Who made the call to OPRA to list the options?" I asked.

"Ah, you know about that and so you should," Jean-François said. He managed something resembling a smile for the first time in my direction. "The call was made from Washington to ensure compliance," was all he volunteered on the subject and then turned to Margaretha, indicating this part of the conversation was over. It was hard to like this guy.

Again I reflected on Johan's brief remark back in November 2007, when in between sentences he advised me to get rid of Bear Stearns and Lehman Brothers. So with Bear out of the way I was curious about Lehman and said, "What can we expect with Lehman Brothers?" Not directed to any of the three in particular, I noticed a distinct quiet before Jean-François took the lead, no smiles this time, making me self-conscious I had overstepped an invisible boundary.

"Lehman will be a meeting topic with a few other names. As with Bear, it will be interesting for all to follow the developments," was all he offered and then dismissed me and the topic alike by ordering another bottle of wine.

Meanwhile, Yuri had been more interested in mixing spirits than to partake in the conversation and was busy downing another Chivas as the waiter refilled his wine glass. I assumed his brand of smokes to be an indigenous Belarus product, with a 1950's kind of trendy name, intending to imbue its user with class and style. 'Golden Gate' is what the red and white package displayed. It depicted a stylized image of the famous San Francisco bridge and in the red part, on top, it informed all who cared about the inferred international flair of the product, 'American Blend Red.' It smelled coarse, nothing like any American blend I had ever smoked.

For the next forty-five minutes or so I ate some more of the bread, drank lots more bubbly water, and resisted the increasing urge to urinate. I just didn't want to get up and miss anything of interest. The rest of the discussion though, wandered off to family topics and persons known to them, but not to myself, so I just sat and hoped for more juicy information. At some point though, when I could not hold it no longer, I did get up, found the bathroom and had something resembling a religious experience when I finally peed.

During the drive back, Yuri exchanged a few words with the driver, after which he announced that we would be entering the building through the tunnel. There was no slurring of words, no mispronunciations, nothing in his speech betrayed the large amounts of alcohol I had seen him consume. Exactly how much he drank would become clear during the ensuing days. And what was meant with entering through the tunnel became clear just minutes later.

Instead of driving up Parkring to the bank building, we turned right onto Tunnelstrasse, which as the name suggests ends up in a tunnel, where, at its entrance a Swiss police car was expecting us. As soon as we passed, it turned its blue lights on and stopped all traffic behind us from entering. We drove perhaps one hundred yards, and I could see the oncoming traffic had been stopped as well at the other side of the tunnel by an identical police vehicle.

Alone in the tunnel, our limo stopped, and as we exited the car two grey steel doors became visible, sunk perhaps three feet into the wall. Well camouflaged, I could see how the general public would not take notice of these, but if they did, it would be written off as public work's entrances. Once through the doors, a rectangular hallway lit by fluorescent light brought us to an elevator flanked by two armed guards in black uniforms. After checking our identification against a handheld electronic device, we entered the elevator which took us to the staircase at the ground floor in the building where Gustav had taken me earlier. What a perfect way to enter and exit the building if one does not want to be observed by outsiders.

Gustav had informed me that the welcome meeting was held on the third floor and would start at four o'clock in the afternoon. Having about forty-five minutes to spare after we returned from lunch, I thanked Margaretha, retrieved my cell phone, and wandered outside in the sunny afternoon to make a few calls to the office and Nicole. I spoke briefly with Sharon, who told me about a client calling in and a trade she was able to put together that would settle later in the week. For the rest, all was in order. Nicole was out of reach, so I left a message on her cell phone, saying I'd try again later in the evening.

Returning to the building, I decided to take the stairs to the third floor. The two conference rooms had been joined to form one large area. Seating was unassigned so I took a seat in the back in one of the comfortable leather chairs lining the two conference tables. The two neighbors who took seats next to me offered no formal greeting aside from a courteous nod of the head acknowledging my presence. Margaretha and Jean-François, black case in hand, walked in together and stayed up front. A bit later Yuri showed up, looking as disheveled as before, and found a place a couple of seats removed from me. Upon seeing me, he mumbled a greeting and lowered himself into the chair.

The meeting was well attended, with about fifty people and only a few seats left open. I noticed five Gustavs strategically located around the room, ready to be of service. The presentation itself was succinct, welcoming us and explaining the course of events. It was hosted by a young-looking, well-dressed gentleman wearing nerdy-looking glasses and even though his beige suit was obviously of good quality, the pants were slightly too short, and his odd-looking red bowtie was visibly hand tied, leaving it somewhat askew. The whole ensemble gave him a rather geeky appearance, which under the circumstances I would not have expected. But hearing him speak dispelled the image as he proved well versed and not shy to communicate publicly.

He started as follows: "Good afternoon to you all. I welcome you to the May 2008 steering committee, and may I remind you, all discussions, all participants' identities, and all meeting topics are subject to the Chatham House Rule. Strict confidentiality and anonymity are to be adhered to. Failure to do so may preclude you from being invited back and could subject you to unintended consequences."

He introduced himself as Gary, working for the IMF, the International Monetary Fund, and informed us that he was in charge of scheduling and organizing the steering-committee meetings. The main purpose of this event, he said, was to disseminate and prepare pertinent information for the participants of the annual full assembly meeting, to be held the following month in Chantilly, Virginia. This upcoming meeting would be especially interesting as both United States presidential candidates Obama and Clinton were to appear and meet with the group. Apparently, candidate McCain either already had, or was about to have his own meeting with Baron de Rothschild and a select group of associates in London, rather than appear in Chantilly.

Then, as part of the introduction, Gary said, "One of the main concerns we have been hearing across the board from our members is the anxiety felt about the situation with American International Group, known as AIG. I am here to assure all of you that at the moment steps are being taken that will eliminate counterparty risk as far as AIG is concerned, including those with open credit default swaps still outstanding. As with Bear Stearns, the process will be further handled by our Parent and coordinated locally through the Federal Reserve. It will involve the Maiden Lane vehicle to secure funding, which should give each of you a sense of relief. This topic is on the schedule and will be discussed in depth in the coming days."

Bear Stearns again. Our Parent? And what the hell was this Maiden Lane vehicle he spoke about? For the rest he mentioned that the Lehman issue would be on the schedule and that the future of the GSE's, the Government Sponsored Enterprises would be discussed. The third day's meetings would deal with loan facilities and financial support to the various factions the group had decided to back and representatives of those factions would be present as well. That should prove to be interesting, I was sure.

Dinner was catered at the premises for those wishing to take advantage of it and to not be exposed to the public's eye while dining in the city. I had chosen to stick around and perhaps learn more than what I had heard so far.

After the meeting, I took the wide stairs down to the first floor, admiring the art on the walls in the stairwell. Where the walls on the first floor were covered with old masters from the seventeenth and eighteenth century, the stairs exhibited modern art. Aquarelles from Chagall, Dali, a larger fresco tempera by Pakistani artist Jamali, a large collage by Richard

Hamilton, prints by Joan Miro, Renoir, Pissarro, Kandinsky and many modern oils I didn't recognize. A few charcoals by Picasso from his earlier years, during what is referred to as the blue period.

One particularly attractive landscape by Cézanne quietly hung on one of the two landings between the second and first floor. I stopped to admire the small painting as I let others pass by. Not larger than twelve by fifteen inches in the frame, it hung alone, framed by the wall itself. As I stood there taking in the blocked landscape, admiring how with just a few brush strokes the movement of a tree came alive and the corn fields flowed in the wind, a voice startled me.

"I always amaze at Cézanne capture the natural feel of scenes with that imprecise movements of brush." His accent accentuating the L's and thick, rolling R's, Yuri stood behind me. Perhaps three steps up on the stairs, one hand in his pockets, the other holding a smoldering Golden Gate, he was disheveled as before but now with his shirt loosely tucked in and his jacket unbuttoned. Smiling at me, I was confronted with the Stonehenge formation, which was the product of a lifetime of dental neglect, the finer details of which I must have missed at lunch.

"I love Cézanne," I simply said.

Then after a silence Yuri surprised me again. "You know he not friends with other artists because to stay original and not have other ideas?"

I actually did know that and was impressed this sloppy guy from out-of-the-way Minsk knew it as well. Just goes to show appearances are not everything.

"Let's drink," was Yuri's solution to our newfound mutual appreciation of art. He stepped by me and stomped down the stairs, cigarette smoke curling up in his wake. We found the same spot at the bar where we had met earlier unoccupied and sat down. This time the place was well populated and the center of much animated talk and laughter. I had mineral water and Yuri, true to form, Chivas. For the amount of alcohol I had seen him consume, he remained absolutely clear and lucid during the ensuing discussion.

I asked him what he knew about the Maiden Lane I had heard about during the introductory meeting we just attended.

Yuri downed his glass and asked for a refill, lighting a new cigarette with the butt of the old one. "Maiden Lane is from Federal Reserve to smooth purchase of Bear Stearns by JP Morgan. Maiden Lane get credit from Federal Reserve of New York to buy toxic portfolio of waste mortgages from Bear."

"Excuse me?" I tried to follow Yuri's words, but this sounded a bit too odd. "Waste mortgages?"

"Yes, you know, bad portfolio, toxic waste mortgages," Yuri clarified. Ignoring my smile, he carried on as if he was not interrupted. "This Maiden Lane happen right now and not yet public knowledge. Result is JP Morgan buy Bear and not have to buy bad portfolio and Fed give guarantee of zero loss to Morgan. Not bad deal, no?" This time he smiled, openly proud he knew about it and admiring how fiendishly smart the transaction was structured. He sipped his newly filled glass.

In order to be clear about what I was told, I rephrased. "So the Federal Reserve finances Maiden Lane, who absorbs the problem loan portfolios from Bear and then guarantees a zero loss to JP Morgan, who in turn receives the OK to buy all the good assets from Bear at ten dollars per share?"

"That's it" Yuri answered. "They try buy Bear at two dollar per share, but was trick to get to ten." He smiled and then added, "Make private the gains and make social the losses. Smart move." He grinned again.

I recognized the ingenious way to shield a Federal Reserve owner (JP Morgan) from exposure to losses while allowing it to basically steal a company (Bear Stearns) for a mere ten dollars per share and transfer the risk of the bad assets to the public. It occurred to me that Margaretha had been correct when she stated I would gain knowledge not available anywhere else.

My head was spinning, but not wanting to seem too eager, I managed to ask nonchalantly if everybody else in the room knew about this in advance.

"This is reason we meet. Sometimes not much notice, but is good opportunity for everyone give new information on markets, conflicts, and that stuff. In January we already know about Bear problem. In February we learn about Bear Stearns option play and receive offer in part-taking. It's up to you if you want in or not. Plenty more, you'll see."

"Gary mentioned not to worry about the AIG thing and that the same system would be used. What's the deal with AIG?" I said. I remember feeling apprehension about wanting to know too many details and perhaps being too inquisitive. But Yuri was willing to let me in on what he knew. Obviously, having been cleared to attend the meeting was proof enough I deserved to know the details, I surmised.

Yuri continued, "AIG can be big problem if Parent not help. Lots of business here with AIG." Yuri waved his arm around the room as he said the last words, implying just about everybody at the meeting was exposed to AIG in one way or another. "In February we know already and get caution. And we get advice to short stock and reduce holdings. You will see, same thing as Maiden Lane as for AIG. Then no losses for nobody here, and everybody get money back from Fed." Big smile.

"Whom do you refer to when you say, Parent? Gary, the IMF guy doing the meeting, just now talked about it as well." My question interrupted Yuri's train of thought, but I had been wanting to know whom they were referring to, even though I had a good idea. Still, his answer took me by surprise.

"Parent is benefactor," was Yuri's mysterious answer. "Benefactor is who decide on policy and direction we follow."

"You mean the Federal Reserve," I corrected Yuri.

But it was Yuri who corrected me. "Federal Reserve only part of bigger group who follow directives of Parent." He looked at me and said nothing further.

But this intrigued me, and I wanted to know more, so I asked, "Are they here, our Parent, during this meeting?"

"Always present every meeting, either in person or agent," Yuri said.

I thought for a moment and offered, "So it is safe to say the Parent are those people who control the companies that own the Federal Reserve, Bank of England, the Banque National de France, and the German Bundesbank."

"Only some of them. Others too," Yuri said. Then he made an interesting point. "Money not enough to make directives. Need legislative to make control of international infrastructure, need press to teach people and need enforcement power. So Sia is in Parent too. This way strengthen Parent influence on wider scale."

"Sia?" I asked.

"Yes, Central Intelligence Agency, Sia," Yuri explained and I understood he pronounced CIA as if it were a two syllable word.

"The CIA is part of the Parent?" It hadn't even occurred to me.

"Sia here too and other Agencies. Always at meetings, but never know who is." Yuri said. "We all part of team who work for Parent. Sia has Secret Team that work in field and do covert stuff and so they are Parent enforcement, like army."

I was quiet and let the information sink in. In the few words Yuri shared, he outlined something that appeared to be a shadow government, with control over banks and publishing, power over legislation and its own stealth enforcement arm. Sovereign boundaries did not apply, and secretly I had to admire the depth of the structure I had become in touch with.

Then Yuri said, "Sometime you see who is Parent. One you already meet, I think." He smiled knowingly, showing off Stonehenge, and waved the barman for another Chivas. "We meet to share information and get direction from Parent. This way we all know same facts and set course that benefit whole group." He sipped his drink and remained quiet for a moment.

Looking around, I was struck by the peaceful ambience of the room. It must have been around five thirty or so, and dusk had set in. Subdued lighting made the place look appealing and warm. The two French doors at the far end were still open to the garden beyond. Outside lights created an inviting and intriguing atmosphere, differing from the elegant opulence within. The bar was still a popular place to hang out, but so were the leather sofas and arm-chairs.

I saw Jean-François sipping brandy in one of the comfortable chairs, his black narrow brief case neatly tucked under his legs against the chair. He was flanked by Gary and Margaretha. The three were sitting alone engaged in discussion and I thought it interesting I had so early in the conference met some of the characters in charge, by chance I thought, or so it seemed at least.

Perhaps a total of twenty-five of us were still around, enjoying the quiet beginnings of the evening. As quiet and peaceful as the surroundings seemed, it portrayed a stark contrast to what was going on inside of me. Too many questions with not enough answers, too many implications without any explanations.

Yuri broke the silence and changed the subject. "What your expertise? You do fixed-income, I am correct?"

So far I had done most of the asking and had not spoken about myself much, for obvious reasons. I took Yuri's question as one of general interest in an attempt to get to know me, without more profound overtones.

"I trade primarily international fixed-income sovereigns and as such have a good view of multinational trends in interest rates and geo-political risk because of the account base I deal with." It is amazing how we can rephrase what we do and make it sound more impressive according to the circumstances. I could have said, "I sell bonds to institutions and I speak with a lot of foreigners who tell me stuff," but that didn't have the ring the first sentence had and judging by Yuri's reaction my original words were well chosen.

"I understand," he said as I wondered what exactly it was he understood. Already busy ordering his fourth, or fifth, I lost count, refill for his Chivas, I felt free inquiring in return. Not sure how to phrase my query it came out as, "How about you? What is Belarus' position?"

Yuri sipped his drink and thought a moment before answering, "We are at advantage because of geography."

His accent was thick, and I had a hard time understanding what he meant. "What about your country is so special?"

"Not country," he corrected me. "Country location. It looks not obvious on a map, but Belarus capital, Minsk, is crossroads to Eurasian Economic Community. Like direct path to Middle East. We are broker many times to bring together groups who in public can not speak together. We make financing from our Parent to old friends, you know, old allies," he said, clarifying.

"You mean friends of the United States?" I asked.

"Yes, old friends in Afghanistan, Pakistan, Iran from long ago. But now too many eyes, too many scrutiny to work together. Here we step in and get help from Secret Team if we need. Sometimes funds need move physically by courier, or assets need move East from West or back around. This is where we help." Yuri's statement made me think of the "Hawala," or sometimes called "Hundi," the invisible and untraceable underground banking system used by Al Qaeda and associated groups.

I remained silent, pondering the ramifications of what Yuri said, when he quietly added, "You learn and look past politic and ideal horizon, and you know today fighters are friends in past. Much your country's enemies were financed, trained, created by your money, by your army, by same Secret Teams only decades ago."

Notwithstanding his accent, his words made good sense. I liked "ideal horizon" and translated it to "ideological horizon" in my mind. He continued. "Just as administration somewhere says some group has become enemy, does it mean we stop do business with them? No make sense at all that. Our Parent has done business with all these peoples in a past and still do and will not stop for long time come. No better way to know all players in a game when all depend your resources. This why I say look past the politic horizon. We are New World Order. We have no boundary, no border, no politic alliance. We superside national limits. We have one goal which unites us. This is true open society."

"Supersede, you mean" I corrected Yuri.

"Yes, yes, superside, supersede. You know what I mean, like pass over, go over limit." Yuri stubbornly and impatiently rebutted. All I could do was smile.

He was quiet after these words and drank his Chivas and smoked his international smokes. Then he said, "Jean-François part this framework. He may act as all his idea, but United Nations structure through why all this functions and possible is."

Yuri looked me straight in my eyes as he was speaking. Aside from getting tangled up in the intricacies of English grammar, there was no sign of alcohol. This guy surprised me. His image and alcoholic behavior belied a smart mind and keen understanding of what was going on. I was at a loss where to go from here. What Yuri told me was that the Parent, the Benefactor, whomever they are, through their associates and banking connections were directly involved financially with those we have conflicts with, either diplomatically or militarily. To learn that our Federal Reserve was just a part of this bigger system, this framework that involved the CIA, the United Nations and obviously the IMF, was a revelation to say the least.

I was appreciating the full extent of why the Federal Reserve was created outside of the United States government. It was not just the financiers backing the Federal Reserve's will, it was the government's desire just as much. Otherwise it would not have happened.

I didn't know at that moment that what was to unfold was a banking crisis of such magnitude that the Federal Reserve, under the guise of saving the universe, would be able to "rescue" the world by buying control in the major banking centers for just pennies on the dollar, similar to what transpired many times earlier. And incredible as it may seem, that was only a part of a much bigger, much more dangerous and larger involvement I was to learn about.

What a perfect way to influence world events and never publicly have to take responsibility for it, while still reaping the results. What a beautifully orchestrated, incestuous relationship, where Congress allows the Federal Reserve to follow its own agenda with the money of the citizenry of the United States, even if it conflicts with the overall policy of the government. In return, it supplies Congress with all the funds it wants, so it can finance and promote its own political agendas and promise untold benefits to the people, thus buying the votes to stay in office and assuring the longevity of the Federal Reserve at the same time.

"Remember Gary talk about representatives visiting?" Yuri interrupted my thought process.

"You mean those who will show up Saturday?" I offered.

"Yes, yes, Saturday. One will be here tomorrow." Yuri beamed, clearly proud about something. "He is good example of mujahedeen from Sia training. First paid by your Congress and now our Parent financed. They are Taliban now you know, so not so popular in Oosa." Yuri said still smiling.

I figured Oosa to mean USA, tipped off by Sia being CIA. I had to get used to that.

The next words clarified what he was proud about. "Oosa taught them and pay them and now fight them. But financing is still there, that not change. You like have dinner with him tomorrow?" From nowhere Yuri sprang the question on me.

"You know the guy?" I asked with surprise.

"I am sponsor him show up here. It shows system works well. Organize by United Nations, finance by IMF, and move by EAEC and CIS, with Sia Secret Team help. Not good come alone from Afghanistan, if not for combined efforts. Too many people after him." Yuri smiled, obviously impressed with the facts he laid out to me.

"Why bring him in at all if he is such a risk?" I wanted to know. I realized Yuri just confirmed my suspicion of the existence of the Hawala, the underground system to move funds and assets.

"Show system works to those who pay. Also show how easy is move assets, even when difficult politic and ideal boundary are passed. It makes trust. No trust, no pays. Very simple, yes? We have to make confidence and conviction. It is necessary ingredient to growth." With that Yuri downed his Chivas and stood up, expecting me to follow suit.

"Growth into what? What's the goal?" I insisted, ignoring the physical cue that this part of the conversation was over.

With his thick L, Yuri said, "Let's eat," ignoring me in turn. He emptied his tumbler, extinguished his cigarette and started to the dining area.

What about AIG and Lehman, I thought. I had not asked him about that yet. How did the CIA, United Nations and the IMF fit in, and what other Agencies did he refer to, and how was Jean-François involved?

Too many questions. I stood up and followed him through one of the four French doors lining the left side of the great downstairs room. The four conference rooms that made up the left wing of the building had been opened and converted into a dining area with enough seating to accommodate the entire conference, perhaps half were occupied.

C H A P T E R 10

I sat next to Yuri during dinner and met a few other participants. One was a skinny, tall London banker in his mid-forties with hair slightly too long named Nigel Kirby. Another was a very wealthy, overweight businessman from the Netherlands whose name I forgot and like a typical Dutchman rolled his own cigarettes, and the third was a managing director from Goldman Sachs. He was very good looking, with perfect hair and aware of it, likewise from London, who addressed me so arrogantly that Yuri jokingly referred to him as the new aristocracy. The conversation was light, and no mention was made of the topics previously discussed in the meeting. I looked for Jean-François and Margaretha, but they were nowhere to be seen.

At one point, when the Goldman pretty boy informed us all that an increase in United States interest rates was imminent, I couldn't stop myself. Without raising my voice and backing my reasoning with facts, I proved him wrong using his own arguments, much to his dismay. And when he attempted to dispute my line of reasoning, I received unsolicited support from the London banker, Nigel, who, while shaking his head to get the hair from his eyes, shut the Goldman Sachs man up.

"Say, old chap, you obviously are an equity man," Nigel said. "Why don't you listen to Stephen, who seems to know what he is talking about, and learn something about fixed income and the dynamics of money supply?" I loved Nigel and noticed Yuri smile as he obviously enjoyed the intellectual demotion of the new aristocracy.

Not wanting to stay after dinner and watch everybody drink and smoke, I decided to walk the few blocks back the same way I came that morning. After an easy and welcome walk in solitude, I arrived at the hotel and entered the lobby, where I was greeted by Margaretha's voice beckoning me over to the bar where she was lounging with Jean-François. A last espresso was not a bad idea, so I changed direction and joined them in their corner. It had comfortable leather chairs and low light to create a semblance of intimacy and privacy. I sat down.

I liked Margaretha. She was smart and attractive, and her outgoing personality made it a pleasure speaking with her.

"Stephen, we're all staying at the same hotel, I see. Great choice." She smiled as she addressed me. "Well, what do you think? Do you believe you may benefit from what will be discussed?"

"Just this evening Yuri invited me to join him for dinner tomorrow with his guest from the Middle East. That should be interesting." As I volunteered the information, I thought I saw Margaretha exchange look of concern with Jean-François, but I dismissed the observation and continued. "I understand how we take care of each other by sharing news and insights into financial and political events. What I didn't realize is the vastness of the international scope of the group and how it surpasses, even contradicts political and social alliances and conflicts alike," I said.

Margaretha had composed herself and whatever I thought I had seen in her eyes, was gone. She smiled, disarming me with her dimpled, coquettish look and complimented me. "Very well said and very concise. It is the nature of whom we are and what our goal is."

"That is the second time today I have heard members refer to our goal, and without wanting to appear ignorant, my belief of the goal is the overall and foremost survival and prosperity of our Parent. Am I correct?" My question was in a sense hypothetical and not addressed to either of them in particular. But it was Jean-François who responded.

"The long-term and admittedly utopian view is one where ultimately there will be one government, with one currency, and one rule that will govern this world. That is the final goal you hear us speak about." Although he looked at me as he was speaking these words, I had the faint impression he was more humoring Margaretha's interest in me than gracing me with an answer. I then noticed he was playing with a sleek, little black object between his fingers which I recognized as a USB thumbdrive, but I paid no further attention to it.

"That goal is an impossibility to reach in our lifetime," I concluded as a matter of fact.

This time Jean-François truly addressed me for the first time as he placed the black drive in his suit jacket's side pocket.

"Time is not of the essence," he said. "What is, is the notion that the fundamental operating structures are organized properly, that the right legislative, regulatory, and financial systems are ready and functioning if and when change becomes a necessity. Look at the United Nations. It took almost a century to get it right. Whole nations and political systems had to alter course before it was a well-performing, integrated international authority. You are correct that most likely it may not happen in our lifetime, but it may in our children's, or their children's, and then again, it may be sooner."

Jean-François looked at me with distinct arrogance and after a few moments asked, "Tell me Stephen, do you have children?" The last question offered with just a hint of a smile, the word "you" accentuated as if he were privy to something unknown to me.

The tone of his voice sat wrong with me and I didn't feel like letting this haughty sob know anything about my personal life. And in a sudden burst of irritation I remember thinking 'None of your fucking business whether I have children or not,' and thought of telling him so. But, "My son is in his late twenties," is what came out.

I was tired and wanted to call Nicole and retire to the privacy of my room. Too much to digest, too much new information and I was done being treated with disdain by the frog. So I said, "Good night, Margaretha, and to you, Sir." I shook both their hands and turned to leave.

"Good night, Mr. Stephen Vinson." Jean-François took time to deliberately state my full first and last name, after which he said, "I hope Anthony is enjoying his stay in Pfullendorf."

I froze, and looked back at the Frenchman.

After a pause I demanded, "How do you know who and where my son is, and what is it to you?" My voice was lowered and cautious, understanding the veiled threat in his statement.

"Mr. Stephen Vinson," again the full name. "You show up here from nowhere. Your institution has no dealings with the Federal Reserve System. Your ownership is indeed valid, but it is not of a corporate nature, so contrary to what you stated, you don't represent a company. Your invitation is confirmed and duly authorized, no doubt aided by your family credentials, which reach those who initiated these summits[4], plus the fact of your father's involvement in various United Nations platforms[5]. But that means nothing to me. Who you are and what you are doing here concerns me, and what I am saying is, you are being watched. That is all."

---

[4] HRH Prince Bernhard of the Netherlands being one of the two founders of these conferences in 1953—the reference was made to my father's friendship and association with the Prince.

[5] My father chaired United Nations committees in his line of scientific and naval expertise, oceanography, continental shelf exploration and military justification of international waters.

Margaretha's hand moved on Jean-François' arm while he was speaking in an attempt to dampen his affront. But to no avail, and the gist came through unmistakably. He had made his point loud and clear.

Jean-François was not yet finished. "Oh, and by the way, I thought it interesting to learn of your past run-in with Interpol, some years back. It seems you have been involved in many different occupations, haven't you?"

I could feel the blood drain from my face in a mixture of fear of discovery and anger at this snobbish and pretentious Frenchman who had chosen to check up on me. Nobody had ever brought up my previous brush with Interpol. I thought it expunged, or cleared off the books. It had been so long ago, close to thirty-five years. And how he found out Anthony's location was a mystery.

And all of a sudden I didn't feel safe. A sudden pang of regret went through me for allowing myself to get into this mess, and now somehow involving my son as well. Not knowing how to respond and not wanting to continue the line of discussion for fear of regretting my words later, I turned and went to my room. As I did, I could hear Yuri's words to pay attention so I would notice who the representatives of our Parent are. I believe one of them had just made himself known to me.

I had not been in my room ten minutes when my cell phone rang.

"Dad, where are you?" Anthony's voice was hurried.

"In Zurich attending a conference. Why?" I came to the point. It wasn't like him to dismiss greeting me.

"I don't know what is going on, but somehow another service inquired about you through the chain of command. Not sure who they are. All I know is they have the respect of my commander, and that is special on its own."

"Any idea what they wanted to know?" I could feel my pulse quicken and felt a knot forming in my stomach.

"It was weird. My CO called me in and asked me to confirm your home address and who you work for and what kind of work you do. They never asked anything like this before, and when I wanted to know why they needed the info, I was told it was just a routine inquiry. Dad, I am not naïve, and I have been around a bit and this was no routine inquiry. I actually stated my doubts about this being routine and was told it was not my place to doubt the origin of the request." Here Anthony stopped as if to gather his thoughts and then went on. "The origin must have been someone or something that made my commander act as my superior, and he has never pulled rank on me before. We went through BUD/S together, for God's sake. Something jarred him, and he doesn't usually get jarred."

"I don't know who's asking, Anthony, but something is going on here on my side. I can't go into details right now, but I'm involved with a group of people I should have stayed away from, and now I'm in too deep to slip away. Just tonight they made it clear to me they know who and where you are, and that spooked me."

Anthony remained quiet for a few moments. He then asked, "You in trouble, Dad?"

"I don't know, Son, I just don't know. Perhaps I am."

"What's going on, Dad? Did something happen?" Anthony interrupted me, and I could hear the alarming concern in his voice.

"It scared me when they brought you into the picture." Was all I said and from there Anthony took charge.

"Understood. This is what we'll do just to be careful. We will work out a way to communicate away from prying eyes and ears. Hang up and wait for a text message I'll send you tonight. We'll take it from there—I love you, Dad." And with that he was gone.

"I love you too, Son." I knew him well enough to know he was worried and that he wouldn't leave a stone unturned to help me.

His text message arrived about five minutes later and consisted of the URL of a website and the instruction to buy and download the software offered at the site. After following his directions exactly, I texted him back a simple, "done." I had purchased a professional steganography application, using advanced encryption standard (AES) 256bit. The software hides files of all kinds, including text messages in common pictures. The hidden message or file can be encrypted and retrieved only when both the sender and receiver use the same password. Using AES 256bit virtually precluded anybody from breaking the code, resulting in it being used by the NSA/NCS for top secret information encryption.

The only thing Anthony and I needed was a password known to us alone. For this I chose a word only he would know the existence of, without me having to verbalize it, or send via text or email. Just in case anybody was monitoring our communications. So my resulting text to him read as follows: "password = the way of the ....." I knew this would make him smile, and he would know the answer without a doubt. When still in single-digit age, I would talk to Anthony about a magic time, when he would learn how to use special powers and be taught spells and charms that would make him strong and mighty. This magic time I would refer to as "the way of the *dwarf.*" I knew I was correct when I received his reply "lol—perfect choice."

We tested the software a few times by sending random pictures to each other via email, embedding text in each picture, which we would then return via text message to confirm accuracy. After being assured the system worked, we had established a line of communication that only he and I had access to. I felt much better, even though my immediate situation hadn't changed. I then used the new system to briefly explain the share mix-up, the resulting invitation and my illegitimate attendance at the conference. His response was to the point, inasmuch that he acknowledged my predicament, but advised me to continue on as if nothing was wrong and to let him know of any developments. We agreed to stay in close contact for now.

Next I phoned Nicole, but I didn't explain anything about what had happened. She was preoccupied with some minor mishap at work, which took most of the call. Even though she and I were close, I couldn't shake the feeling that for her it would matter little if we were to break up. I couldn't blame Nicole for not seeing a future with me. I had discouraged her from doing so in the first place.

It was late when I finally turned the TV off and tried to sleep. My mind wouldn't let go of Jean-François' ominous tone when he said, *"You show up here from nowhere..."*

I tried imagining the potential consequences of being discovered, but couldn't possibly conceive where all this was going. It was late when I finally did fall asleep.

Thursday morning was another beautiful day, but I woke up with Jean-François' threat looming over me. I had coffee in my room and watched the news about the financial collapse of the subprime mortgage market, the losses in bank and insurance stocks and the presidential election which was getting into full swing.

AIG was discussed, and the possibility of a default seemed frightfully close. The ripple effect on the markets would be disastrous. AIG was one of the largest insurance companies in the world, and just the previous day we, at the conference, were informed not to worry about counterparty risk with AIG. Counterparty risk is the risk one takes transacting with another company, the counterparty. The risk is whether it, the counterparty, will be around in the future to see the deal through, and the longer the duration of the transaction, the higher the perceived risk. A huge derivatives market emerged insuring this particular risk, and that specific insurance is called credit default swap (CDS). The fact AIG was being talked about in terms of default meant it could take many other companies with it on the way out. I was curious to learn how just yesterday the introductory speaker, Gary, was so certain all those with outstanding claims and CDSs would be OK.

The doom and gloom that came across the television didn't improve my mood, but I had already made up my mind to continue attending the meetings and ignore the Frenchman's attempted intimidations. As he stated, my invite was valid and so were my ownership credentials. I was not about to quit with the prospect of so much new information right in front of me. This whole thing fascinated me far too much.

But I couldn't ignore a certain nervousness while walking up to the building's entrance. My mind imagined the armed guards would deny me access and publicly humiliate me by removing me from the premises. When nothing unusual occurred and I was politely granted access, I still caught myself being on the lookout for Jean-François once inside. He was not to be seen though, and the unease dissipated quickly.

The morning consisted of meetings with two officials from both Fannie Mae and Freddie Mac. Both of them were introduced as return invitees to the gathering. They were professional and impressive in their delivery and demeanor. Two administrators sent on a mission abroad to inform this rather astute group of bankers, wealthy industrialists, and behind-the-scenes controllers of power on the financial condition of their institutions.

Notwithstanding the expert presentation, the meeting was rather dull. It became interesting when one of the bureaucrats nonchalantly stated that "shareholder value had been sacrificed as a result of the initiative to own and control the subprime mortgage market." He then asserted that the objective was in the latter stages of completion and that the resulting intervention would be timed and triggered by the stock values approaching zero. One of them referred back to a previous meeting in September of 2007, where these same gentlemen were invited and had discussed the positive outcome of the then-suggested short positions in both companies.

Again, the seemingly detached approach of the discussion floored me. What was being relayed in very few words was the fact that both Fannie Mae and Freddie Mac had been planning to own the subprime mortgage markets all along, knowing perfectly well it would compromise shareholder value. In addition, anticipating the decline in price, it was suggested to take advantage of it.

Both these companies were trading in the mid-twenties at the time of this meeting, which was already down over 60% or more from their highs. The suggestion offered, though, was that both stock values would deteriorate even more, most likely to zero, with the obvious understanding that serious profits could still be made while taking advantage of this privileged information.

The next speaker was the CEO of a lobbying firm whose primary goal had been to influence and convince Congress to leave the rating agencies alone. The point, in essence, was to allow them to do their business without restrictions. The rating agencies would be instrumental in aiding the congressional pledge to have minorities and lower-income groups become homeowners and thus, part of the American Dream. The fact that they would become homeowners at the very end stages of the housing bubble, with highly inflated and unrealistic home values, was not acknowledged, or noted as detrimental. By that time the electorate votes were already cast anyway and consequently placed in power those who had promised homeownership for all.

None of the lobbyist's presentation was about the social, moral, and ethical implications of the subprime market and the financial destruction it would create. What was discussed was how the participants of this select group could benefit and profit on the insight offered. A change in environment was on the horizon, and those who expected business as usual should heed this warning and sell any structured subprime investment vehicles in their portfolios while a favorable rating was still to be had.

Again, I was struck by the blatant distribution of insider information.

The meeting continued with questions being asked and answered, and I took time to get up and stretch my legs. Margaretha was present, and even though she saw me when she walked in, she avoided looking in my direction and sat away so that I couldn't see her face. It then occurred to me that I hadn't seen either Yuri or Jean-François. Nigel, the British banker, sat close to me. Upon entering the conference room, he had made it a point to greet me, and we briefly exchanged some small talk about markets and our mutual business.

"I'm going downstairs to get some coffee. Care to join me?" I asked Nigel. I wanted some time to pick his brain and find out how familiar he was with these meetings and the type of information being disclosed. He agreed, and both of us descended the stairs, passing Cézanne on our way down and a few participants on their way up.

FEDERAL

We were alone at the bar in the main room. Aside from the two of us, I noticed a few personal Gustavs at attention on the sides. The time was about eleven thirty in the morning, and I requested an espresso while Nigel ordered a Bloody Mary. A bit early for alcohol I thought, but I made it none of my business.

Nigel was a perfect example of the British upper class, well-bred and educated, with a skin tone so light it bordered on anemia. A narrow face with hollow cheeks, a small dark mole on the left. Teeth yellowish and big, exposing the gum line when he laughed, in disarray as was the norm. Tall and lean, perhaps even skinny, he wore an obviously expensive single-breasted suit with a studied nonchalance that emphasized its elegance. The dark-red bow-tie, although somewhat old fashioned, looked in place and style, as did the color-coordinated pocket square. Speaking the Queen's English, he had the uncanny ability to alter perfectly good words and add syllables by accentuating vowels, as only the British know how.

I learned he had been schooled on the Continent, which is the UK's way of referring to being abroad in Europe, across the Channel. A high-end boarding school in Gstaad, Switzerland, followed by Cambridge and a degree from the London School of Economics. When he inquired after my education, I told him about my attendance at a small public school in Southern Wales, which sufficed to gain his respect and impression that he was speaking to a peer. Even though the information was correct in its essence, the whole truth about me having been expelled from the school and ultimately the country, to end up eventually in a psychiatric hospital, would have altered the image I intended on communicating.

"I am impressed at the type of information being relayed," I said. "This is my first meeting and I am more than pleased with the contents so far."

Nigel waited with his response, as if to weigh the words for maximum effect. He finished his drink and ordered another. Turning to me he said, "The fact is we are just getting started. There is much more to come. Today we are touching upon some financial markets and following up on recommendations made during previous meetings. What comes tomorrow should be bloody more interesting, as it will touch on political trends and macroeconomic changes to come. That is where we will see a bigger picture, the next twenty to fifty years. Knowing and anticipating this is where the real fortunes are made." He took a sip, and both of us stayed quiet for a moment. He went on. "I must say, I enjoy these meetings—they are concise and very informative without wasting a lot of time. All the information from these three days is compiled and then offered to the full assembly meeting next month in Chantilly. But why wait if we can get the goods bloody well right now?" He smiled while moving his head back, freeing the hair from his eyes.

"How long have you been part of this?" I asked. "And how did you get involved in the first place?"

"It's a grooming process, as you well know. In time, those who decide choose from the ranks whom they believe have what it takes to make the right decisions. Looking back, I now realize that every position, every special project I was involved in, every time I made a career move, I was being watched and tested, if you will. Ultimately, it was just a matter of time until I was invited. This is my third year participating, and I'll say, it is exhilarating. How about you old chap?" Nigel looked at me genuinely interested in finding out about me.

"My company owns a small block of Federal Reserve stock and as a result I was invited." I answered as a matter of fact, without trying to make much of the issue. Judging from Nigel's reaction, or lack thereof, the answer was accepted at face value and not given another thought.

"I find it interesting," I went on, "how the Federal Reserve, which in the United States is such a huge and independent system, is only a cogwheel of a huge global network. A big cogwheel, but a cogwheel nonetheless."

Nigel replied, "Don't underestimate it, though. The Federal Reserve is the blooming flagship of the whole operation, if you please. When it was created in 1913, it was done as a sister operation of the old Bank of England, which operates identically. It was expected and anticipated that the Federal Reserve would ultimately overshadow all banking systems in the alliance because of the sheer size and enormous potential of the US economy. Obviously, they were right. Without the Federal Reserve's existence, we would not be where we are right now, and our influence would not be bloody half of what it is today."

I didn't respond as my thoughts drifted back to the United States. It occurred to me that the general population in the United States, or anybody else for that reason, had no clue what-so-ever. They had no idea at all what the Federal Reserve was and how they manipulated the funds of the people of the United States. Nor did they know of the activities it was involved in. I was certain that if they did know, the uproar would be so enormous it would be the end of the system. Little by little, I started to see a bigger picture, where seemingly independent organizations like the Federal

Reserve, the Bank of England, the International Monetary Fund, the United Nations and scores of other smaller institutions were all part of a larger network, controlled and managed by a small group of extraordinarily wealthy financiers, industrialists, and very powerful families.

As I was thinking, a question that had been nagging in the back of my mind for some time came up. "What I don't get, though, is why would the Federal Reserve continue to print more money when that action ultimately will kill the currency? I get the inflation part of it and the residual interest effect, but it seems the continual issuance of more debt will have a destructive influence on the currency over time. It seems that would be counterproductive to the Federal Reserve or any debt-issuing institution like it."

Nigel smiled and said, "Don't be surprised to see an ocean of debt being issued over the next couple of years, in the United States and in Europe alike. Every bubble in any Keynesian economy when it bursts is ultimately transferred to government spending. The current blow-up of the housing market and the loss of asset values is deflationary, which is a government's nightmare because there is no remedy against deflation. Debt increases, then incomes decrease and it has to run its course. In order to fight it they will act with massive fiscal intervention, true to the Keynesian intervention principles. It is the perfect excuse to take control of whole industries, to overhaul the economy and to print more money than they can ever dream of paying back."

"And if the intervention does not work, if the debt can't be paid back and the currency fails, what a perfect excuse to introduce a new currency in combination with other countries and create a one-world currency with its own debt-issuing institution. Mirroring a Federal Reserve but on a global basis," I surmised.

"You are getting the picture," Nigel said laughingly. "Not too bad at all. You are beginning to see the future and how we are going about getting there."

"Socialize losses and privatize gains. Do you really believe it will work out that way?" I asked. "I mean, the process of currency failure, whatever method is used, can not happen without untold suffering and massive loss of personal asset values. I would assume that populations will resist, maybe even violently protest. What makes you think they will accept a new currency offered by those who destroyed the previous one?"

Nigel flicked the hair from his eyes as he answered. "To start with, you have to believe in the solution. You have to believe beyond a shadow of a doubt that the final solution is the right solution. Then you will be able to accept the sacrifices necessary to arrive there." He was quiet for a moment while he sipped his drink. "Many bloody awful conflicts in this world have been orchestrated as a means to obtain certain goals. It is exactly the suffering and destruction these conflicts leave in their wake that are the convincing factors to the populations that change is necessary. We control the conflict and we control the solution."

It reminded me of Cloward and Piven, who in the 1960's wanted to overload the welfare system in the United States with the intent to bankrupt it. In the wake of the destruction they would be able to reconstruct a new and better government, eradicating poverty by instituting a guaranteed annual income.

Whereas their approach has not had the desired effect as of yet, a recruit of theirs, George Wiley, used the same principles in conjunction with community organizers (read agitators) with more success. It is thought that his tactics of overwhelming welfare offices with demands, ultimately aided in the bankruptcy of the city of New York in 1975.

Nigel agreed when I mentioned this and reiterated that controlling the conflict makes you control the solution. The only reason that Cloward-Piven and the New York initiative were not successful was because they were ahead of their time. The legislative changes needed to promote the desired transformation hadn't occurred as of yet. "But today, that isn't far away," he assured me.

CHAPTER 11

Lunch was catered for those wishing to stay in the building. Both Nigel and I chose to remain, and as we walked into the dining area in the left wing of the building, I spotted Yuri. After the previous night's verbal encounter with Jean-François, I wasn't sure what to expect from the few people I had met so far. I was cautious with Yuri, wondering how he would respond to me. But to my relief, and judging from his reaction, he either didn't share the Frenchman's thoughts or was not aware of them.

"Stephen, you sit with me," he bellowed across the room. Same suit, I was sure and same shirt. For all intents and purposes, he looked as if he never went to bed and had spent the night drinking, which is what he was doing while motioning me to his table.

"I see you met Yuri," Nigel said laughingly as he followed me.

Yuri shook my hand while his other clutched a tumbler of Chivas. Both he and Nigel exchanged greetings, and we sat down for lunch. And I remembered drinking just as Yuri did, and I remembered how it felt in the mornings after not having slept nights. And I remembered how in the end it just didn't work for me anymore. Not before I lost a second marriage and most things dear. I remembered well, and it was those memories that keep it green for me. Seeing Yuri, however well he may have seemed to function, I knew what he was doing, and I knew the obsession inside. But none of that mattered that afternoon while we had lunch.

"Tonight dinner with my friend, yes?" Yuri reminded me after lunch. I hadn't forgotten the invitation he'd extended the previous day and was actually looking forward to the encounter. I concurred and agreed to meet him at the conclusion of the day's sessions at the bar where we had first met. It was there where he headed after lunch, when both Nigel and I returned to the conference room upstairs to continue with the subsequent meetings.

The topics covered that afternoon were market oriented, inasmuch that they concerned themselves with information on how to profit on specific events that were to occur in the near future. The Bear Stearns option play was brought up as an example of how to profit by pooling funds for those who participated, while anonymity was maintained.

There were three speakers, one from Goldman Sachs, another from a large German trading house and a third official from the SEIU, who discussed companies and industries they felt would exhibit big moves in their stock values over the coming weeks and months. Some of the names suggested were Fannie Mae and Freddie Mac, and it was intimated that the Russians were in the process of selling large quantities of both stocks in an effort to bankrupt the two institutions thereby placing additional financial pressure on the United States.

Other names offered were the three big automakers in the United States. It was the union official from the SEIU who, in no uncertain terms made it clear that a push to take over the automobile industry would be staged in the coming year, depending on the result of the election. The representative made an interesting point in that a long-term process of union control was about to come to fruition.

He told us that the basic philosophy all along had been that the legislative and executive environments in the United States would ultimately accommodate a union-driven and organized market. This couldn't have happened without a carefully orchestrated campaign, with origins in the early twentieth century and the push by the progressives' movement. His point was that all the pieces of the puzzle were in place and through the power of the unions whole industries would be placed under pressure, thereby reducing their stock values to near zero and forcing a collapse.

With the right administration these collapses would then be taken advantage of in the name of bail-outs, as opposed to bankruptcies and reorganizations. Bailouts, it was touted, would save the jobs, and it would be a "peoples' victory." The real victory would be for the unions and the government who in the process would take control of major portions of the US commerce at pennies on the dollar. According to the official, the coming administration would accommodate and finalize this process. We were encouraged to take advantage of the forced decline of the automobile, healthcare and insurance industries.

Nigel sat next to me and I could tell he was as fascinated by the information as I was. It was laid out to us, detailing how everything was prearranged and organized. I knew this was price fixing, insider trading, securities manipulation, fraud, and front running, just to name a few of the laws that were being broken. People go to prison for this, and it was discussed here as if no laws applied, as if there was no danger of it being publicized and blown wide open.

Leaning over to Nigel, I commented, "This is sensitive stuff. Doesn't anybody fear exposure?"

"I don't bloody think so," he replied. "We're a very select group, remember that. But even more important, suppose somebody were to make this public. Do you really believe the public at large would listen or even care? Anybody exposing this would immediately be ridiculed and labeled with a conspiratorial paranoid disorder. Their lives would be taken apart and destroyed and their credibility wiped out. Those in government have no interest in exposure because they benefit from this, and the press is part of us."

Nigel smiled and went on to say something that reminded me of Johan, who phrased the exact idea in near-identical terms not six months earlier and I wondered if they knew each other.

"What is important to understand is that people in general are simple in their desires and that as long as you feed them what they long for, they will follow right along," Nigel said. "Give them their TV, religion, food, home, sex and alcohol and they are mollified and believe they are free. Threaten those daily comforts, and you have discontent. Disrupting it creates public disorder. Take it away, and you risk revolution. They don't want to hear anything that threatens their day-to day lives. All we do here is plan the future so that the masses have their opium, and I am not just referring to religion."

He chuckled at his own remark, taking Karl Marx's famous quote that "religion is the opium of the people" into a broader context.

"The point is, let them try to expose this. Few would believe it to start with and the price to pay would be too high."

I understood Nigel's statement well about planning the future. Having been a trader in many commodity groups, I gained somewhat of an appreciation for how essential products move around the world. Trade policies, international accords and agreements are not set up to secure the flow of goods for a nation just for today or tomorrow. They're designed to protect the uninterrupted access, availability and distribution of these products for the next generations. When we go to the gas station and expect there to be gas for our cars and fuel to heat our homes, when we go to the grocery stores and expect there to be bread, milk and food in varieties that boggle the mind at times and when we expect drugstores to carry any medicines we may need, very, very few of us ask this simple question, "How do these goods just show up? How is this done without interruption, from day to day, week to week, month to month, year in and year out?" Instead, it is taken for granted that they are available. And whereas it is exactly this attitude that is part of the reason why it actually works, a certain naiveté of not caring how it is done is the greater component of the public's attitude, just as long as it is.

One thing is for certain, nothing is given away. The goods and products we need don't just show up because of the benevolence of the human race. The reason we have access to them is because it was set up that way a long time ago. As today, we are preparing and safeguarding the continuous delivery and supply of our basic livelihood, not just for us, but for our children and theirs in turn. The process of assuring this continued availability is messy, difficult and ruthless at times—a practice generally not visible or known to the public at large. It's often distasteful and unpleasant because there is no room for error—the basic needs of a nation are either supplied, or they are not. There is no in-between.

The fact is, we are continuously three days away from disaster. If our infrastructure crumbles and there is no fuel to create electricity, or for trucks or trains to deliver goods, cities will run out of food in only a few days. Riots will break out and hordes will roam the streets looking for sustenance. In the end, people will eat each other. As a population we have forgotten how to make or create our own nutrition. If it is not in the grocery store, we are lost. As a result, when international agreements don't fulfill these necessities, when other nations have differing goals for the basic commodities they need or offer, sanctions are applied, tariffs are raised and oftentimes wars are fought.

So Nigel's remark about planning the future was not lost on me. What was becoming clear was to what extent this planning was orchestrated and pre-arranged and how blatantly it was laid out with the obvious intent of this very select group's benefit.

A short break was announced before the last ninety-minute session of the day was to start. The local time was three o'clock in the afternoon, so at home it would be nine o'clock in the morning with the day ready to start.

I retrieved my phone and once away from the building, I called the office. With my assistants Sharon and Kevin on the phone, I spent about five minutes catching up and I was reassured all was under control and all settlements had gone through. I was pleased to learn that they both had been able to transact some business in my absence with a few local clients. In response to Sharon's inquiry about when I would be back, I told her most likely the following Monday and with that hung up.

Next, I called Nicole trying to get a hold of her before her day started. I had been missing her and was looking forward to hearing her voice. But as she answered, her irritated tone took me off guard.

"Stephen, what is going on?" Her voice sharp and demanding.

"What are you talking about? I'm just calling to see how you're doing."

"I don't appreciate getting calls in the middle of the night by strangers asking me where you are and what you are doing, especially from a woman." An audible sigh of frustration came through the line, followed by, "I don't know what you are involved in, but for some strange woman to have my number and to…"

"Nicole, Nicole, hold a minute, just listen to me for a second," I interrupted her loudly, ignoring her barrage while trying to get her attention.

She shut up and managed an exasperated, "What…?"

"I don't know what is going on and I don't know who is calling you at night. Somebody is checking up on me and not just through you, but through Anthony as well. Please, tell me when did they call and what did they ask?"

"She called twice last night and wanted to know if you were with me. When I asked who was calling she said her name was Mary and that she works with you. It made no sense for her to call at three thirty in the morning, so I told her it was none of her business and hung up on her. Then she called again about ten minutes later. She insisted she needed to know where you were and I just told her that if she works with you then she should know, which pissed her off. So I hung up on her again." She paused and I could hear her breathing and I knew she was upset. Without waiting for me she went on. "Stephen, I don't appreciate women calling me looking for you in the middle of the night, who is she?"

"Sweetheart, ple…" I started but didn't get far.

"Don't sweetheart me, who is she?" she insisted abruptly.

Losing my temper to an extent, I raised my voice. "Goddammit, I am telling you I don't know. Something is going on behind my back and it is coming from more than one side and you have to believe me when I tell you I don't know who she is or what she wants. Why didn't you call and ask me?"

The line was quiet for some time before she answered, "Whatever you do, make it stop. We'll talk more when you get back. I have to go now."

Her voice was cold and detached and there was no good bye when the line went dead.

"Fuck this," I muttered under my breath. I didn't need this bullshit. The implication there was another woman involved angered me. There never had been anything of the kind in our relationship and even though I could understand her feelings, the unprovoked and implied guilty verdict was undeserved and not something I had expected. This, combined with the uneasy atmosphere caused by Jean-François' comments the previous evening, left me with a pit in my stomach.

It was with these feelings that I entered the conference room to partake in the last session of the day. Nigel was already present and I took my seat next to him. Still no sign of Jean-François. Margaretha was present in the front row and had been able to avoid my gaze successfully so far.

A gentleman in his early to mid-sixties, with combed-back grey hair, stepped up onto the platform. He was dressed in a dark linen suit with a darker grey t-shirt, the long sleeves ever so slightly extending from under the jacket at the wrists. The shoes appeared Italian, black woven leather, seeming well-fitting and comfortable. Impeccable image. Not too flashy, very European and very tasteful.

He was holding reading glasses in one hand and a folder in the other as he stood still, looking back at the room. A cleanly shaven tanned face, square jaws with deep lines in the cheeks that earlier in life could have been dimples. Strong and weathered, there was no smile present. His mouth too wide for the face, attributed to an unforgiving disposition with dark eyes piercing like a hawk from under thick eyebrows.

He looked very familiar to me, but I dismissed the notion, not being able to place him within the context of the meeting. I was told to expect an official of the Federal Reserve Bank of New York. What surprised me, though, was the cultured image this man portrayed. Not that the Federal Reserve Bank of New York and culture are antonyms, I just expected a more stuffy banker type of personality. This man's approach impressed me and I was looking forward to listening to him.

Not six feet tall, his posture alone had an arresting effect. It took no more than a few seconds for the room to quiet, which he left that way at least for another five until he spoke.

Then it hit me and I knew who he was. "Is that van Buren?" I whispered to Nigel.

110

FEDERAL

Next to me, he responded quickly, not wanting to disrupt the beginning. "Yes, it is. I like this guy. He is absolutely bloody brilliant—this is going to be interesting."

The intro was short and to the point. "Most of you know me. For those who do not, my name is Austin van Buren, and today I have been asked to represent the Federal Reserve Bank of New York."

Uneven teeth, contrasting the cultured image while adding a somewhat predacious edge—with perfectly manicured nails. He paused, looked around as if to gauge the effect his first statement may have had.

So this was Austin van Buren. The legendary, infamously powerful and wealthy hedge-fund manager. Behind the scenes for most, but very much known in financial and political circles, this billionaire had the muscle and clout to singlehandedly move markets and political tides alike. It was even rumored he was the authority behind the liberal left, the progressives, and it was he who set policy and direction and decided who would flourish financially and politically and who would not.

I leaned over to Nigel and asked quietly, "Why is *he* representing the Fed?" There were many more questions, but this was all I could muster at the moment.

Nigel dismissed me, not wanting to miss anything. "Shh... just listen, and it will make sense. He has power and direction and clarity of vision."

Austin continued, the voice deep and melodious without hesitation, clearly accustomed to publicly addressing sizable groups of influential people.

"We are in the midst of historic times. Many outside this group don't realize this as of yet and I believe even some who are here may not either. We are witnessing events that never before have occurred in the financial history of our time. The interconnectedness of this global economy has reached a point where decisions made on microeconomic levels will have major effects on macroeconomic systems, continents and oceans removed. A homeowner's choice not to pay his mortgage in Nebraska may cause a bank in Iceland to become insolvent. The resolve to pay off the note on a car rather than trade up to a newer model by a woman in Texas may cause layoffs in factories in Germany. The fear of a store owner in Florida that buyers will spend less will cause banks in London to cease issuing credit and this lack of credit will cause companies in Europe and the United States to fail and place even more people on the brink of bankruptcy the world over. These are all events we are witnessing today and whereas they may be regarded as the cause of our financial difficulties, they are in fact symptomatic of a larger and more troublesome dilemma."

He paused, placed the folder on the ebony lectern, opened it, and removed a few of the papers. Using his reading glasses he studied the information for a few moments and then replaced the sheets. His left hand casually draped in his jacket's side pocket, he stepped away from the podium and went on.

"The post-Second World War unprecedented economic expansion in the United States and its allies found its root in the expansion of credit facilities to a Western population tired of war and strife and ready to settle down and build a new society. The two industrial complexes competing with the United States, Germany and Japan, had been destroyed, making the American industry the supreme survivor, eager to facilitate a nation and a world ready to absorb all its products and financial services. Sixty years later, this credit explosion and the consequent liabilities it created in all levels of society has run its course. The mathematical formula discounting future income through the issuance of credit by anticipating higher wages and price structures is flawed simply because the inflation-based system it relies on will not stimulate increases in consumer demand ad infinitum. It can not do so simply because the consumer group creating this demand is shrinking, and thus its historical push on asset values falters accordingly. As such, industries seeking to move their production need to discount its final value to the consumer. But today, even this price erosion is insufficient to create a modicum of demand. Such is the basis of the problem we are faced with, the attrition of asset values in the face of escalating debt. Combine this with the reluctance of financial institutions to issue credit and we have the makings of unprecedented economic instability."

He delivered the words with finality, matching the intonation with the intended importance of the message. It had somewhat of a Greenspan-esque effect, a mixture of pontifical delivery varied with a portentous choice of language.

Weighing his words and pausing before continuing, he emphasized the next statement.

"It is in these times that opportunities are fostered that only rarely present themselves. The ability to take advantage of these rare occasions can only be appreciated through identification of the coordinated organization that caused the instability in the first place. Even though the origin of today's financial instability goes back over a quarter of a century, the building blocks of its creation were carefully planned. They were staged in concert with popular political agendas, promoted by a press largely owned and controlled by us, in order to produce the opportunities that present themselves to us to date."

That caught my attention. It was as if I could hear my own words spoken to Johan in Basel some six months earlier come back to me through this speaker.

Austin continued. "The prospects in front of us are not limited to depository and commercial assets, but on a larger perspective a currency potential is at play as well. It will involve both the North American and European monetary systems, even though this timeline may be opaque as of yet." Greenspan-esque all over again.

"I will elucidate on this further. The more immediate issue concerns the current consequences of today's credit markets' disequilibrium. The recent fallout we have seen so far has been the infamous Bear Stearns failure, which members of our group absorbed. This bankruptcy was well publicized, but many more depositories in Europe and in the United States have quietly failed, thus allowing us to accumulate assets at values otherwise impossible to obtain. However, not all failures are going to be absorbed as easily. To note, and I caution you to be careful, the credit markets were shaken on January 23 this year when rumors of a Lehman Brothers insolvency surfaced. Even though these reports were denied and markets normalized to an extent, I am here to clarify that the initial warnings were correct and that any positions with Lehman as a counterparty, any open positions in its stock, or any exposure whatsoever to this name should be treated with utmost prejudice. No facility will be offered here, nor will it be absorbed within this group."

I actually remember January 23, 2008. A Wednesday, the bond market opened with the ten-year Treasury Note gapping lower in yield at 3.281%, over twenty basis points down from the previous day's close of 3.484%. Rumors everywhere about a Lehman insolvency, and the markets panicked. But as van Buren correctly relayed, the story was discredited, and the markets returned to a sense of normalcy. Numbers seldom lie though. A warning had been sounded, a warning that evidently should be heeded, I was just told. Looking sideways, I noticed Nigel looking at me. "You remember that?" I quietly asked.

"Some bloody chap at Goldman leaked the story trying to impress a female trader at another desk. She in turn told a few large clients and fund managers, and the rest is history," was Nigel's response "They fired him that same morning." So he knew as well and obviously a lot more. Considering this train of thought, my mind was redirected to van Buren's voice.

"I want to address one more point prior to touching on the currency topic. We have been hearing about AIG and questions have been posed demonstrating the concern felt about this matter. I understand the combined corporate and individual exposure of our group to this institution is considerable and therefore I am here to confirm to you that similar measures that were extended to the Bear Stearns acquisition will be applied here. Substantial funds and structures will be made available through a Maiden Lane type of vehicle, which should sufficiently reassure each of you that not only will your principal be safe, but your total investment will be honored."

Nigel leaned over as Austin paused and whispered, "I like that, *'individual exposure.'* Everybody here knows the president of the New York Fed personally owns AIG stock, so you bloody well know a bail-out is coming." I had heard the same rumor in the market, that Timothy Geithner was long AIG in his personal holdings and that therefore the bailout was a foregone conclusion. I thought it intriguing having it confirmed in this group of insiders.

Van Buren had been striding back and forth while speaking, but then stood still phrasing his last sentence. He had the undivided attention of all. The finality and confidence with which the information was relayed impressed me. It left no doubt about the outcome of the events. I was learning about the actual behind-the-scenes mechanics of how the financial world really operated. Hands went up and voices interrupted each other in efforts to pose questions. A single gesture of van Buren's hand was all it took to restore quiet.

"I understand there are many questions, and we will have time for these. Prior though, I beg your patience and allow me to finish. It will complete the vision that I want to impress upon you."

He stopped briefly emphasizing the last sentence, and deliberately filled a glass with water from a carafe. Again, he looked around as if to gauge the impact of his words. He took a sip and continued.

"The economic downturn currently in progress both in Europe and the United States will be dealt with on traditional Keynesian principles. Significant economic intervention is to be expected in an effort to jumpstart growth and aggregate demand. Two issues of importance will have to be taken into consideration. First, the upcoming presidential election will produce a president with great Keynesian convictions, among other qualities, which we will discuss tomorrow. Second, is the understanding that no matter what size of fiscal stimulus is applied, it is the opinion of this forum that it will not create the desired result." A brief pause.

"The lack of liquidity in both the European and American financial systems is systemic and can not be seen outside a prolonged period of deleveraging. Even though intervention attempts will produce brief periods of perceived growth and productivity, our general view is that the current existing burden of deficits will stifle any possible expansion, and any increases in deficits through quantitative easing types of interventions will only exacerbate the predicament. Regardless of any intervention attempts, without the necessary unwinding of the complex debt structures currently in place, any sustained increases in both consumer demand and industrial production are deemed unattainable. However, as will become clear, vast resources will be injected into the economy anyway. There is no reason why fiscal stimulus can not be applied as a mechanism of redistributive change."

Interrupting himself, he removed his jacket and draped it nonchalantly over the lectern, exposing a trim and strong physique. This guy knew how to create an impression and was not shy in doing so. He took another sip, deliberately shuffled through some of his papers, and waited prior to moving on. His remarks about Lehman reminded me again of my discussion with Johan in Basel, and I wondered about Johan, how much did he really know?

What Austin had just told us was that they knew that throwing gigantic amounts of money at the economy would not help, but they were going to do it anyway, disguising redistribution of wealth as fiscal intervention. The speaker disrupted my musing.

"The previous time the United States faced a similar deflationary environment is better known as the Great Depression. At that time, the Federal Reserve restricted funding into the economy and actually tightened the money supply considerably. This one event, this tightening of the money supply, is thought to have been the cause of the Great Depression. Today I insist our actions will differ drastically."

I was hearing it right. Austin van Buren just indicated he would insist on the Federal Reserve acting differently. Quite a statement for anybody to make, let alone somebody who was not employed by the Federal Reserve to start with. I was privy to an immense display of power, all relayed in one simple sentence.

He continued. "We find ourselves in a position to accelerate and activate the next stage in our long-term goal of global governance. As a side note, you will find the next president of the United States to be sympathetic to a variety of ideals that will overlap, if not match our objectives."

"What new president?" I thought. Was this guy actually telling us he knew who the next POTUS was going to be? But he didn't elaborate.

"If part of our ambition is the globalization of financial systems, then we should look at the European Union as an example. In contrast, the European Central Bank does not share our power and ability to issue currency, but I will return to this later. This, by the way was the main reason for the United Kingdom not joining the euro. The Bank of England is a bank of issue, as is the Federal Reserve." He stood still, took a sip of water and proceeded.

"When founded in 1993, the essence of the European Union was to create a uniform multi-state society providing for the free movement of its residents, goods, and trade within the community. Of the twenty-seven member states, so far sixteen have agreed on a uniform currency, the euro, which became effective in 1999, thereby creating the Eurozone. This couldn't have been done without the standardization of judicial, financial, and commercial structures and oversight across the various borders. It is exactly this standardization that is the requisite we are looking for. Not only a European, but a global union that would eventually include the North American currencies."

He picked up a few sheets of paper from the lectern, read it over and continued.

"Consider these four areas of activity. One, the United Nations as a basis. Two, the Federal Reserve, IMF, World Bank, and BIS as financial oversight systems. Three, the acceptance of the International Criminal Court with super-sovereign jurisdiction and its enforcement branch, Interpol. And four, the ratification of the United Nation's Rome Statute by the next United States administration. We are witnessing progress readying us for the next phase."

He had no qualms about giving the appearance that he knew who the next administration was going to be. Whether he did or not, I had known for a long time the power of the Federal Reserve over presidential elections. But to realize the Fed merely reacted to forces and people even more powerful was a revelation I had not expected. I wondered if I was the only one present who was surprised about this. He went on.

"A multi-front approach has been carefully orchestrated, and financial turbulence is needed to happen simultaneously in Europe and the United States. The United States will compromise vast amounts of funds dedicated to various bail-outs and interventions. Such will be the scope of issuance so as to ultimately undermine the confidence in the currency and remove the United States dollar as the number-one reserve currency. The world's number-two reserve currency, the deutschmark, is the backbone of the euro. Very much against the wishes of the Germans, certain nations were allowed into the Eurozone even though it was clear from the onset that their fiscal responsibility and ethics were far removed from the expectations and norms of the participating Northern European countries. It was through our insistence that these nations became part of the Eurozone as they are instrumental in the development of our objective. Even though stringent measures were put in place safeguarding fiscal accountability and defined debt ratios, we were certain some of these financially weaker and less-disciplined entities would ultimately not be able to maintain control. Therefore, they will either covertly or openly fall behind, which is according to plan."

Being familiar with the European cultures, I remember wondering in 2000 when Greece qualified for admission into the Zone, whether it was wise. Everybody in Northwestern Europe understood that Greece as a nation adhered to a different discipline about its financial affairs. Apparently, as I just learned, the powers behind the scenes convinced the right people to make it happen anyway.

Austin said, "Consider the European Central Bank not being a bank of issue. The resulting interventions will have to be burdened directly by the participating nations, making their initial protests a much despised reality. This will underscore the need for a European Central Banking system of issue, such as the Federal Reserve and the Bank of England. And a similar lack of confidence in the euro as in the United States dollar will result. Whether these events are to be paired with hyperinflation, currency failures, sovereign bankruptcies, massive unemployment and perhaps even military interventions can not be foreseen from here. It will definitely create deeply felt fissures on both continents. This will be our impetus to introduce a one world currency, accepted by the multitudes as the solution to end their suffering and restore peace and calm once again. What better way to fulfill one's destiny than through the careful creation of crises and to offer the masses restitution that fits our long-term goal of global financial governance?"

Austin bowed his head slightly, acknowledging the audience, stepped off the small stage, and left the conference room. A private "Gustav" announced Mr. van Buren would be back in twenty minutes to address any questions. As the rest of the participants stood and milled about, the room filled with a low buzz of voices conversing.

I remained seated. Here I was listening to a foreigner representing the Federal Reserve telling me how they conspired and manipulated the systems with the intent for the world's major currencies to fail in order to create a new world currency ruled by central banking systems controlled by them, while they determined the next presidency of the United States. Nobody would believe this if I told them. If I hadn't been present, I would not have believed the depth of the deception either.

I walked downstairs and retrieved my cell phone from Gustav. It occurred to me that I had turned the gadget off when I delivered it upon entering the building. Receiving it back the phone was on and not locked any longer. Perhaps I had not shut it off correctly, I told myself, partly dismissing the issue and partly making note to be more aware next time.

Once outside in the gardens, it informed me of two voicemails and one text message. The voicemails were from the office, and the text from my son Anthony was only one word, "email." The stega software we used to communicate was installed on my laptop only, so I had to go to the hotel to communicate with him. It would have to wait till later. Checking the messages, I learned both Kevin and Sharon had been trying to reach me about some settlements. No news from Nicole, and even though I hadn't really expected a call from her, the fact there was none bothered me.

CHAPTER 12

I didn't return to the question session of the meeting that afternoon. Speaking first with Sharon, I was assured business was well. She remarked that Nicole had been trying to reach her during the day, but for some reason they hadn't been able to make contact. The two women knew each other, and oftentimes Nicole would learn about my agenda and updates on my timetable from Sharon, and a sort of friendship had developed over the years. But considering my unpleasant encounter with Nicole earlier in the day, I was wondering what it was she was after, if anything at all.

My discussion with Kevin had a different spin. He had received a message over Beta, the industry-standard settlement communication system between clearing houses and brokerages, asking him to recap the transaction that delivered the Federal Reserve stock into my account. As long as nobody had claimed an imbalance, or delivery mistake, there was no need for a recap. Evidently none had, so the error had gone unnoticed for all these months. Until now that is, and the fact that the request coincided with Jean-François' open confrontation about my attendance, made me suspect the two events were connected.

I needed to slow down the discovery process and avoid being exposed as an illegitimate participant. I was familiar enough with the operational side of my business to know that the Beta query was a computer driven probe, albeit initiated by human intervention. More than likely, a few hundred of these requests had gone out to various dealers with whom transactions had been executed that particular day. Ultimately, through checking, rechecking, and re-matching, the error would be narrowed down to only a few possibilities and then corrected. By not responding to the request an interruption would occur in the final reconciliation and hopefully give me some time.

First thing I asked Kevin was, "Did you already answer?" to which he answered negatively, wanting to wait for my input first. With a distinct feeling in my throat, as if a noose was fastened around it, I told him, "Don't respond. Leave it open and don't do anything on this issue until I approve it."

Kevin hesitated, not wanting to object to his boss, yet knowing he had to say something. "Are you sure that is the right thing to do? I can't ignore this type of request."

At that moment my cell phone beeped and another text message arrived from Anthony. For a second time he prompted me. "Check email—urgent." However much I wanted to return to the meeting, I had to go to my hotel to retrieve his message. He would not emphasize it, were it not important.

So I wound down my conversation. "Kevin, I repeat, don't respond. This is a first request only. Remember too that this is my personal portfolio, so technically speaking it does not involve you. I do appreciate your concern though, but when you receive a subsequent notice, or anything else, just call me. And this must stay between us, you understand?" I had always trusted him and had no reason not to do so now. But this was the first time I asked him to do something that could be construed as against regulations. There was no time anymore to worry about trusting him. I was in way too deep and could feel a shift in my reality. I didn't like the way it felt, a certain dread that I was on the edge of the abyss staring into a deep, dark hole.

Whatever I had involved myself in was starting to unravel. I had decided, however, that the information and knowledge gained at the meetings was worth staying, regardless of Jean-François and the noise he was making. More was to be learned at the evening dinner with Yuri and the next day's meeting when the presidential elections were to be discussed. I was determined to go the distance and find out all I could before I'd be barred from doing so.

While most made their way back to the third-floor conference room, Jean-François crossed my path as I was leaving. I returned his gaze and our eyes locked for a split second. "No love lost between the two of us," occurred to me as I exited the grounds and walked the few streets to my hotel. Once in my room, I booted up my laptop, retrieved Anthony's email, which consisted of a generic panoramic landscape and separated the embedded text from the picture.

"NCS[6] origin of investigation in you—HUMINT directive joint CIA/Interpol—utmost care suggested. These guys don't play nice. We should discuss options in case you need help. Can be there within two hours. Intel suggests jihadist ops in your area for high-level meeting. Not sure this connected with you, but considering the type of attention you attracted thought you should know."

His warning to use "utmost care" made me uncomfortable, as I had no idea how to apply that in my current situation, and for him, in special ops himself, to tell me to be careful meant it was serious. I told him about the dinner meeting I was about to attend with Yuri and his contact and that I would be in touch later in the evening. I refrained from informing him about Yuri designating the visitor as Taliban, not wanting to escalate events before I knew the details, but remark about Jihadist ops was not lost on me. The fact he was only a few hours removed from me was a sense of relief as Pfullendorf was only seventy miles or so north of Zurich.

Leaving my laptop at the hotel and walking back, I wondered about Anthony's indication of jihadist ops in the area and if it was connected with Yuri's contact. Obviously, he thought it relevant enough to let me in on this information.

After going through the security scrutiny, I entered the Parkring building and walked into the bar. By now, Yuri had become a fixture and I noticed him in the corner sitting at one of the tables with three other gentlemen. The place was crowded and smoky.

I weaved my way through the crowd and came up to his table. It was then that I noticed two of the three men could have been twins. Eastern features, both shaved heads but bearded, brown leather coats down to their thighs, which considering the weather was a bit much. Each had similar sunglasses, one wearing them, the other placed on his forehead.

The moment I approached, both raised and inserted themselves between the table and myself. The movement was quick and smooth and done without attracting the attention of others around us. It was very effective and clear in its message—"You will not get any closer without approval."

---

[6] NCS – National Clandestine Service – previously the Directorate of Operations, main organization for handling HUMINT (Human Intelligence) from within the CIA.

The one with the sunglasses on his forehead had his coat buttoned only at the bottom, giving me a clear view of two sizable handguns, one under each armpit. I was sure his twin had similar credentials, but chose not to flaunt it. The third man at the table exchanged a few quick words with Yuri in a language I didn't understand and then curtly addressed the men in front of me, who parted ways and let me through.

This third man sitting next to Yuri was of indeterminate age, perhaps in his late-twenties to mid-thirties. He must have clout, I thought, being allowed armed guards inside the building. Dressed in a business suit, he looked relaxed and comfortable. A slight body structure, lean and almost somewhat frail looking, his facial structure told a different story. Deep lines and weathered dark skin with nearly black Asiatic eyes belied his image. This man had been exposed to discomfort and was accustomed to hardship. His gaze had a forbidding and uncompromising caliber, a trait rarely found amongst older men, even rarer in those his age. In striking contrast, his mouth had a gentle curve to it, lined by a black, well-trimmed goatee. Jet-black hair, long and tied in a knot fastened on the top of his head, created the unusual image of a man not at home, but at perfect ease. As he reached to greet me, I noticed there was nothing frail about him and his hand was hard and callused.

Yuri introduced him as Mohammed, omitting any further credentials. He greeted me in perfect Oxford English without even the slightest hint of an accent. I sat down as Yuri looked at me and inquired after the meeting,

"How was van Buren? He has good grasp of what happens and delivers good message. You like him, no?"

"Yes," I replied. "The information he offered was very impressive."

Ordering tea, I noticed Yuri now had the bottle of Chivas on the table which he used to refill his glass. Mohammed was drinking tea as well. The twins drank nothing.

Mixing Golden Gates with Chivas, I watched as Yuri inhaled deeply from the delivery mechanism (this is what the tobacco companies refer to as cigarettes) and let the smoke slowly drift from his mouth, creating a sort of misty effect around the still standing remnants of the Stonehenge formation. I had to look away to avoid becoming engrossed in the absurd vision I was having.

It was Mohammed, though, who intrigued me and I was waiting for an opportunity to query Yuri about who this guy was, but I had to be patient. I was hoping dinner would afford a moment where I could corner

Yuri. He informed us that it was going to be on the second floor in one of the private conference rooms and that a select group would join us.

I noticed two other men lingering at opposite sides of the bar, untouched drinks in front of them. These two were less obvious than the twins with their leather coats, but they were part of Mohammed's protection. Positioned strategically, they could see who approached, entered and left the area. Both bearded and wearing sunglasses with distinct Middle Eastern complexions. Hair too long, the coat jackets buttoned up, jeans and black high-top Cheetah sneakers, they were not present for the conference. Neither moved until Yuri finished his last Chivas and stood up.

He led the way, followed by the twins flanking Mohammed as much as possible, with me in tow. As we passed the bar, the two black high-tops followed behind me. It was all done very casually, but I could see these guys were well trained and knew exactly what they were doing.

A second-floor conference room had been converted into a dining room and the table was set for eight. An open bar in the corner was made available for those wishing to use it, which was not wasted on Yuri. Two personal "Gustavs" were available for whatever we deemed necessary and waited quietly in a corner, ready to make the event run smoothly. The high-tops never entered the room, but the twins did and took their positions on each side of the door.

Yuri headed for the bar and as he was pouring his drink, I seized the opportunity. Standing shoulder to shoulder with him, acting as if I was interested in the assortment of spirits offered, I asked him quietly, "Who is Mohammed?"

Yuri waited with his answer until his glass was filled with just the right amount of Chivas and ice, took a sip and turned to me. "Full name is Mohammed Haqqani." Observing me to see whether the information had any effect, he offered nothing else, just the name.

My eyes widened in amazement. If this was who I thought it was, then this was a very big deal. "The Haqqani from Pakistani Waziristan?" I probed incredulously.

"You right. Not bad you know this," Yuri complimented me. Eyebrows raised and a gleam in his eye told me he was impressed, just as I was when he volunteered his thoughts on Cézanne.

"So this is Maulavi Jalaluddin's son?" I insisted to be sure.

"Again, you correct. I am impressed." Yuri continued looking at me. He smiled, realizing I was aware of the enormity of the situation.

I knew who Maulavi Jalaluddin Haqqani was. How I found out about the man was through an unrelated event. Not six months earlier I had seen an excellent movie and became intrigued by the story. Based on actual events, I spent considerable time and effort figuring out the true account behind *Charlie Wilson's War*. It chronicled the events of CIA Operation Cyclone during the 1979 – 1989 war between Afghanistan and the USSR. The operation arranged for support to the Afghan mujahedeen fighters against the Russians. Then Texas Congressman Charlie Wilson (played by Tom Hanks) spearheaded the initiative. Maulavi Jalaluddin Haqqani, Mohammed's father, was one of the main mujahedeen fighters receiving weapons, logistics, training, funds and intelligence from the CIA. As was Osama Bin Laden.

After the United States' withdrawal from the region in 1989, the remaining mujahedeen factions radicalized and ultimately ended up in control of Afghanistan in 1992. First as a mujahedeen government, then in 1995 through Pakistani influence, the Taliban took over. Haqqani served as minister and military commander in both regimes, while working closely with the Pakistani Inter-Services Intelligence (ISI), until the United States' 2001 invasion into Afghanistan. It allowed him to set up an Afghan and Pakistani network of fighters, finances and support groups. It was generally believed it was the Haqqani Network that gave protection to Osama Bin Laden and helped Mullah Mohammed Omar, the Taliban leader, escape when his arrest by US forces was imminent in Afghanistan in late 2001.

Ultimately, the massive Haqqani Network joined forces with Al Qaeda and commands over ten thousand Taliban fighters. The network is believed to be so powerful as to pose imminent danger to the United States forces in the area and is actively overseen by both Maulavi Jalaluddin Haqqani and another son, Sirajuddin (Siraj).

Haqqani Sr. has twelve sons by two wives. Siraj acts as second in command of the network and is a member of the Quetta Shura, comprising the top echelon of the Taliban. Another son of the old man Haqqani is Mohammed. Not a top Taliban leader, but certainly working his way up in the ranks, he was known as a competent and dangerous warlord.

And here he was, sitting in a chair not ten feet away from me, being served a cup of tea. I could feel the hair on my neck stand up when I realized Anthony's warning about jihadist ops in the area. This whole conference and the dinner invite had taken an eerie turn in a direction I would never have been able to foresee.

Two others had entered the room. One of them I was already familiar with, Margaretha, who came up to me and acted ever so friendly, as if the earlier encounter with Jean-François hadn't occurred. Offering me her cheeks, I lightly kissed both in very European fashion and played along by being charming and pleasant.

Margaretha then introduced me to the other person, Ileana, a woman perhaps in her mid to late forties. Dark hair to her shoulders, nondescript features, other than her light-green eyes, which made you look twice, just to be sure you were right the first time. She had a pleasant demeanor and indicated she was an official of the Eurasian Economic Community (EAEC) from Moscow. I guessed her presence at the dinner was for assisting Mohammed and his guards through the system. Trying to speak to her was futile. Even though her English was proficient, her accent was thick, and she didn't smile for fear of exposing a badly repaired, but slightly better version of Yuri's Stonehenge. So I left her alone.

A knock on the door, and the twins allowed three others in. One gorgeous woman, perhaps in her mid-twenties, and two men, one of whom was Austin van Buren. This was Yuri's gig and he took pains in introducing everybody. I had my fifteen seconds with Austin exchanging polite greetings, but it was obvious his interest was not with me. After shaking my hand, he turned and walked over to the other side of the table where Mohammed was seated. Rising, the two shook hands, kissed and embraced. It was obviously not a first visit and both were very comfortable with each other.

This turn of events intrigued me, but in retrospect it made sense for Austin to know Mohammed. Their discussion was out in the open without any attempt to be discreet.

"How is your father?" he asked the young man. "I wish him well and am sorry we couldn't meet this time around, but perhaps at a future date."

"Allah willing, indeed a next occasion," Mohammed answered. He said that a life of war and fighting and living many times under impossible circumstances had left its mark on Haqqani Sr. "But Allah be merciful and will allow for a last visit perhaps."

Yuri introduced me to the third person entering the room as the IMF resident representative in Belarus. Named Jürgen Rothenbach-von-Holtz, I sensed an overbearing personality matched by his body type. Large frame, over six feet tall and likely close to three hundred pounds, he was massive. Bushy, dark, uncooperative hair combed away from his forehead, which seemed small with his hairline too low. A wild, shaggy uni-brow on a thick, protruding eyebrow ridge finished the look of a Neanderthal in a nice suit. Shaking his hand, which easily was twice the size of mine, I noticed dark, thick hair extruding from under his white cuff-linked shirt. A beast, I remember thinking. Yet this beast was the only one in the room who seemed to have any interest in me, so we chatted for some time prior to sitting for dinner.

Jürgen explained that although he was currently living in Minsk, his home was Nurnberg, Germany. Our conversation turned interesting when we realized our experience in banking was similar. After the London School of Economics he ended up on the repo desk with Goldman in London, from where he moved into collateral trading. Although I had never done repo, collateral was right up my alley and we figured out we had some mutual acquaintances. From there, the IMF had taken an interest in him and groomed him at their headquarters in D.C. prior to sending him out in the field.

"Of course I know Austin quite well," he responded to my inquiry if he knew Austin. "We work together on many occasions organizing fund transfers in and out of various regions."

It was only a day earlier that Yuri remarked to look past politic and ideal horizons to understand that financial arrangements don't just cease to exist merely because a new administration somewhere changed its views and alliances. Austin's openly friendly and familiar overtones with Mohammed, and the fact he knew Haqqani Sr. personally, made this abundantly clear. The business and financing arrangements among the parties in the room were alive and well, notwithstanding the fact we, the United States, were at war with Haqqani and all he stood for. Once more, what better way to be on the winning side of any dispute than to finance both sides?

While speaking with Jürgen, I kept half an eye on the interaction between Austin and Mohammed. I knew I was being exposed to potentially explosive information and wanted to capture as much as possible of the situation as I could under the circumstances. Both were engaged in discussion and it occurred to me what a great story it would be in any newspaper with a picture of these two men speaking so amicably, a billionaire hedge-fund manager representing the Federal Reserve Bank of New York with the son of the head of the Haqqani Network. No wonder no cell phones, PDAs, laptops, cameras, or gadgets of any kind were allowed.

Austin stood up, embraced Mohammed, and informed him he couldn't stay for dinner as planned.

"It was an honor, and I look forward to meeting you tomorrow at the hotel," he said.

Acknowledging Yuri and Jürgen with a short bow of his head, he left the room. 'What meeting the next day and at what hotel?' I made note.

I never did get introduced to the mid-twenties beauty who entered with Austin and Jürgen. No one else either for that matter. It was interesting to observe that she and Mohammed knew each other, which made me think this was not the first time he had ventured in this direction. While he was speaking with Austin she quietly stood about three feet behind his chair without any intent to interrupt. Clearly, she had been well instructed how to behave in this rich and varied cultural panorama. After Austin's departure she took the chair on Mohammed's left and remained quiet. Mohammed offered the only recognition of her presence when she sat down, he looked at her and managed an ever-so-slight smile, to which she responded by lowering her eyes and avoiding his gaze. Well trained. Very expensive.

She was stunning and it took some effort not to stare and offend either her or Mohammed. Her evening dress was formal, deep blue chiffon with open arms and back. Tight and stretched around her body, I couldn't detect anything separating her and the garment. Bare shoulders and arms displayed strong muscles with great definition. Any more would have been masculine. Perfect breasts standing at attention offering enough of a profile through the fabric to pique the imagination, without being too obvious. Full lips, curved in a gentle natural smile, betrayed sensitivity and strength of character. The same intensity resounding in her blue eyes, but kept in check by her desire not to be overtly aggressive. Long straight dark blond hair with highlights framed her face, touching her shoulders. The only justification of her presence was for Mohammed's pleasure. No other reason. She made no attempt to speak or engage anybody else and never spoke, apart from the few occasions when Mohammed addressed her. Even then, her words were whispered and only for his benefit.

Jürgen sat next to me during dinner, and we talked about some of those we knew in the business and the general outlook of the markets, which was not good. Then, during a quiet part while all were waiting for dessert and after-dinner drinks, coffee in my case, I addressed Mohammed with a question that I had been pondering all evening.

I had misgivings asking this man anything directly, though. The Haqqani Network was known for its brutality and cruelty. No more than a tribe of organized criminals and thugs who under the guise of creating a religiously pristine society extort, plunder, rape and pillage their own in an attempt to grab absolute power and control of the region. Forget the fact that Jalaluddin Haqqani was dubbed the "embodiment of goodness" by Congressman Charlie Wilson in the 1980's. He was just dressing up the story in order to get support for Operation Cyclone and give the Russians a bloody nose. The truth was that these guys were cold-blooded killers with an appetite for savagery and viciousness. All this while touting Sharia law, a brutal medieval interpretation of the Koran, as a means of control, compliance, and public submission.

As far as medieval was concerned, I have always found it interesting comparing Islam with Christianity. The Islamic year started in 622 CE. Therefore, in 2008 the corresponding Gregorian calendar year count was 1386 (1429 / 1430 in the Islamic year count, as the Islamic calendar year is eleven days shorter than the Gregorian). Islam regards all non-muslims as infidels who should convert to Islam. More radical groups use beheadings and other less-than-pleasant practices on infidels, while denying all women any rights whatsoever. Further, there is no separation of religion and state and Islamic clerics and caliphs rule all facets of life.

Where was Christianity at the end of the fourteenth century? All who didn't follow the Catholic Church's doctrines were branded as heretics who needed to be converted to Christianity. More radical followers burned non-believers at the stake, dismembered, disemboweled, or tore them apart, and women had no rights whatsoever. There was no separation between religion and state, the pope was all commanding, and the Church and its priests decided on all facets of life.

So for all intents and purposes, Islam is perfectly on track. They are where they are supposed to be according to the learning curve experienced by Christianity. The problem is, they live among us and blackmail us with our own politically correct need for tolerance into tolerating their intolerance. To further complicate issues, oil made them rich and powerful, capable of obtaining big-boy weapons which they are not afraid to use. So I thought twice about asking this current-day medieval thug a direct question. But I did so anyway.

"Sheikh Mohammed," I addressed him with the formality due a tribal leader, "there is something I have been wanting to know for a long time and this will likely be the only occasion I will ever get at obtaining a direct answer." He turned and looked straight at me, wondering what was to be asked. I noticed he disliked the uncertainty of not knowing what was coming next, and the arrogance in his eyes openly admitted the fact he knew himself superior.

"I have been told that at some point in the 1980's your father visited the White House and had a private meeting with president Reagan. I have always been curious about this, is it true?"

Mohammed's gaze penetrated me. Not answering, he kept his eyes on me as if to gauge the real intent of the question. Finally he said, "My father's business is just that, my father's business." The short sentence was delivered in staccato with a finality not to be argued with. It caught the attention of the table, and suddenly the room turned quiet. Still his eyes didn't move away from me, and the intensity of the stare with the un-cooperative answer had its effect on me.

I forced myself not to look away or swallow and betray my unease. Taking his cue, I replied. "I meant no disrespect and hope none was taken. My curiosity overtook me, and I gave in to the occasion. Please disregard my inquiry."

I did not flinch and returned his look while I spoke. Then, considering the topic closed, I turned my attention to the coffee in front of me as if nothing of importance had transpired.

The tension waylaid and the table returned to life, it was Mohammed who ultimately interrupted and continued the subject.

"Many people have had an interest in our territories for centuries. Some want to give us weapons and money, or offer training and intel, and others want to give us their government, their way of thinking. The price is always the same. They want to control us and our country. But after their interests have waned, when they tire of war and death, their politics change, or their money runs out, long after they have gone, we are still there. Fighting for our Dīn, our way of life. And our Dīn is not for sale, not subject to change or open to argument." He stopped and sipped from the cup in front of him. All the attention was on him, and for maximum effect he waited as if to consider how to deliver the next words.

"To answer your question, Mr. Vinson, my father was invited by your president Reagan, and he did visit him in your White House. He was not impressed."

Another pause and more time for the cup in front of him. The patronizing tone and delivery of the statement was not lost on me. I thanked him and decided to drop the subject. It was Jürgen who after dinner put the issue in perfect perspective. "Similar to all who publicly denounce your country, they sure are right there when the dollars are being handed out, and the Haqqanis are not shy asking for more all the time." I liked Jürgen.

At about ten o'clock we wandered downstairs, following Yuri's direction into the bar. I had no desire to stay any longer, so I bid my goodnight to all, including Mohammed, who reciprocated absentmindedly as he finally started to pay attention to the mid-twenties blond. I found my Gustav at the entrance, retrieved my cell phone and declined the offer of a car to drive me to the hotel.

Summer in Northwestern Europe has long days and short nights. Still dusk out, the evening was warm with a slight breeze. Similar to early mornings back at home, quiet with only an occasional car passing and wind rustling the trees. But the knowledge I gained at dinner disturbed the calmness of the walk back to the hotel. I now was certain I had slipped into territory I had no business being in.

CHAPTER 13

The first thing I did when I returned to my room after dinner was send a steganographic email picture to Anthony. The encrypted message read, "Had dinner with Mohammed Haqqani. Is here in town with at least four bodyguards."

My cell phone rang almost immediately. It couldn't have been more than sixty seconds since I sent the email and I saw it was his East Timor number.

His first words were, "Do not mention any names, absolutely do not. Understood?"

"OK, OK," I agreed, and he went on.

"The guy you had dinner with, do you have ANY idea who you are dealing with?" His voice was urgent, though firm and under control.

"Yes, I do. I am aware who and what he is. It fits with your warning earlier on." I stopped for a second, not sure how to convey the next message. "The whole situation is getting more strange by the minute," and as an understatement I added, "I am far from comfortable with this."

"Send me where you are staying by our usual method. We are not far away, so expect us tonight." He hung up. A sense of relief overcame me knowing Anthony was taking control. What that meant I had no idea. I just felt grateful knowing he would be here.

It would be two to three hours at best before he would arrive. So I had a moment to project what the results of the situation I found myself in could be. It was fair to assume I would at some point be compelled to leave, perhaps even with very short notice. So I decided to pack my suitcase and be prepared for such an event, just in case.

About an hour later I stretched out on the bed and turned on the TV for distraction. My bags were packed and I had left out the few things that I would need in the morning. There were no messages from the office, or Nicole, which was fine since I had no desire to call her either. Around midnight I must have dozed off with the TV still on.

A single knock on the door startled me awake. Two thirty in the morning, and it took me a few moments to gather my wits about me. Checking the peephole and seeing my son, I opened the door, and Anthony walked in carrying a small briefcase. He said nothing and gestured with his index finger to his lips for me to be quiet.

From the case he produced a small black wand, perhaps four inches long, which he turned on with a switch on the side. He worked the room methodically from floor to ceiling, the electrical outlets, lamps, coffee-maker, refrigerator, bar and bottles and glasses, cabinets in the bathroom, each ceiling tile, closets, and linen drawers, all the while in absolute silence blanketing every surface with the rod.

He froze when a tiny red light flashed while inspecting my clothes draped over a chair. Gently picking up my pants, shirt, tie, and shoes, he isolated my suit jacket when the red dot turned solid. From the left pocket he produced the gold button I was presented with by Gustav upon my arrival, which I was to wear at my discretion. I had used it only once and then forgot all about it.

Anthony smiled as he looked at it. It took him perhaps two seconds to take the top off, and to my astonishment he exposed a tiny transmitter snugly fitted inside, silently conveying my whereabouts to whomever was at the other side of the signal. No microphone, just a beacon signal. He held on to it while checking the rest of my room. On a notepad on the desk he wrote, "Anything else they give you?" upon which I produced the ID card and the biometric password generator from my pocket. The ID card produced a similar light, but the password generator was exonerated. I then passed him my cell phone, to be sure it was not tampered with and it turned out to be clean. But I was sure it had been inspected by someone at the conference and I told Anthony so. His observation was interesting. "They were probably looking for phone numbers of those close to you. Intimidating a loved one always has a more profound effect than a direct confrontation." And I thought of Nicole.

When he was secure that nobody was listening in on us, he relaxed and hugged me. "These serve to keep track of your whereabouts," Anthony informed me about the card and gold pin. "Just hold on to them," he said, handing the items back to me. "Better not raise any suspicion that you know what they are, for the time being." And again the sensation of a noose slowly being tightened around my neck overcame me.

Then he said, "Herder's with me. He's downstairs getting a room for us." Anthony looked good. Tall, broad shouldered, confident and relaxed in civilian clothes. At least three to four inches taller than I am, at six feet four, he was not somebody you wanted on the wrong side of you.

We ordered coffee and some snacks from the night menu and waited for Herder to show up. Again, just a single knock announced his presence.

Upon entering the room, Anthony briefed him.

"The room is clean, two locator beacons, no listening devices." Herder's acknowledgement was a short nod of the head. Where my son was tall and broad, Herder's physique was less pronounced, less obvious and not as tall. But he shared Anthony's level and unwavering look in his eyes. In his late twenties, perhaps early thirties, his eyes were steel blue with thick lashes a woman would kill for. A boxer's broken nose and an old scar through his left eyebrow told a story of physical altercations, but there was none of the bravado or arrogance that so often accompanied these physical trophies. If anything, Herder's demeanor was held back, even resembling humility. With a typical army-style crew cut, his blond hair was matched by a slightly darker goatee, softening and somewhat disarming his appearance. It was the way he carried himself, though, that betrayed a suppleness and confidence, the result of strength and fitness.

Anthony had spoken to me about his friend, and this being the first time meeting him, I could see what he referred to when he told me Herder was a one-of-a-kind individual. Fluent in seven languages, including Farsi, Arabic, Russian and a few European ones, he held an MBA from Wharton and a PhD from Berkeley in applied mathematics. Moreover, he was a fifth-degree master in Kajukenbo, a third-degree in Aikido and proficient enough to be a US Special Forces instructor in SERE training. That was just the stuff I knew about and I guessed there was much more I would never know.

He introduced himself and came right to the point.

"We arrived here in two cars. There are four of us in total. The other two are staying nearby. When they get here we want you to tell us the whole story, how and why you came here, who are the people you met, what the facility looks like, security, guards, protection, entrances and exits, anything that went on. We need to know all you know. We need to know about your visit with Haqqani, who is with him, where he is staying, and anything you observed about his guards."

I looked at Anthony, who had been standing on the side listening to Herder giving me instructions.

"Anthony," I asked, "what's the plan, what's going to happen?"

"First we need to be brought up to date, like Herder just said. In the morning you have to go about your business as if we are not here, as if nothing happened. It is imperative nobody realizes anything could be out of the ordinary. So tomorrow follow your schedule as planned. We will be busy finding out what we need to know. There are two objectives at play. First, to be sure you will be safe and if necessary evacuate you. Second, apprehend Mohammed Haqqani. That is why there are four of us here."

Anthony looked at me while contemplating his next words.

"I'm not sure how you pulled this off, Dad, but it's certainly intriguing. You may not know this, but this Haqqani guy is a high-value target. We had intel of the movement of assets and a lot of chatter about a top-level meeting, location only specified as the Zurich area. Then from nowhere I receive an inquiry for stats on you through the chain of command, originating from NCS. They want to know last contact date, employment, travel characteristics, known locations and associates if any, and it was not a request either. It then took all of a few moments to put your conference location together with the jihadist intel to figure you could possibly be involved in something big. We were ready to act yesterday and basically waiting for more information from you, which you supplied."

Herder's cell phone rang. He listened and without answering hung up. "They're on their way up," he announced.

A few minutes later, two of Anthony's colleagues knocked and entered the room. If there was a common denominator among the four men now in my room, it was the fact they were all self-assured and at ease. An unusual mixture of traits betraying they had nothing to prove while at the same time emitting a low-level, but profound physical sense of danger.

All were in exceptional shape, and each had prodigious levels of expertise in martial arts, languages, electronics, weapons, explosives and God knows what else, fitting in with the other's proficiencies so that this diverse four-man group was an extremely lethal army all on its own, a modern-day ninja clan.

At about five o'clock in the morning, after having explained about the share-certificates mix-up, the letter invitation and folder with its background, the reception at the conference, the security and password generator, the surplus of guards and after answering question after question, I was spent. But they needed to know about the people, about Yuri, Jean-François, Margaretha, Nigel, Austin and about the four bodyguards with Mohammed. I had to give a near-perfect description of

Mohammed and they quizzed me about the firearms. They asked who else might be armed. Where Mohammed was staying I couldn't answer, but I did say I knew both Jean-François and Margaretha to be in the same hotel we were in at that moment. I explained the encounter with them in the bar the previous night and how Jean-François made no bones about the fact he knew where Anthony was at the time.

The fact Jean-François was informed about classified information caught their attention. This was information of the type he couldn't possibly know through his professional involvement with the United Nations. I was not very helpful answering their inquiries about him. I had only seen Jean-François once that day when I left for my hotel and just didn't know him well enough. It was clear, though, they were convinced there was much more to the guy than was obvious.

Herder interrupted me, asking, "The Austin van Buren you mentioned, is he the hedge-fund manager?"

"Yes, he is. He represented the Federal Reserve, which I thought was odd."

"I know him," Herder informed us. "Aside from being ultra-wealthy, he's very involved politically and basically sets the tone and policy at the UN. I'm not surprised he is at these meetings. For all I know, it is his influence that defines the goals."

I caught the nuance between "I know him" and "I know *of* him" in Herder's statement, but held back from asking how he knew him. Instead, I talked more about the CIS and EAEC, the virtual Hawala it created, and the continued secret funding of groups and nations we now called our enemies or were publicly at war with in order to provoke or maintain international conflicts. I went on to tell them about the currency and stock manipulations that forced financial destruction so as to offer solutions that only suited the elite at the expense of all.

And I explained the discussion I had with Kevin where he indicated the initial stock trade may be exposed as erroneous, and I told them about Nicole's nightly phone calls with people asking for me.

It was when I remembered Yuri's chat about the CIA being present, that I was interrupted by Anthony. "What exactly did he say about the CIA?"

If I did not have their full attention before, I certainly had it now. So I explained what Yuri informed me, that they are always present, but you'll never know who they are and that they act as the enforcers for the Parent. "He gave them a specific name, something like Special Team, or so. I don't remember exactly." I said.

"They're called Secret Teams." Herder said quietly. "Did he mention other groups to be present as well?"

"Yes, actually he said that the Sia, as he pronounced it, were always there and other Agencies, but he never said who the others were." I answered. "What's the deal with the Secret Teams?"

"It's CIA and NSA. We know they employ small paramilitary tactical groups who take care of issues, or arrange situations and events to prepare for specific outcomes." It was as if a forbidden topic was brought up. As Herder spoke a soberness came over the room. "And if they work for what you call the Parent, then it makes sense for them to be here."

It remained quiet for a few moments. Then Anthony added, "If the Parent employs them, then they are formidable indeed. It's akin to having your own army while nobody is aware of it. All outside of military oversight or chain of command. They are independent and as the name implies, they're secret and very, very lethal."

Nothing else was said on this topic, but it was obvious the information had struck a nerve and made an impact on them the nature of which I was not privy of, but noticed nonetheless.

At six thirty that Friday morning I was done talking. Tired and drained, I sat back. Anthony's other two associates were quietly talking to each other, comparing notes on the Mohammed information I had supplied. Much like Herder, these two men would not stand out in a crowd other than their demeanor which belied unusual poise. Dressed in jeans, loose shirts and low cut athletic shoes, both were comfortable and ready for action.

I showered, shaved and felt considerably better after doing so. We agreed I would get in touch after the first meeting and then decide on what to do next. I knew Anthony and his team would spend the morning trying to find out where Mohammed was staying, which more than likely was a safe house somewhere in the Zurich area.

They exited my room one by one, trying not to draw attention and when Anthony left he told me to be careful. He said something else as well, which has stayed with me because of its poignant truth. He told me to prepare for change.

"Dad, you're tangled up in something that will take on a life of its own. You uncovered information that some very powerful people will not want to see become public and they will go out of their way to make sure it won't. I have the feeling your life will turn in a direction you may not be used to. All I am saying is, better be ready for a change."

I knew he was right.

CHAPTER 14

Friday, May 16, 2008

The cool air with the lake effect made the walk to the building almost chilly. Rain was in the air and expected to arrive in the afternoon. This was typical weather for the region. Springs can be warm and sunny. Then skies turn milky white with a cold wind and rain and it will feel like fall. Knowing the weather from experience, I had brought an overcoat just in case.

Once inside and through security, I felt conspicuous, knowing two beacons were keeping track of me. I wondered who else was subject to that, or was it just me? Gustav took my cell phone and coat and I proceeded over to the bar. It was still morning, about eight thirty and the meeting would start at nine in the third-floor conference room. But I wanted to meet with Yuri prior and had a good idea where to find him. Find the Chivas, find Yuri.

Not only were many of the participants already present, it amazed me how many were in the bar working on a morning buzz, just like Yuri. You had to hand it to the guy, not missing a beat he was nursing half a tumbler of Chivas on ice. I suspected he may have changed his shirt and suit, but as I drew closer the suspicion faded. He was a mess, tie loosened, shirt wrinkled, badly tucked in at the waist and one button under his tie had become undone unbeknownst to him. His pants were a few sizes too wide and hung under his belly, kept up by a pair of suspenders, visibly strained by the effort.

But he was lucid and clear headed. Speaking to a couple of guys he noticed me, waved me over and introduced me to two very prominent money managers. Very wealthy and very well known, so it was no surprise finding them here. The discussion was about the upcoming meeting and they were excited to find out what the US presidential election information would prove to be all about. Austin and Jean-François both were hosting the meeting, I learned.

While heading to the stairs on our way to the third floor, I had a chance to thank Yuri for the dinner the previous evening.

"Last night was an honor. I appreciate you inviting me. I was impressed with the whole operation, bringing in Mohammed, his entourage. He certainly seems like a man to be reckoned with." My intent was to bait Yuri into divulging more information, and flattery usually has good results. I was not disappointed.

"Yes, was good evening, very successful. Show efficient and effective of infrastructure we made. We want older brother Siraj, but was not possible. You know, Mohammed not yet very top animal, but he will be in future," Yuri offered. I was sure he meant "top dog," but did not pursue it. His attempt at English idiomatic correctness made me smile and added a touch of innocence to the otherwise loaded subject matter.

"What time is Mohammed going to speak tomorrow, and what topic will he discuss?" I wanted somehow to find out about his schedule, without appearing too nosey or creating any type of suspicion. So I just kept asking innocent questions, hoping for an opening.

"Tomorrow about conflict management, from start of the finance support to what they receive now and how no change over time happened. Now politic climate is turned against them. Will be interesting, hear from him how they go from mujahedeen with Sia help to then be Taliban. Now financial movements gone through system of the United Nations."

Yuri stopped for a second, looked at the wall of the staircase and said just one word, "Cézanne," while pointing with his eyes and raised eyebrows up to the painting, which was the object of our first discussion. He went on as if the interruption hadn't occurred. "You see yourself how Austin is with him. Not first time, not last time they meet and he very well know old man Haqqani."

One thing Yuri said intrigued me. Right there for the first time a direct indictment was made how the funding to these factions was organized. "You just said through the systems of the United Nations. Are they directly involved?"

"Somebody has to be managing institution and make coordinating movements of the monies and peoples. From United Nations it goes to my districts and then reaches targets. Jean-François and Jürgen works together on this." Then as an afterthought Yuri said, "You know, me and Haqqani meet this afternoon with Austin and Jean-François about tomorrow talks."

I could tell he felt proud being an integral part of this program. That being the case, I knew he would want to divulge more as long as I phrased it correctly, playing into his pride.

"Oh, that was the meeting Austin was referring to when he left last night. You mean you will be there as well?" I asked the question nonchalantly, wanting him to emphasize the point as if his involvement impressed me.

He was out of breath climbing the stairs and paused at the top, not wanting to enter the conference room gasping for air. "Yes, in JF's hotel," Yuri managed, abbreviating Jean-François' name. "Same hotel as mine," I thought. I left the issue alone, knowing enough. This was what I was hoping for, something that would give me an idea where and when Mohammed would be, but I would have to wait to pass this information to Anthony until after the meeting.

The conference room had two entrances, and as I wanted to sit in the back, Yuri and I entered through the rear door. I could see Jean-François standing, the ever present black briefcase in hand at the front row in discussion with Margaretha.

As he noticed me, he interrupted himself, following me with his eyes. Arrogant and with a pithy little smile, as if to tell me "I know about you," I kept eye contact until he finally looked away. It made me uncomfortable and I told myself to keep my cool and that anything I read in his eyes was my own paranoia speaking back at me. We then sat down next to Nigel and the fund managers.

From his jacket's side pocket Jean-François produced the small USB drive he played with the evening of our confrontation, plugged it into a laptop on the ebony lectern, and waited until Austin entered moments later.

Jean-François started by telling us about an event that occurred late the previous year, when in December 2007 a rookie United States senator from Illinois introduced a bill known as the Global Poverty Act. This bill, if passed, would require the United States to pay 0.7% of GDP, or close to $100 billion per year, to the United Nations in order to eliminate poverty in the world. This sum would be in excess of the humane aide the United States already dispensed. The United Nations would have full discretion as to how and where these funds would be allocated. The bill had only limited support, most notably from Senator Joe Biden, who moved it through the Senate Foreign Relations Committee of which he was chairman.

One of the last sentences Jean-François voiced was, "Even though the bill never materialized, the original sponsor, the Senator from Illinois, Barack Hussein Obama, made his allegiance known in favor of the United Nations and the type of redistribution of wealth that resonates with our redistributive convictions."

This caught my attention. Substituting "redistributive" for "socialist," I had been wondering about the whole socialist movement, and it seemed to me that those in the United States who are the most ardent supporters of this thinking are some with the most money or power. All of it earned in non-socialist environments. It seemed that in a capitalist society most are capitalists, while in a socialist society only the very top are capitalist. All may embrace socialism, but the elite are nowhere near to being one themselves.

My reflections interrupted, I was brought back to the meeting as Austin van Buren stepped forward and took over where Jean-François left off.

"Senator Obama's 2008 effort didn't originate in a vacuum. In 2006, I was instrumental in developing the Millennium Project, taxing wealthy industrialized nations 0.7% of their GDP to a common fund. This fund was to be managed by the UN, which would oversee the fiscal distribution to less fortunate populaces. This would favor the underclass of the world to develop and transcend out of poverty through an open society into the new world."

He followed this with an interesting observation, stating that, "A profound conflict exists between capitalism and the open society. Karl Marx's ideal of communism, with communal redistributive mechanisms, would have worked were it not for the fact that the communists in charge placed their own interests ahead of the people's." And with those words he affirmed my earlier comparison between capitalist and socialist.

The remark was ended with, "A distinct difference exists today. With this candidate at our disposal, we are now capable of enacting real change. There is an innate need to heal the centuries-long damage inflicted by industrialized nations on less fortunate ones in this world. The 2006 Millennium Project and Senator Obama's 2008 Poverty Act sought to remedy this harm done and address the inherent conflict between capitalism and the open society. Thus creating a world wide Open Society Alliance with a United Nations controlled International Central Bank in charge of redistributing the contributions from wealthy nations to poorer populations."

Pacing the floor, he was silent as if searching for words. For maximum effect, he stopped in his tracks, looked the crowd straight on and said, "If we learned anything from both these efforts, it is the evidence that collective interests can only be served if and when the sovereignty of nations is subordinated to international laws and institutions. The strongest opponent of this idea originates in the United States of America." The sentences were uttered in a crescendo, where the last statement came across loudest, voiced full of passion.

"In light of this knowledge, and to underscore the need for the required judicial alterations necessary to fulfill these goals, only one presidential candidate has demonstrated similar visions of fundamental societal transformation."

The suspense was tangible as Austin delayed delivery of his next words and just for effect he prolonged the tension until he said. "As such it has been decided the nomination of the Democratic National Convention in August this year to be in favor of Senator Barack Obama. This information will be further discussed with both Mrs. Clinton and Mr. Obama during next month's full assembly meeting in Chantilly, Virginia, to be held from June 5 until June 8." Little did I know that Senator Clinton, while attending the Chantilly meeting, was to suspend her campaign on June 7, 2008.

Just like that, it was laid out why and how the process was decided. If I ever had any doubt about it being influenced and manipulated, none was left any longer. The actual vote of the people was no more than a formality confirming a decision made by others for reasons disguised from the public. I found it perplexing how a sense of individual choice and fairness was nonetheless maintained, while the process was controlled and calculated by a media machine under orders to promote and advance a foregone conclusion.

Turning to Nigel I remarked, "Both Clinton and Obama support the United Nations. Why Obama?"

Nigel's response was remarkable. "Only Obama is committed to follow Austin's full agenda. And, he is vulnerable where Clinton is not. There are inconsistencies that can be turned into advantages." The statement was delivered without hesitation, as if the information were public knowledge.

Austin continued before I could fire off another question and answered my query as if he knew what I was about to ask. "We are fully aware of potential compromising data regarding Mr. Obama's past. We feel that through proper information management and news dissemination, this can be limited in scope and potential damage minimized. The success of this nominee is all but assured due to these reasons. First, Mr. Obama's ethnic background will guarantee an African American vote. He will be hailed as the final answer for a minority that historically has felt second class. Second, the message we feel that will most likely get him a liberal and independent white vote is one of reconciliation and compromise. A sense of a new beginning that feeds into a cultural culpability established in the white community for acts of the past. Third, it is our belief Mr. Obama represents a new generation and will resonate with a younger and more idealistic populace, an electorate which so far has refrained from participating in elections due to a lack of personal identification."

He looked around while formulating his words.

"Finally, Mr. Obama will have the benefit of our unlimited infrastructural, financial and media support to run his campaign so that he will be victorious," confirming Nigel's statement.

The room was crowded and it was obvious the information had found its mark. Not a noise was heard and I could feel the anticipation with which the next sentence was expected.

"One has to see a larger context within which to evaluate the soundness of the Senator Obama choice. Not only will he deliver that which his predecessors would not, he also shares our convictions in redistributive change and compliance with the overriding judicial international authority of the United Nations. His ethnic and religious background will bridge a gap that thus far we have not been able to fill. It has always been our goal to create inroads into the African and Muslim nations and increase the scope of our financial and banking influence. We feel that our candidate will be most beneficial in this aspect."

He stopped and looked around. If his words so far had been eye-opening, what he was about to share took me totally off guard.

"Our mandate to the president will be for the United States to ratify the Rome Statute, thereby initiating submission of United States sovereignty to the jurisdiction of the International Criminal Court, both domestically and on the battlefield, thus granting Interpol, the ICCs law-enforcement arm, limitless access to the United States. These are the fundamental and integral requirements for the framework that will be the basis of the new one world community. An open society with one government, one currency and of course, one banking authority."

'Our mandate?' I repeated the words in my head as if to gain clarity on the enormity of the statement. They mandate *our* president? Nigel's earlier remark about Obama being vulnerable started to make more sense.

Whatever these issues are, they obviously compromise the presidency. It allows those with power to mandate, to dictate policy and in return fund their candidate into the presidency. It made me think of president Woodrow Wilson who in 1913 was supported by the bankers into the presidency as long he would sign the Federal Reserve Act.

Austin's voice demanded my attention again. "We are adamant and will not encourage United States border enforcement, north or south, as we believe it to be counterproductive to the ultimate assimilation of the communities on the North American continent. This will act as a precursor to the anticipated multinational currency, financial and judicial mergers."

Another pause, and he walked from left to right and back. He stopped, stood still and faced the room.

"Furthermore, our directive will allow for a nuclear Iran. Under the guise of producing peaceful nuclear technology, the region will rightfully suspect the motives of the Iranian regime and initiate an arms and nuclear-technology race the scope of which can only be financed by our group. This is our long-term interest and historically the decree from which we operate. We finance nations and their armaments on each side of the conflict."

"Yes you do," I thought. "And by doing so you secure yourself of always being partners with the winners, no matter who they are." Once again Johan's remarks from months earlier were brought up and I wondered between a possible link of this group and my friend.

Austin was not finished. "We will insist on a lesser dependence and alliance between the United States and Israel, thereby creating access into an otherwise restrictive Arab community. This will prove to be a necessity once a nuclear Iran is a reality. In addition to the continuous Shia/Sunni conflict in the area, the politically disruptive reduction in the United States/Israeli coalition, combined with the destabilizing effect of a nuclearized Iran, will spur similar needs for arms and financing support by its Arab neighbors. Our vast financial resources will be called upon in those nations sensing a need to protect themselves against the perceived overpowering Farsi thread."

I was as spellbound by the subject matter as was the rest of the audience. This knowledge was as powerful as it was explosive. This is where international political strategy originated and where the leaders of the world received their orders. I witnessed how, why and by whom policy was set and the fearsome, ruthless and draconian results they foretold. I could only imagine the profit potential knowing these policies in advance and being able to set up portfolios and trading systems in anticipation.

Austin cleared his throat. "Since the 1947 inception of the state of Israel we have purposely worked to build a conclusive financial and military supremacy of Israel in the midst of an otherwise Arab region. This was only our interim goal, the creation of a strategic imbalance of power in the Middle East. Subsequently, we supported Israel during the 1967 and 1973 wars. The intent was to provoke the Arab nations into retaliation, which they could not do successfully without financial support of unprecedented proportions."

Austin looked around readying the audience for the point he was about to make.

"A mechanism was needed to infuse the oil-producing Arab states surrounding Israel with enough resources to address and equalize this arms and weapons imbalance. Our next goal was a production boycott. Such was our advice, impetus and counsel to the cartel, OPEC, that a supply restriction would address this inequity in their favor, resulting in the 1973 Oil Embargo. The embargo and its consequent drastic increase in the price of oil was the desired mechanism for a massive transfer of wealth from the industrialized nations needing oil to those selling it. These new riches were the source for a Middle-Eastern increase in military power and an arms race that was financed, manufactured and procured through our systems. This was the final goal, reaching an arms equilibrium in the region. A precarious balance, I may add, but nonetheless maintained, supplied and controlled by our group. Here we see how strategic use of resources and supply dynamics can cause seeming disruptions, which over the longterm are beneficial to us."

Looking around, I observed that this concise history lesson was news to many present, as it was to me. I had never even considered that the West conjured up the 1973 Oil Embargo. But I understood the brilliant, devilish rational behind it. Create an imbalance, then provoke and engineer the embargo. Enrich the petroleum-producing nations, which in turn use this new wealth to buy arms and weapons from the same countries the embargo was meant to target. Truly a mastermind in redistributive thinking. It was the Western populations who financed the Arab nations through the increased cost of crude oil, gasoline and diesel fuel. This same money came back to the West in the form of arms and weapons sales to the oil-producing nations. But it came back to the bankers and military industrialists, not to the people who actually paid for it through the increased prices of gasoline, heating oil and gas. Redistribution of wealth while nobody was aware of it. Brilliant and absolutely unscrupulous.

"In light of this," Austin continued, "we are witnessing another unprecedented and more pronounced rise in the price of crude oil. It is imperative to regard oil as a mechanism through which redistributive change can be effectuated. We have allowed for certain Middle Eastern parties to finance their purchases and activities from us through these price increases. Increases, I may add, largely staged and created by members of this forum. As early as the fall of 2003 we notified you through these meetings of imminent price accelerations, and many of us have had ample opportunities to take advantage of this."

All the talking had created small deposits of an off-whitish substance in each corner of his mouth. It had somewhat of an unsavory effect, which I am sure was disregarded by most due to his tenure and status. But much like being confronted by oncoming headlights in traffic and not being able to look away, my gaze was drawn to his lips and how the white matter elastically moved with each word spoken. The tiny flaw made him appear more human and brought him down to earth a notch.

"It is vital you realize with the coming announcement nominating Senator Obama as candidate for the presidency, that these same syndicates who benefitted from the recent increased value of oil will be denied continual use of this source of income. Since 2003 our intent has been to modernize these more surreptitious Middle Eastern groups with arms, tactical tools and surveillance equipment, using oil as the vehicle of their wealth creation. It was imperative we control this arms supply in size, timing and origin so as to maintain a degree of leverage over these otherwise volatile individuals."

He let the words sink in so that everyone understood how detailed and thorough the plan was.

"It is our belief that our interim goal of financing a rearmament of Middle Eastern factions has been realized. Therefore, a continued financial support through our means of wealth creation will no longer be a necessity. We suggest you implement exit strategies, combined with short positions within the coming thirty days, after which drastic decreases in the value of petroleum products and its derivatives are to be expected." [7]

Another eye opener. Again, it hadn't occurred to me that the previous years' incredible bull run of crude oil, from $30 per barrel in 2003

---

[7] Crude oil prices topped at $147.27 (front futures month) in July 2008, then crashed and continued to drop until January 2009, when a low of $33.20 was registered.

to over $140 in 2008, was a manipulation orchestrated by this group in Zurich. Regardless, as Austin pointed out, this bull market was about to end. I didn't want to, but reluctantly I had to admire the superb genius behind this scheme.

Gary, the event scheduler, still sporting the red and somewhat askew bowtie, stepped up and told the group to take five minutes. A low buzz filled the air, voices conversing with much excitement as both Austin and Jean-François left the area.

As they exited, the rear door behind me opened and somebody entered the conference room. He remained standing in the back, observing the gathering. Most of us, including me, were unaware of his presence.

Insisting on learning what Nigel meant earlier, I took advantage of the intermission and asked, "What inconsistencies were you referring to about Obama?" as we stood up and turned to make our way out.

But before Nigel could answer I found myself face to face with my friend Johan from the Swiss Institution. It took me perhaps two seconds to recover from the initial shock of seeing him and at first I questioned myself if it really was him, immediately followed by an alarming sense of being caught in the act. Then as I wondered why he was present, I realized he was a senior trader at one of the largest and most influential international financial institutions in the world, whose chairman of the board was the same as the chairman of the Federal Reserve. So come to think of it, why would he NOT be there?

But I was the only one surprised at our encounter. He was looking at me, eyes intently fixed on mine, void of any wonder at the encounter. I stood up, shook his hand and professed my joy in seeing him, trying not to let my initial shock shine through. But his response was a simple statement indicating he wished to immediately speak with me outside the building. No pleasantries, all business. This was a different Johan.

The sense of urgency in Johan's request didn't go unnoticed, so I forgot about the question I just posed to Nigel, complied with Johan's request and followed him.

"What is it you want to discuss?" I asked.

"Wait until we're outside," was his only response.

I didn't like his tone and I had the feeling bad news was about to come my way. We went downstairs in silence, retrieved our cell phones and my coat, and left the building. Dark clouds had gathered threatening rain, but none fell so far. A cold wind from the lake added to my sense of foreboding.

FEDERAL

Johan had brought his car, a Mercedes with Corps Diplomatic license plates. I took the passenger seat and as we left the building grounds I observed the guards at the gate salute the diplomatic status and its owner. We drove in silence down the street and parked the car in an empty lot close to the lake.

He was quiet for a moment and then started.

"Before anything else, you have to tell me something. Are you aware of the trouble you are in?"

Following my gesture implying "No," he went on. "How did you end up at this conference, and why would a guy like Jean-François have an interest in you? He initiated an inquiry into you and told me about your presence here. I know him very well and he is not somebody you want against you. Right now he is."

I had known Johan for over a decade and he had never crossed me, nor I him. We were good friends and had trusted each other with very personal information about our lives. Aside from being a great friend, I respected him and I believed this was mutual.

All this went through my head as I made up my mind that he deserved to hear the truth. So I told him about the stock mix-up and the letter invitation and the folder and ending up at the meeting. I admitted I had been wrong taking advantage of an innocent mistake, but that my curiosity had taken over.

Johan's facial expression went from surprise to disbelief while I was speaking. In the end his eyebrows furrowed and a severity overcame him.

"I appreciate your candor," he said. Then he confided in me, "This is what happened. I received an unusual phone call late last night from FINRA at the close of business in the States, requesting background information on you and a detailed description of all transactions for the previous twelve months executed with you. I'm outside their regulatory reach, so I can stall their requests, but ultimately I will have to cooperate because we transact in the US as well, as you know. The point is, I made a few phone calls trying to find out what the issue was and I found out FINRA to be the least of your problems. You're about to be charged with securities fraud by the SEC in conjunction with the Treasury Department and the enforcement arm of the NYSE, which is part of FINRA. The charges will be transferred to the Interpol Financial Fraud division for them to investigate and pursue according to directives issued by the United Nations ODC." He looked at me, questioning the impact of his words while I was at a loss for any.

Not grasping the full impact of what he was saying, I just asked, "You said Jean-François started all this? Why?"

"You crossed him and invaded his territory and they do not take lightly to intruders. I think you will experience the influence and power they can muster when antagonized," was Johan's answer. Then he added, "I wouldn't be surprised if they checked in on your family, or others close to you. It's how they operate, subtle pressure at first from the outside to unhinge you."

The two events, Nicole's female caller and Anthony's request for information about me all of a sudden made sense. But it was what Johan said earlier that needed further clarification, "Who is the UN ODC and why a securities-fraud charge?"

"UN ODC is the United Nations Office on Drugs and Crime. It acts as a liaison between governments on crime issues. It assists international law enforcement agencies and enforces the UN Convention against Transnational Organized Crime. It is charging you with falsifying credentials, invasion of a private company under false pretenses and obtaining restricted and classified information. This may potentially result in a charge of treason. The fraud stems from your absence of correcting a known securities error and using it to your advantage to gain confidential data."

As I started to realize the severity of the situation, my mouth parched and with some difficulty I said, "This is ridiculous. I am not a criminal, even less part of organized crime. Johan, what's going on? And why is Interpol involved?" I couldn't believe what I was hearing and it scared the shit out of me. Had it not been relayed with such seriousness, I would have laughed at it. But I was not laughing now. Not at all.

"It is being treated as an international breach of national security and a potential act of terrorism. This way other foreign agencies are allowed in. So Interpol is involved as the law-enforcement arm of the UN. They will want Interpol to be the lead because it is not as visible and is less scrutinized. They also have unrestricted entry anywhere the ICC is recognized, including the United States. You have to appreciate that in the US they are not subject to the freedom of information act, so they can not be forced to disclose their activities and basically can do as they please." Johan looked at me quizzically, trying to understand his own sentiments. "I know you and I know you are no criminal. At the same time I am taking a risk in warning you. All this will come down at the open of business New York time, which is in about three hours," he informed me.

"What's that going to mean for me right now?" My voice cracked as a sickening feeling had crept into my stomach, and I could feel a trickle of sweat form in the nape of my neck. There were many other things I wanted to ask, but the immediacy of the issue struck home, and I needed to have an idea of what I was up against.

"I assume Interpol will issue a warrant and they will be looking for you."

"What is the deal with Jean-François?" I asked.

No answer from him. He remained quiet and stared outside. Rain had started and blurred the windows. As it obscured the view, I felt my prospects dim similarly. I could see him ponder my question but still he didn't answer. Then he looked at me, and it was evident what he was going to say troubled him.

"You have been exposed to information not meant for you. Very, very few find out what you learned, for obvious reasons. We have had infiltrators in the past, and they were always dealt with. If not physically, they were destroyed financially and socially, or at the very least rendered ineffective and powerless."

Just like that, with the word 'we' and that one sentence, Johan exposed a gap between us unknown to me thus far, a distance unsuspected, but now opening wide and ominous and I started to understand how involved he actually was.

"When the inquiry came and I learned what agencies were involved, I knew Jean-François was part of it. It took one call to him to know you were here. He is an official of the United Nations, but more importantly he organizes these meetings and decides who attends, who comes back, and who does not. He clears the information to be shared. He and Austin, whom I am sure you have met, control the money flow to and from those we support and finance, although Austin is the senior. They are part of the nucleus of power, otherwise referred to as the Parent. They both are as powerful as they are dangerous, and you opened a hornets' nest."

"If Jean-François knew, then why allow me into the meeting at all?" It didn't make sense for him to let me in and expose me to even more information, while at the same time making moves to get rid of me.

"To keep you within reach. You were targeted from the moment you walked into the conference. I know you had lunch with him and Margaretha. That was no coincidence. She was the one who approached you initially, correct?"

"Yes she was," I said, "right after I arrived." And I realized that what I had thought was an interesting development meeting some of the organizers of the conference, had been a deliberate set-up to get close to me.

"They work together." Johan explained as a matter of fact. "Better to know where you are than have you disappear. I also know Jean-François is arrogant and believes he can handle anything and anybody, which is his weakness. Jean-François may be your trouble now, but never underestimate van Buren. No one crosses van Buren without incurring his fearsome wrath. He is too wealthy and powerful to be confined by laws or borders. He controls Jean-François, and he is the force behind all the activity you have witnessed."

"How about Yuri?" I asked. "He was there at lunch." I was curious where he fit in, if at all.

"I know he was, but he's not part of the inner circle," Johan answered, "and he's not your problem."

My turn to be quiet now that I was told who my real foe was. The news was not just bad, it was horrific. What I had just been told subjected and influenced every facet of my life. My business was in serious jeopardy, if not destroyed. A securities fraud indictment meant the suspension of my licenses, without which I couldn't function professionally. The loss of my livelihood scared me, but the loss of my freedom scared me more. The loss of both terrified me, let alone the implication that my life may be in danger. For a second I contemplated informing Johan of Anthony's presence, but immediately decided against it considering Johan's voluntary admission of his intimate involvement with the group.

I had trouble speaking and made an effort to control myself. "Jesus, Johan, what can I do?" was all I could muster.

His look conveyed compassion and concern. The fact he had gone out of his way to warn me spoke volumes. He was taking a risk in doing so and I loved him for it.

"Should I try to speak to Jean-François? Would that make a difference?" I was grasping at straws, trying for a way out where intuitively I knew there was none.

"You have a bit of time before any order becomes reality," Johan said. "The speed and ferocity with which all this will come down all depends on Jean-François and speaking to him will not make a difference. You know too much and have learned things meant to stay hidden. I know he will not take the risk that you will make this information public. That should tell you enough." Again he looked at me with concern. There was a tone of helplessness in his voice when he said, "I don't know what advice to give you, Stephen, other than stay out of their way, disappear. I have seen this before and it will not go away. They may be ruthless and play hardball in business, but they are downright merciless at protecting their turf. I was planning to be at the conference Friday and Saturday, but learning about you I came earlier. I know what they are capable of, and you are my friend."

I knew what he was telling me. This was goodbye. Not much else to say. I had been warned and given a few hours' notice before my world would cave in on me and realized I had to move on.

"Thank you, Johan, my friend. I love you for what you have done for me here." Then as an afterthought, it occurred to me how big a risk he had taken, so I asked, "Will you be OK? Doesn't warning me place you in a precarious position?"

"I know how to handle Jean-François. Don't worry about me. Nobody knows what we discussed, and I am not without resources. Besides, after all these years I am quite certain you don't truly realize who I am." Johan looked at me knowingly, as if to hint at some secret not available to me.

We hugged in the car and the last words Johan said were, "Be careful, Stephen. Perhaps our paths will cross again, 'til then, God bless you my friend."

I stepped out of the car into the rain and didn't look back as I heard him drive away. With all the feelings I was experiencing, a sadness about the finality of this goodbye overcame me. It meant more than goodbye. He understood my life was about to undergo a drastic alteration and he would not see me again on the other side of a business transaction. His farewell confirmed what was about to happen.

But I couldn't linger or get carried away by emotions. I was given a few hours' notice and I needed to use this time the best way I knew how. I called Anthony and without divulging any of the news, I told him it was urgent to meet me in my room in ten minutes.

Both Herder and Anthony were in the bar of the hotel. Without acknowledging me, they waited until I had entered the elevator and then followed me to my room.

It was an effort relaying the information efficiently and not becoming emotionally charged. There were two points to consider. The first one was about Haqqani having a meeting that was to occur in my hotel that afternoon with Austin van Buren, Jean-François, Yuri and perhaps others. The second was my personal news, the impending indictment and its repercussions. I explained what Johan had told me about Jean-François and Austin, who they were and how they dealt with intruders.

First thing Anthony said was, "Johan is a good guy. You have a real friend there." He then stood up and paced the room as he spoke. "Couple of things that are priority here. First we have to get you safe and out of sight. They will come looking for you here at the hotel once warrants are issued. So you are checking out and you and your stuff stay in our car. Give me both beacon transmitters and we'll dispose of them so that they will think you're somewhere else. We should be gone and on our way north by tonight. Second is Haqqani. We already found out what room Jean-François is in. We need to know when they are in the hotel, so we will position our car, with you in it, in view of the entrance. You let us know when you see either Jean-François or Yuri arrive and we'll take it from there. Nobody knows the four of us are here, so I don't think any additional security is in force. The only unknown is how quickly they'll act on the accusations about you and how many will show up to enforce it."

As a second thought he added, "There are too many moving parts at work. The NCS is making inquiries, the SEC is charging you and transferring it to Interpol, with all communications coordinated through UN-ODC. I'm assuming bureaucracy will take effect. We just may have more time than we are aware of, but let's not count on it to be on the safe side."

Noon. I didn't bother checking out. The hotel had my credit card information that they were perfectly capable of charging. I didn't want to start leaving a timeline of my activities or alert others of my doings, so I just left the hotel. My bag was in the Audi S8 Quattro that Anthony and Herder brought down from Germany. Windows blacked out, it was impossible to look inside the vehicle. A powerful and high-tech performance four-door sedan, it offered speed and comfort in equal parts.

I settled in the back of the car, with the others in the front and ate some energy bars they bought earlier. The car was parked on a side street about sixty yards from the hotel entrance, so we had a good view of the comings and goings through the doors. Anthony's two other associates, whom I hadn't seen since leaving the hotel that morning for the meeting, were nowhere to be seen. The response I received inquiring about them was a quick "They're around." Getting the hint, I left the subject alone.

FEDERAL

My phone rang. Answering it I found myself speaking to my friend Carol, who lived across the street from me in Florida. Aside from taking care of my dog Sparky, we received each other's mail while out of town, which over the years had worked out fine for both of us.

It was about one o'clock in the afternoon for me in Zurich, and due to the six-hour time difference it was about seven o'clock in the morning for her.

Her voice was hurried with an undertone of concern. "Stephen, where are you?"

Not wanting to offer too much information, I answered, "I'm still abroad. I should be home in a couple of days. Why, what's the matter?"

"Do you know what is going on at your house?"

Alarmed I answered, "No, what?"

"There are cops up and down the street and three black SUVs in your driveway. They are taking out boxes full of stuff, as if you're moving."

At a loss for sensible words I asked, "What do you mean, as if I'm moving? What boxes? They're taking this from my home? Who is doing this?"

My remarks caused the two in the front seats to turn their heads and pay attention to my conversation.

"Stephen, when I saw them they were already inside, so I thought you had come home and something was wrong and you called the cops. When I walked over I was stopped, and they weren't joking either. I was held back and told it was a formal investigation, and when I asked if you were OK they asked me how I knew you, how long I knew you, what my business was, if you had been in touch with me, on and on. That is when I saw the boxes coming from your house being placed into the SUVs, and your computers as well." Carol was upset. A second later she added, "How can they just take anything they want? Your computers are your business! Stephen, what should I do?" The situation scared her, and she understood I was in trouble. I was touched by her willingness to help and her sense of powerlessness knowing there was nothing she could do.

"Could you talk to any of them? Did they say anything?"

"I wasn't even allowed onto your driveway. It was the Broward Sheriff's Office holding me back, but the SUVs had FinCEN logos on them and the guys taking your stuff had 'FinCEN Officer' written on their shirts. I have no idea who they are. What happened, Stephen? What's going on? What did you do?" Her voice cracked asking the last questions.

"It has to do with my work. I am involved in something I was not aware of, and now they are investigating me and making it seem like I am some kind of criminal and I tell you that I'm not. Carol, you may have to keep Sparky a bit longer. I'm not sure what's going to happen next, but don't believe anything you hear. It's better for you not to call me again. I'll call you when I can and give you an update. But this thing is not looking good and I'm afraid there are people who are interested in making it appear like I am a real bad person."

I paused, not knowing where to go with the call. "Hold on to my stuff if you can. But if anybody causes you trouble, just give them the mail. It doesn't really matter anymore. Thank you, Carol. Thank you for calling me and for taking care of Sparky and everything. I have to go now. I'll be in touch later."

With that I hung up. I hadn't even asked how my sweet Sparky was doing. Both Anthony and Herder were looking at me.

"What is FinCEN?" I asked.

It was Herder who informed me without a moment's pause, as if reading from an encyclopedia.

"FinCEN stands for Financial Crimes Enforcement Network and is part of the Department of the Treasury. They enforce, among others, the Bank Secrecy Act, which oversees financial institutions. It not only deals with domestic financial crimes, but also with terrorism and terrorist financing. They report to the office of Terrorism and Financial Intelligence, or TFI."

Anthony looked serious. "They are not fucking around with FinCEN being involved."

Then after a slight pause and articulated with a much lower voice, Herder said to me, "They operate a police force outside the generally accepted law-enforcement systems, very effective and very stealthy."

"And they won't waste time," Anthony said. "Next they'll freeze your bank accounts, place a lien on your home, cancel your credit cards and put a hold on your passport. FinCEN doesn't screw around. They mean business. Plus they can use the infrastructure and assets of the DEA, FBI, CIA and a few other lesser-known agencies."

My home being raided, I dreaded to learn what was going on at work, but I needed to know and the only person I hoped who would tell me anything was my assistant Kevin. "I want to check with somebody and see what more I can find out," I told my companions. I dialed his cell phone hoping for him to answer. The phone rang and was answered on the third ring.

"Kevin, this is Stephen. Can we talk?" I said.

His response was immediate and hurried. "Stay on the line, hold on a sec." I could tell he stood up, and walked through several doors. A bit later he informed me that, "I went out in the hall. What is going on Stephen, where are you? This place is crazy this morning. I was called early this morning at home and told to report to work immediately. When I came in there were black SUVs outside with BSO everywhere. One guy dressed in black with a FinCEN logo is at your desk and others are in a closed-door meeting with management. They told me not to leave, hand over all your files and pending trades and they want to meet with me and Sharon as soon as she's in. I can't stay gone too long, they're watching everything I do." He sounded scared.

"What are they telling you?" I asked.

"Nothing. They wanted to know when was the last time I heard from you and I said yesterday. Stephen, what's happening?"

It was as if a fishnet closed around me, all my avenues were being cut off. No use talking any more, nothing I could do about it anyway.

"Kevin, I don't want you to get in trouble. Tell them I called and when you told me what's going on, I just hung up on you."

"OK, but what's going on?" he insisted.

"Remember the Federal Reserve shares mess-up? The thing blew up on me and I can't stop it. What you need to tell them is that you advised me several times to correct the issue, but that I told you specifically that it was a personal transaction and that I would take care of it myself and that it was none of your business. That way you will not be in any trouble." Then before disconnecting, I added, "Whatever you hear about me is not true. Not true. I have to go, Kevin. You take care." I didn't want to stay on the line and explain myself. I had heard enough.

Anthony and Herder didn't need to be filled in on the conversation. They understood the raid on my home coincided with one at my work.

"Jesus, Anthony. What am I going to do?"

I struggled not to break down, but I couldn't shake a sense of desperation. Not to go home anymore? How about my Sparky and Nicole? What about my home, my safe haven that I had built over the last thirty years? How about my friends and the life I had carved out for myself? A sense of disbelief overcame me. This could not be true. The magnitude of my loss was too great, too all encompassing.

I could see my son was worried and concerned about me. The totality of the implications was starting to sink in and never in my life have I felt the way I started feeling that early afternoon. At a loss himself what to say, he looked at me and I knew he felt my pain.

The sound of the rain on the roof and windshield was interrupted only momentarily by the wipers refocusing the view every three seconds. The beautiful weather of the previous days had made way for dark-grey clouds and a cold rain that kept people off the streets.

The silence was interrupted by Anthony responding to a voice in his earpiece.

"Roger, out," was all he said. Then to fill us in, "There's movement at the back entrance. Two men corresponding to your description of the twins were seen entering the hotel." From this I gathered Anthony's other two partners were at the rear of the hotel. "We don't think Haqqani is present yet. These men may have been sent to clear the way. Be on the lookout for your guys." I assumed Anthony was referring to Austin, Jean-François and Yuri as my guys. He went on. "We are going to try to separate Haqqani from his four goons. The best time to act will be at the moment he arrives or when he leaves. While he is inside the hotel, the operation will be more complicated. We'll have to improvise according to how situations present themselves. When events develop, best for you to stay in the car which will be your safest spot. Understood?"

I nodded in agreement, knowing the last sentence was addressed to me only.

It occurred to me that I was about to see my son in action for the first time ever and it impressed me. They were loading clips with ammunition, threading suppressors onto the extended barrels and stashing filled clips in easy-to-reach pockets. Each had two-long bladed knives sheathed upside down, attached closely to their chests and two of the silenced guns. Turning to me from the passenger seat, Anthony handed me a USP .45 ACP H&K semi-automatic.

"Dad, hang on to this, just in case." He knew I was no stranger to firearms, having owned them most of my life.

About twenty minutes later a black limo, similar to those at the conference, drove up to the hotel.

"Contact," was all Anthony said. The street being nearly empty in the rain, the car stood out, and the three of us watched intently. A doorman with an open umbrella approached, but he was left waiting at the car door. Finally, two men exited, one from each side. I recognized them as the black high-top Cheetahs from the previous evening who stood outside the dining room and sat at the bar. Clearly, Haqqani was in the vehicle. The two bodyguards remained at each side of the limo, visually scouting the area. Once satisfied, they motioned inside the car for others to exit.

First Yuri, then Jean-François stepped out into the rain. Austin followed, and both he and Yuri were escorted by the doorman inside, while the Frenchman stayed at the vehicle, using the black thin brief case to keep his coiffure dry. Still no Haqqani.

"Flank vehicle." A single command picked up by the microphone on Anthony's throat. The order was short, followed by Herder starting the engine and accelerating toward the hotel, which was ahead on our right. Facing us, a similar Audi S8 approached, occupied by Anthony's other two partners. The hotel entrance about equidistant between us.

It took less than two seconds to place the S8s on both sides of the limo so that each Audi's passenger door opened facing one of the high-tops. Even though the black-sneakered guards were outside to provide protection and prevent potential problems, they obviously were distracted by Jean-François, or had assumed an all clear. The sudden ambush took them by surprise.

Violence is usually associated with chaotic sounds and loud noises. What happened next that rainy Friday afternoon transpired in silence, aside from an occasional order issued, or moan uttered. The first outburst of gunfire lasted no more than a few seconds and the sound was sufficiently hushed by the suppressors that it attracted no attention. The second was equally muted, but lasted slightly longer.

The two Cheetah-soled goons sagged fatally wounded against the side of their car and slowly descended onto the pavement. Three shots apiece in rapid succession from Anthony and his associate in the opposing Audi had done the job even before our cars had come to a full stop. The limo was on our right, between the hotel entrance and us. Anthony was out of the car convincing the limo driver not to take off and to unlock all doors. Herder opened the vehicle's rear entrance and Mohammed Haqqani's face became visible, looking at his attacker while reaching inside his jacket. In a flash I saw his eyes, and there was no fear present, nor surprise. Just determination and resolve not to be on the losing end of this encounter. In that same split second, I saw the limo door at the opposite side being opened and one of Anthony's associates from the other car reach in. Appearing in slow motion, he staggered, dropped his weapon, reached for the roof of the vehicle with one hand and with the other for his neck. Blood gushed from a wound and through his fingers, spurting inside the compartment, covering Haqqani. In an effort to say something he moved his lips, but instead of sound, blood gulfed from his mouth. He dropped to his knees out of view. Then from my vantage point, through the limo and the opposite open door, through the other Audi's open windows, I saw the twins running from the hotel entrance, guns in hand toward the enfolding scene. It had been one of their bullets that had struck my son's associate, even though I never heard the shots.

Anthony took his attention off the driver, facing the twins who were bearing down on the scene. Seeing an opportunity, Haqqani moved to exit his limo. And even though Herder was still there, I decided to enter the conflict. I chambered a round in the .45, exited my Audi and targeted the Afghan in my sights.

"Don't move," was all I said pointing the barrel at the top of his sternum. He looked at me and smiled as if the parts of a puzzle just became connected. Arrogance and contempt in his eyes as if to say, "This time it's you with the gun. Next time it's me."

All this activity, from driving up to the limo to me exiting the car, hadn't taken more than six seconds, during which Jean-François hadn't changed position. Standing on the hotel side of the limo, he found himself in the crossfire between the twins coming for their master and us. In shock and total terror, wedged in between two vehicles, he froze, still holding his black case above his head, shielding him from the rain. But nothing could shield him from the two bullets that struck him nearly simultaneously, one just above his left eye and the other in his chest, right at the solar plexus. I watched as he went down without a sound.

Within moments, my view became strangely occupied with the limo moving up in front of me and subsequently, the ground rushing into my face. I never felt the first bullet hit me in the stomach, nor the second or third enter my right lung and shoulder.

Later that afternoon, I died in an industrial section of town on the outskirts of Zurich.

CHAPTER 15

"In a freak accident three people were found burned to death in their car on the outskirts of Zurich in the early morning hours of Saturday, May 17. The remains were identified as Mr. Jean-François de Beauvais, a French official of the United Nations residing in Genève, Switzerland, Mr. Stephen Vinson, an investment banker from Fort Lauderdale, Florida, United States and a third person whose identity so far remains unknown. A preliminary investigation has concluded that the unidentified driver, for reasons unknown, lost control of the vehicle under the E41 overpass and Überlandstrasse and collided at high speed with the overpass pillar. Upon impact, the vehicle burst into flames, consuming its occupants. The cause of the collision remains under investigation, but foul play has been ruled out. Employers for the identified have not volunteered information regarding the incident, other than expressing regrets over the loss of life and condolences to those left behind. At the time of the incident, Mr. Vinson was the subject of a Treasury Department investigation, which due to the occurrence is expected to be closed as inconclusive, according to insiders who requested to remain anonymous. Officials declined to comment on the nature of the investigation, and calls to Mr. Vinson's employers remain unanswered."

This was the extent of the coverage in the newspapers emanating from the events in front of the Zurich Sheraton Hotel on Friday, May 16, 2008. Any further investigation, or subsequent reports following up on new findings, never made the news. Public interest, if any, in the incident died as quickly as it occurred.

After the three bullets hit me, my son had decided it was more important to get me and his partners out of harm's way and potentially save our lives, than to apprehend Mohammed Haqqani. His day would come at some point. The two Haqqani bodyguards I referred to as the twins had come running from the hotel entrance once they realized what was occurring and it was their firepower that caused Jean-François' death and the injury to Anthony's man. His wound, although very bloody, had missed the artery and didn't prove to be life threatening. It was not clear where the shots originated that hit me, but more than likely they came from Haqqani himself.

With Anthony and his team's changed priorities, the twins were able to gain access to the limo and protect their boss, at which time they sped away, leaving the other two guards and Jean-François for dead on the rainy street.

In the aftermath it was Herder's suggestion to place Jean-François and the two high-topped guards in one car and stage an accident where I would be one of the people perishing in the vehicle. His reasoning was that in the event I survived my injuries, my life would be in serious jeopardy by those pursuing me. My livelihood, my business, was already destroyed through the Treasury Department's action and my assets were in the process of being frozen, if not seized. The opportunity was there at that moment, a small window to be taken advantage of and it was the perfect way to disappear.

So my IDs, passport, wallet, cell phone, and personal papers were placed on one of the guards. He was dressed in my blood-soaked clothes and given my two beacon transmitters. My suitcase was placed in the trunk with my computer. Aside from what extensive DNA testing could prove to the contrary, it was I who died in that car that fateful night. Jean-François' attaché case was never found in the wreckage.

My recovery was slow and painful. Anthony had taken care to place me with a surgeon's family whose son had seen action down range with him in Afghanistan. When the young man was wounded and captured, it was Anthony's team that went in, rescued him and ultimately saved his life. This time, when Anthony reached out for their help, they never wavered and in return offered their home and expertise without question.

After I arrived, the doctor performed three separate operations on me in his home, his wife acting as the anesthesiologist and nurse. First to stop internal bleeding and close up my torn stomach, again to repair a collapsed lung and remove bullet fragments and a third time to patch tendons in my shoulder. I had lost large amounts of blood and for weeks it was not clear if I was going to survive the ordeal when one of my internal injuries became infected.

When finally the fevers subsided, my wounds started healing and I was out of the danger zone, the painful process of rehabilitation started. Walking, breathing and even just sitting up would hurt and exhaust me.

FEDERAL

Food came in small quantities, initially intravenous, then liquids and finally small amounts of chewable items. Stretching my shoulder was agony. The bullet had gone through and through, and had torn ligaments and muscle in the process. Day after day I would attempt moving my right arm higher and higher, measuring progress in fractions of an inch. I would rotate and stretch until the pain made me nauseous.

But improvement came, albeit slowly. My wounds healed and little by little I regained some flexibility and stamina. Pain, always the companion, served to prompt me of my limits and guide me in my progress.

The doctor and his wife never knew the kinship between Anthony and I, nor did they ever inquire. Not once was I asked what happened, who I was, where I lived, or where I came from. For a full five months they welcomed me in their home and cared for me, fed me, bathed me, taught me to walk, eat and live again. And they were there when I would descend into the darkness of loneliness and despair. I ached to share my thoughts but knew the knowledge could ultimately harm them, so I stayed within myself and let my body heal.

I didn't venture outside and expose myself to daylight and the prying eyes of others. When their friends came to visit, I remained in my room and stayed quiet. Some evenings I would sit in the backyard and look at the stars and sky and imagine my Sparky next to me. I'd close my eyes on those few occasions and I could feel the fresh air and hear the wind in the trees and I imagined early, early mornings back home in Florida, more than a lifetime ago.

In my mind I was at peace with the anonymity of my existence, with a single purpose to mend my wounds and come to grips with a new and unfamiliar life ahead of me. The peace of my solitude numbed the fear of the obscurity of what life was to become. As if I was given time to adjust, time to learn and adapt, time to get ready for the unknown.

At other moments my emotions would fight and incriminate me for my fate. I played the events over and over in my mind: when I received the letter and folder, my decision not to change the simple mix-up of the shares. Was it all worth it? A question whose answer escaped me.

I learned I was in Ravensburg, a small, sleepy town in southern Germany. Rolling hills, farms and dense forests make up the scenery of the land. My temporary home was on the edge of town, a quiet dead-end street lined with stately old homes surrounded by even older trees, tucked away in the woods. Comfortable and tranquil, it gave me refuge and felt like a sanctuary.

The doctor and his wife were contemporaries in age, but they treated me as if I were their son. This was the closest I have experienced anybody give unconditionally and I will always be grateful to these kind people. Perhaps at some point in time I'll be able to express this and repay them for what was given me so freely without query, objection or complaint.

Occasionally, the television would show the United States presidential race. The European news anchors would comment on their favorite, Barak Obama, and I would see the machine in action. McCain and Sarah Palin made headlines as well and received great attention as male/female presidential contenders.

But the biggest show was the senator from Illinois himself. Addressing Berlin crowds in July, harking back forty-five years to when JFK so famously reached out in the aftermath of the erection of the Berlin Wall and declared his support for the West with his words, "Ich bin ein Berliner" and was loved ever since. But Obama was no Kennedy.

In October 2008, Anthony came to visit as he had done once before, about three months earlier. During that first visit we had taken care of the trusts, companies and bank accounts I had control over in Europe, which had remained undetected by authorities. I transferred all power to him and set up a mechanism through which I could access funds and information using passwords, while assuming my son's identity. This second visit he had news.

Drinking tea, we sat together, appreciating each other's company, when Anthony said, "As anticipated, the media and those who knew you generally accepted your death, but those who initially were after you did not. The Treasury Department and FINRA closed their files regarding the securities fraud claim due to your death. They are no longer interested in the matter."

"Then who is still pursuing the issue?" I asked.

"We're worried about the UN and their enforcement arm involving FinCEN. Even though the Treasury Department dropped the fraud action, this deals with terrorism and terrorist financing. Two things occurred. First, the bodyguards were identified during an in-depth investigation of the accident and were tied to Haqqani. This was instigated and executed by the UN ODC taskforce and not by local law enforcement, so it was left out of all official reports. Secondly, that meant that unofficially your death was discredited and your disappearance is now being used to orchestrate terrorist ties to you. They are doing everything possible to separate Jean-

François from the terrorists he was found with and they are calling the incident a terror attack against the United Nations. Of course they will be implicating you and the Haqqani guys and maintaining that Jean-François was a target and victim."

He was quiet for a few moments. Then with puzzlement in his voice, he said, "What isn't clear is who is actually after you. It's being done very quietly and discreetly and neither Herder nor I can get intel on who or what agency is behind it. We believe this is privately staged, but whoever it is, has access to UN ODC data, including Interpol, and the ability to execute active enforcement decisions at the highest level."

Whatever this news meant to me, I found myself worried and I needed to know its implications. "This means I have people actively looking for me?" I asked.

"Those who want you are the same whom you call the 'Parent' and most certainly they will have enforcers after you."

Anthony searched for words in an attempt to be as clear as possible, "It won't be general branches of international law enforcement, though. More than likely they will employ professionals, like the Secret Teams we talked about. My guess is they first want to assess how much you really know and then trump up charges against you, or even worse, just eliminate you."

'Eliminate me?' I thought. I wouldn't stand a chance if they ever caught up with me. I had been active in martial arts in my late thirties and early forties, even received a black belt in tae kwan do and another in ai-kido. But that was fifteen to twenty years ago and I hadn't kept it up. Now five months after the injuries I sustained, I was still in pain and in terrible physical shape.

We sat there without speaking for some time in that tranquil backyard. The sun already low, announcing dusk and an evening chill. But fall was still showing its colors with trees shining in gold, red and yellow, the final rays of the day lightly warming the air. Just the hush of a breeze rustling leaves, a dog's bark in the distance, a small plane's murmur above were the only sounds as if the world held its breath, drawing out the moment in silent suspense before night would fall. 'Serene,' I remember thinking, contrasting the news I received and the implications it held.

"There are a few more things we have to discuss, Dad." Anthony interrupted the silence, gaining my attention. "Do you remember the black brief case Jean-François had with him that last day?"

The thought had actually occurred to me on a few occasions, but in the absence of knowing what happened I had dismissed the issue and nearly forgotten about the fact he was holding one that fateful Friday.

"What about it?" I asked.

"Well, it was never found in the wreckage because I kept it when we left."

Anthony smiled making the last remark, as if proud of the accomplishment. I remembered that smile and a wave of melancholy overcame me, looking back at Little League baseball and seeing that same smile full of pride when he made a hit or a good catch. How I loved those years and their simplicity.

"What was in it?" I asked, my curiosity piqued but at the same time not really sure I wanted to know, feeling a sense of trepidation, much like Pavlov's dog must have experienced. The last time I learned about something not meant for me, it held consequences I was not ready for.

"What I have is a CD and paperwork. The CD is mostly encrypted and needs work, but the paperwork has invaluable data of how assets are moved through the system, the Hawala. People, safe houses, special transports, passwords, bank accounts, contacts, couriers, sleeper cells. A wealth of information that I can use without tipping anybody off. This assures me we will get the Haqqanis at some point. Even better, we learned who is at the top and runs the show and whom they are connected to. Some of them you already met. But you will see for yourself."

I felt pleased for my son, but I couldn't muster excitement about the subject and missed the implication of the last sentence. It had cost me too much, and I feared that what he'd told me was just more trouble. Where I had hoped my disappearance to be definite and at least give me an opportunity to build another life somewhere, I now knew otherwise.

Anthony looked away, and I saw him reach inside his pocket to retrieve an item. Having found what he was looking for, he continued. "Here is something else for you, Dad." He handed me a USB thumbdrive, small and sleek. The black gadget felt comfortable in my hand. "This too came from Jean-François. It is encrypted, and I kept a copy of it. I believe it contains communication files between him and others, one of whom I know is Austin van Buren. I am still working on the encryption, but I thought it could be of interest to you when it's unlocked. You and I are the only ones who know of its existence, and we need to keep it that way. Let's not expose others to it, not even Herder."

"Herder doesn't know you found it?" I asked. I took the sleek little black device and kept it in the palm of my hand. Smilingly, I mused about the turn of events, remembering Jean-François playing with it in the hotel bar that evening in Zurich an eternity ago, and then seeing him with it at the lectern preparing to speak. I was skeptical about gaining any use from it, but I wasn't about to guess the future and accepted it from Anthony without question.

"I found it in Jean-François' pocket when we dragged him into the car. I never told anybody. It may be nothing, or it may be something. Just hold on to it. Then there is this."

Anthony handed me a large, thick envelope. "Here is all the information from the briefcase, plus some money that you'll need to get around. There are papers and the encrypted CD. I bought you a new laptop as well. It hasn't been registered and will remain anonymous as long as you don't register it. The papers are worth reading to gain a better understanding of what we are dealing with. You will see what I mean."

His care and concern made me grateful, but worried me as well.

"Why give this to me? Doesn't it make me even more of a target?" I wasn't sure I wanted to know anyway. Wanting to know more had already cost me almost everything dear to me.

"Listen Dad," Anthony said, leaning forward. "First of all, you already are a target because they suspect you have Jean-François' info. Second, if I lose it, or something happens and it becomes compromised, I want to be sure somebody else has it and can use it if needed. You are the only one I can trust with it." He looked at me and I saw emotion in his eyes. We both understood the implications of his words. He then added, "The data is too important and volatile to just stay with me, so I opened a safe-deposit box in Luxembourg that has copies of all of this, including a backup of the thumbdrive."

"Does Herder know?" I asked.

"All he knows is that the briefcase existed. It stayed with me when I took care of you after Zurich. He suspects there was more data in there, but I told him there was little of interest, and I only shared some of the paperwork. He was disappointed, but it was a moot issue after that."

His actions and choice of words made me think the relationship between Herder and my son was not exactly what I had assumed it to be, one of absolute trust and confidence in each other.

"Are you and Herder OK? I mean, it seems like you're keeping him at arm's length," I asked.

"This is too close to home, Dad. Somehow you gained access to facts that at best are beyond top secret and classified and as a result you were nearly killed. Either the UN, or people high up, are after you and want you implicated in a terrorist scheme that we know you were not part of. Your life back in the United States has been destroyed, your business has been discredited, and almost everyone thinks you're dead."

He paused for a moment to formulate his thoughts. "There is a relationship between the importance of the information you unearthed and the length to which people will go to retrieve it. I know Herder is close to the inner workings of the enforcement arms of the UN. So yes, I am careful and protective. Herder doesn't even know you are here, and he won't be told where you are going either."

My eyes opened in surprise. "How did you do that and why?"

"As I said, when it becomes this personal, I've learned that the fewer people who know, the easier it is to maintain control. When we left Zurich, Herder took care of the other wounded man and his partner and returned to Pfullendorf. I was able to get another car and brought you here and kept the briefcase. Nobody knows these people are friends of mine. An hour longer on the road, and you would have been dead for real. I never disclosed where we went, and Herder knows enough not to have asked. He knows you're alive and probably wonders about you, but we never discussed you again."

"But Son, aren't they following every move you make and trying to find me through you? And how did you find out that the UN ODC realized my death was staged? And what does that mean for you? Aren't you in danger?"

Anthony looked at me and didn't answer immediately. Then he explained. "We were brought down to Pfullendorf to do a joint exercise with NATO and UN forces. We trained all of the Smurf special ops, and in doing so I became close to many of them."

I smiled at the Smurf designation for the United Nations soldier. It refers back to the original Belgian comic creatures who were dubbed Schtroumpf in French and translated into Dutch as Smurf, a designation that took hold in English. The four-fingered creatures were characteristically blue, which resembled the color of the UN soldier's helmets. Hence, they are referred to as Smurfs.

"When we came to Zurich, it was on our own initiative. We didn't ask permission, knowing we would be shut down going into another country, so we were quiet about it. Our other two associates were Swiss

ARD10, now working for the UN. We trained the ARD10 and those two in particular, so it seemed obvious to have them with us going into Zurich." He stopped to look at me, remembering that day. It had been hard on me, but I had realized it must have been terrible for him as well. Not only to see one of his partners get shot, but to watch his father just about die and then have to abort an operation to get Haqqani, who had been so close and then slipped away.

I never knew the fate of his partner other than that I was told he recovered. So I asked, "How about bringing back one of your guys shot and hurt? How did that go down?"

"There are training accidents all the time, and at times people die," he answered. "It happens and that is what we blamed it on. No one questioned it."

Not wanting to be sidetracked, he continued. "It was them, the ARD10 guys who initially warned me about the UN ODC, who were quietly looking into the accident and had figured out you were not part of it. What's ironic is that the ODC are keeping this very hush-hush and don't want it to become public. They don't want Jean-François' real story exposed any more than they want to have you walk around with the information. So I was tipped off that his death will be pinned on you, but first they'll need to get a hold of you and eliminate the potential breach of security and that may include you as well."

"Are they aware of the case and what was in it?" I wanted to know.

"As far as we could tell, they have no idea what intel was exposed. That's why they want you, to find out. They know there was an attaché case because Yuri told them, but the whereabouts or contents is unknown to them. But no one knows about the thumb drive, nobody. All they are really sure about is that you didn't die in the car crash. They want you so they can implicate you as having collaborated with Haqqani and killing Jean-François. Then they can ascertain what intel was compromised. They're convinced you control some very incriminating information, partly because they knew Jean-François had it. When it didn't show up and you staged a disappearing act, you became the prime suspect and target. So we have to make sure they don't get close to you."

I came back to something he mentioned just a few moments ago. "Earlier you said Herder does not know I am here and he won't know where I am going. Am I going somewhere?"

"Yes, there is a final issue we need to discuss." Anthony shifted in his chair and pulled his jacket closer. The sun was low on the horizon behind us casting long shadows but still throwing its light on the beginnings of the forest in the far back of the garden. In just a few moments, late afternoon would make place for dusk and drape everything in tints of grey, as if suddenly all color was taken. It cooled quickly in the shade, and it felt like October.

Even so, we didn't move, and my son said, "We have to get you in shape. I want you to be taught by a friend of mine. First to heal further, but more so because you will find yourself in harm's way, and without a doubt that moment will come sooner or later. When it does, you'll need to be able to defend yourself physically, mentally and emotionally."

He was choosing his words carefully, not wanting to sound an alarm, but making sure I understood. He told me that arrangements had already been made for me to be trained and conditioned. I was to leave later that afternoon and would need to pack my few belongings and get ready to go.

Saying goodbye to the couple who cared for me so selflessly for so long was hard, but dampened by its abruptness. Just as suddenly as I appeared, my departure was without announcement that day back in October 2008.

CHAPTER 16

Anthony dropped me off at the station, handed me an address, hugged me, and left. It was difficult seeing him leave. It just hadn't been enough time with him, and I felt lonely and vulnerable watching him drive away. When his car turned out of view, I entered the station and waited for the train.

I travelled with just minimal luggage and a long overcoat with a large hood, which I kept up to avoid showing my face.

I felt odd and unprotected away from the shelter of the home I had lived in for five months. Walking had to be negotiated with care, as it still took my breath away. But I needed no help and was able to move along, just a bit slower than I was accustomed. When the train arrived, I was grateful for the seat and relative comfort it supplied.

The ride was quiet. I had chosen to sit in the back of the compartment where I could observe everybody and be left undisturbed. I opened Anthony's envelope, put the money away and read the short note my son had included with the papers. It explained how to gain access to the safe-deposit box in Luxembourg where the originals were kept. More importantly though, he wrote that he loved me and would always be there for me.

I knew this, but the simple words moved me deeply. The emotion touched off nostalgia, and I had to fight an ominous sense of feeling lost. Folding his note, I tucked it in my wallet, making sure I wouldn't lose it. It was going to take some getting used to living this way, alone, without a place to call home and cut off from my past.

To change my mood, I focused on the paperwork in the envelope. There were reports of meetings, a few handwritten notes, and a couple of memos. One originating from Austin van Buren was directed to both Yuri and Jean-François, where instructions were given to transfer close to $450 million United States dollars from the IMF via the Belarus Central Bank to Mitha Investment Company in Karachi, Pakistan. The note made it clear van Buren was at least an interested party in this Karachi company, if not an owner.

Jean-François had compiled a spreadsheet with a history of transactions from the IMF, World Bank, foundations and other charitable trusts, all dealing with Mitha Investment Company going back about fifteen years. Other notes dealt with the Haqqani appearance in Zurich that May 2008 and detailed the route he was to take in order to arrive without detection. Safe houses, phone numbers, contacts, sleeper cells, and even the Haqqani compound in Danda Darpa Khel, Waziristan[8] were described in detail.

Another five-page document consisted of an email that Jean-François received and it listed in detail van Buren's background, upbringing, education, and affiliations.

The first three pages dealt with Austin van Buren's past. I found out he hadn't always been known by that name. He was born Aurel Bajusz in Debrecen, Hungary, sometime in 1943 during WWII (the exact date was not given). He was the only child of Jewish parents and was orphaned before the end of the war. Cared for and protected by friends of his late parents, he spent the next ten years or so in Budapest, until he was sent to an English boarding school in 1955 at the age of twelve. He excelled in math and languages and was awarded a scholarship to the London School of Economics (LSE), from which he graduated in 1967 summa cum laude in international economics and business administration.

It was during the final years at LSE that he altered his name to Austin van Buren, negating any ties to his past and ancestral heritage. He subsequently entered the business world, focusing his skills on international trade and commodities, and almost instantly became known as an extraordinarily shrewd currency trader and speculator, with a near sixth sense for markets, unparalleled by any of his peers before or after. This rare quality, mixed with an unemotional, many times brutal and merciless approach, made his successes such that it was only a matter of time before he controlled his own company. The Hungarian orphan singlehandedly invented and pioneered the phenomena of the hedge fund. His net worth was estimated to be in excess of £300 million before he was thirty-two years old.

---

[8] On September 8, 2008 the Haqqani controlled Manbạ Ulom madrassa in the North Waziristan village Danda Darpa Khel was attacked by six missiles from US drones. At least 17 were killed, but the Haqqani's had left just prior to the attack. Other attacks would follow.

FEDERAL

From there his empire grew to enormous proportions, with offices in Genève, London, Manila and Sydney. He made New York his headquarters and primary residence from where he managed and oversaw his multi-billion dollar realm. His views and ideas of how the world should be organized came from his tutelage at LSE, being influenced by the thinking and ideas of philosophical scientist Karl Popper and his famous work 'The Open Society and its Enemies.'

So far, the report on van Buren's background was interesting but not of consequence within the context of what I had learned in Zurich. It was in the final pages where I gained insight into why Jean-François would want more information on this man. Mention was made of the various foundations and philanthropic organizations that van Buren controlled and how those companies invested large sums of money in political movements with one overriding theme: to promote those running for office, including the presidency, whose convictions were in line with his open society ideas and the redistribution of wealth. Seven of the foundations were highlighted as the core of a system that was dubbed the Shadow Party. The system was organized to finance, influence and endorse the personal political and social agendas of van Buren himself. Each foundation was identified with bank accounts in the United States, Europe and Far East.

What was of particular interest were the detailed disbursements van Buren made to other companies, United States and foreign-government agencies, and their officials. Dates, amounts, beneficiaries, and account information of both issuer and recipient were neatly tabulated in columns on the fourth and fifth pages. Many of the disbursements were in the six and seven figures, some higher. Gauging from the beneficiary's names and titles, this was not intended to be public knowledge. Judges, politicians and CEO's of public institutions were listed by name with personal emails and telephone numbers. If the receiving entity was a foundation or organization, the relationship to the intended person was clarified. It was obvious van Buren had direct and personal access to the most powerful politicians, industrialists, and financiers in the world and he made prolific use of it.

Whatever reason Jean-François may have had to obtain this incriminating data on van Buren and those he dealt with, he had been highly successful at it.

As the train entered Stuttgart station, I carefully packed the paperwork, envelope, and CD in my duffel bag. I had to change platforms and take the high-speed bullet train to Frankfurt. The 120-mile trip would take less than fifty minutes.

Mingling with the crowd, trying to find my way through the tunnels to the right track, I was confronted again with how alien I felt, how little I had been exposed to other people in those last months. I'm sure nobody paid any particular attention to me, but I sensed as if I stood out, so I covered my face in the hood of my coat. It was an unusual mixture of excitement and vulnerability to be on the move. At a kiosk, I purchased a few newspapers and some coffee and waited the ten minutes or so for the train to arrive. Once inside I opted for the quiet of the first-class cabin, and I sat down in a far corner to read the papers.

Minimal news had reached me by choice. I had had no interest and wanted nothing to do with it. I learned how the presidential election was fairing, how Obama had swept Europe and many back home off their feet with his eloquent charisma and well-delivered speeches full of promise and change. It made the memories flood back into my consciousness, and it occurred to me how far removed I was from that world that once was my center point.

Arriving in Frankfurt I took the short cab ride to the Alte Gasse address Anthony had given me and late that night I moved into a loft above a martial arts dojo. The house, a non-descript white four story structure on a well-travelled street in the center of town, afforded me my own floor with kitchen and bathroom. The building was owned and operated by an instructor Anthony had known for many years who provided advanced training for operators in the art of evasion and close-contact attack and defense strategies. His name was Gervaas, or just Ger.

Although I had been prepped about this instructor's curriculum, I was not impressed when I met him. He wasn't tall, nor muscular, nor impressive in his demeanor. Soft spoken, his voice a bit shrill, and his English just fair. The accent I judged was from either Holland or Belgium, but I was proven wrong when I learned he had grown up in Capetown, South Africa. I was right, though, as far as the accent, as Afrikaans, the local language in South Africa, is an evolved version of seventeenth century Dutch. Adding to his peculiarity was his insistence to add "You see" after most sentences, at times even starting a dialogue with it.

His head was shaved bald which made it shine and reflect the neon lights hanging over the workout mats. His beady eyes were wide open and intense and they never looked away, eyebrows arched up as if in perpetual surprise. He reflected a happy kind of attitude that was matched by a round face and round cheeks that stood out with rosacea. I guessed his age at perhaps late fifties judging from his hands and wrinkled face. But this is where the age determination stopped. I had never before met a person with the agility, speed and lethality this man could foster. A true artist in various styles of martial arts, he had designed his own methods of no-nonsense, very effective attack and defense schemes, which when applied correctly were devastating to any opponent having the misfortune of being confronted with it.

Anthony had told me about him, this non-confrontational, innocent and somewhat simple looking man. He had seen action in Congo, Somalia, South Africa, Bosnia, Afghanistan, Yemen, East Timor, and a few other conflict areas around the world. He was known in the underworld of mercenary special-ops fighters as controversial in his techniques and applications, which were effective, brutal and dangerous. His clientele was select and instructions were never given to more than two persons at a time. But mostly they showed up alone and often at odd hours. It was not unusual to hear the space occupied in the middle of the night. Even Sunday mornings at three o'clock, I have noticed activity.

When I arrived, Ger welcomed me and showed me the space on the second floor which was to become my home for the foreseeable future. Sparsely furnished with only the necessities, I looked forward to some privacy and a place of my own where I could move around without disturbing anybody who was being trained. Even more so, I could come and go without being seen.

From the beginning, he worked with me in a manner I couldn't predict. The idea was for me to strengthen my body, get in shape, gain stamina, and learn self-defense like a street fighter. That first day has stayed with me because I was taught something I didn't expect. I would have thought we'd start with basic defense or attack moves, or learn katas by heart as we did in martial arts. But an hour after I arrived, at about two thirty in the morning, Ger called me down and simply announced, "We start now, you see?"

A single round pillow was on the mat, perhaps five inches high and fifteen inches in diameter. "OK, you see, sit on pillow, cross your legs, fold hands in lap, close your eyes, and don't look up, move, or speak until I tell you to do so."

Sitting on the small pillow as instructed, I attempted to relax, which was not easy. My joints stiff, tendons inflexible and my injuries still plaguing me, I struggled in vain trying to find a pose of comfort. As easy as the instruction seemed to be, I had a very hard time staying still. It was impossible to tell time. I could hear traffic outside. I heard Ger move about. I heard the wind against the door, a rattle in the window, the odd person walk by. But whatever sounds came to me, they all dimmed against the discomfort and a pain that slowly built first in my ankles and my knees, then in my hips, back and shoulders, down my spine back into my hips, down to my ankles and feet and on. I didn't move, and the pain continued, a pain so excruciating, so all encompassing I was certain I couldn't stand it any longer. And against his instructions I opened my eyes to find Ger opposite, staring directly at me not three feet away.

Eyes wide open, eyebrows arched, the happy look I thought I saw earlier gone. Knowing what I was feeling he didn't let me speak.

"Pain is the gateway inside. It only hurts because your mind tells you it does. You see, everything always changes. Look at the pain, stop telling yourself it hurts, and don't give it a value. Close eyes, don't move." With that I returned into myself and struggled to endure.

Time passed slow as molasses flowing. Hours crawled by and the effort not to move my legs, or just my forearm, or my hand, became gargantuan. Whatever I tried to alleviate the agony, failed.

It was Ger's voice finally taking me out of my misery. "Open eyes and stretch limbs, slowly."

I didn't need to be told to move my limbs slowly. Gingerly I flexed, extended, and appreciated the tingling relief, as if hot amber flowed through my extremities.

"That was twenty minutes, not even, more like nineteen, you see. Not bad for a first time. Tell me where it hurt most."

As I explained my ails Ger listened and then simply mumbled, "Good, good, that is good you see. That is all for today, tomorrow morning at nine o'clock you are down here again. Good night."

From that day on I sat every day, sometimes at the beginning of a session, at times at the end. I would dread the distress and feared the time spent on the small round pillow, the Zafu. But I sat nonetheless.

On days when I didn't see Ger, I would sit alone in my loft. He taught me yoga to open my joints, lengthen my muscles, stretch the tendons and strengthen my core. He taught me breathing, how to unlock its power, how to control, restrain and unleash its force. It was vital while sitting. It eased the pain, which then turned to color.

And from color to light, and slowly time evaporated.

Sitting with me, he guided me, refined my Prana, my breathing and slowed the process, slowed it down and taught me to focus my attention to a small area of the body, ever smaller and smaller, infinitely smaller. Until the focus was a single point. Then I became the point, the atom, and felt its sensations, the vibrations. Absolutely still, learning to sit a full hour and beyond, without moving anything, slowing my breath, focusing my attention with greater and greater awareness. The boundary between the world and I would diffuse and ultimately cease to exist, and all I would be was my focus and Prana. Then that ceased in importance. In the void I found a new world and total peace.

Ger taught me about pressure points and nerve clusters. How and where to apply force to create maximum pain, or immobilize an arm, leg, or organ. He taught me where to hit to create dizziness, confusion, unconsciousness, or immediate death and how to hit the Vagus nerve to create a near-fatal drop in blood pressure, causing extreme discomfort. I learned where arteries are close to the surface for direct immobilization when using the knife, where to strike for utmost agony so the opponent can not utter a sound and goes down in silence. I was taught arm, wrist, elbow and shoulder locks to subdue and control a foe, and single digit locks to exit and reverse chokeholds. I learned how to ward off blows and invert the energy against the attacker and I found out which bones break easily with a single jab. Ger showed me how to use everyday objects as weapons, a pencil, paperclip, keychain, glasses, or books. There was nothing that couldn't be used as a deterrent. He instructed me how to protect against a knife attack and showed me how to disarm an opponent using my bare hands. I learned how to overcome being subdued, how to exit joint locks and how to escape after being tied down. I mastered predicting my opponent's next moves based on body positions and balance and I learned how to anticipate blows and attacks. I learned how to trust my feelings, how to listen and how to fight blindfolded, as if in total darkness.

The same breathing I was taught while sitting was applied in the martial art. Each attack was to be a catharsis, an explosion of physical power emanating from my core, combined with a simultaneous outburst of breath and ending inside the opponent. The combination of the physical outburst, in harmony with a sharply focused effusion of air and the single-minded mental clarity of focal objective, created a near unstoppable force. Highly effective, lethal, invasive and emotional but never personal. Breathe in to prepare, visualize the attack and breathe out striking. Breathe in when bringing arms in, visualize and breathe out extending, breathe in with legs closed, out when spread, in with knees up and out while kicking, in when setting up the move, out while executing. In slow motion, over and over, always first visualizing how and where to strike inside the opponent until I obtained total mastery and synchronicity over vision, breath and motion. The process of breathing and visualizing while moving took total concentration and left no room for emotion, which when inserted into a conflict was always the cause of defeat.

Each movement he taught was numbered and I learned to control all of them in slow motion. Slowly because my injuries were hurting, my middle age was showing and my lack of training obvious. Slowly did not mean easy. Ten minutes into the practice and the sweat would be pouring of me. After forty minutes I'd be exhausted, an hour and I felt like throwing up. After two hours I was spent and could move no more. And little by little, stretching and exercising each day, my body adapted and changed. In time he would just say the number and I would go from movement to movement, not losing a breath, always in slow motion with maximum intent. As we progressed, so did my efficiency and speed. Gaining strength and stamina gave me the ability to become fluent and move from number to number, faster and faster, while keeping my breathing even and in pace with my body. At first I became capable, then proficient, and ultimately I reached total fluidity in the art I was taught. Then finally, I experienced the same peace in moving and breathing as I found on the Zafu, the little round pillow.

Anthony visited me twice during the year I spent at Ger's place. We never spoke by phone, so as not to give anybody the opportunity to find out where I was. On both occasions he brought money, so I could pay for my stay and living expenses. Ger was adamant about not being paid for his instructions. Something about an old debt he owed Anthony. But I would leave him cash in an envelope at the end of each month on his desk, and I believe he was grateful, since he never mentioned nor rejected it.

Ger insisted I practice sitting at least once each day. He told me, "You see, if all I teach is violence without an understanding of what is truly important, my purpose in life would be deemed destructive. I believe the universe is predatory, you see, and therefore knowledge of defense sustains life. But it isn't enough to have knowledge of physical defense only. You see, ultimate defense is in the mind and soul. To learn how to deplete our reservoirs of resentments, wants and desires, hates and obsessions, means we can eventually decide what is important and then pick, or not pick our fights with wisdom. You see?"

On another occasion when I asked him how to turn off the thoughts that interrupted my focus, he said, "What we feel and think has no meaning until we give it one. You see, while you sit, thoughts and memories will surface. It is up to you to be indifferent to them, to be equanimous, to cease giving them meaning. It is the meaning we give to thoughts and memories that we identify with, not the thoughts themselves, and it binds us to them and makes us their slave. Without meaning, you see, they will pass and move on and leave us and make us independent of the past, you'll see." He smiled saying the last words.

Living above the dojo made it easy to remain self-contained. I didn't go out much and when I did, it was to buy groceries and necessities, which were all available within a quarter-mile radius. From my windows I could see down Alte Gasse and further down Petersstraße which crossed a small park. Sometimes I would go there and sit on the benches in the early mornings, when the streets were empty and traffic minimal and enjoy the quiet, listening to the wind in the trees. My state of mind was such that I had no interest in hearing news, or finding out what was going on in the world. My injuries had changed the way I looked at things and altered what I thought was important. Gone was my nearly obsessive preoccupation with all the financial markets, with all things Federal. Gone was the adrenaline lust for new deals and new transactions. Gone was the need to earn more and more and gone was the need to acquire stuff, never enough stuff. The simplicity that had entered my life had come unannounced, nearly imperceptible at first, until my realization of its silence and the absence of noise, internal and external, could no longer be ignored. Where I had nine TVs and six computers with sixteen screens in my home in Florida, I was perfectly happy with the small TV I had acquired, which I turned on only sporadically.

The only other objects I had bought were a cell phone and a TomTom GPS. My laptop was the one Anthony had supplied me with when leaving Ravensburg. I took the precaution of using public email addresses, Yahoo, MSN, and AOL. I very rarely sent or received email, and the few times I interacted on the web, I used software that redirected my web traffic through HTTP and/or SOCKS proxies, hiding the location of my activity and adding another layer to prevent exposure.

I had made various attempts using the laptop to unlock both the CD and thumbdrive that Anthony had recovered from Jean-François. The only responses I received were requests for a login ID and a password. Not having either, I decided not to fool around too much in fear of corrupting the data. For my cell phone, I purchased prepaid SIM cards that never requested or verified identity, and thus provided the anonymity I was seeking. When I didn't use the phone, I took the battery out making sure no signal was emitted, and I did the same with the laptop. Perhaps I took my precautions too far, but the price for not doing so was sufficiently high to warrant a somewhat paranoid behavior.

My life was confined to practicing Ger's teachings, the physical and mental components in equal measure. Previously, I would have regarded this lifestyle as boring, but I didn't experience any boredom whatsoever. I became engrossed in perfecting the minute and detailed requirements of my training. I accepted and understood that if I gave my mind time to wander, I would end up regretting a past that was gone, thereby preventing full recovery. So I spent my days doing yoga, refining the numbered moves and sitting twice daily for an hour each.

On the days Ger instructed me, I would spend between two and three hours with him uninterrupted. He never set a fixed schedule, but at the end of a session he'd tell me when to return, sometimes the next day, at times skipping one and at times at odd hours of the night. "To keep me on my toes, you see," he would tell me when instructing me at two o'clock in the morning.

Those eighteen months at Ravensburg and Frankfurt were not just rehabilitation for the injuries. Through the selfless actions of strangers, made possible and facilitated by my son, my life had been transformed. I was preparing, being equipped to move forward into an unknown lifestyle and location. My physical trauma had in an ironic and strange way become my savior and the cause of my transformation.

When I embarked on the road to Zurich I was headed for trouble, even though at the time I may not have been aware of it. But once committed to the action, there was no turning back and I had to face the consequences.

I don't know how many times I asked myself, had I known, if somehow I could have predicted the aftermath, would I still have gone? Would I have been willing to sacrifice my modus vivendi, my home, Nicole, my business, my books and art, my friends, my Sparky, most of my assets, and potentially my life? All to find out about what is behind the Federal Reserve? I don't think so, not without knowing what would be on the other side of the loss. But I could never have discovered what was behind losing all that I cherished without having sustained the harm that came to me that rainy Friday afternoon in Zurich. Looking back, I realized had it gone any other way, I would never have been as prepared as I was then for the new life staring at me. Anthony, in his wisdom, had given me what I needed most, when I was in no position to claim it for myself. It was one of those rare occasions where roles reverse and fathers become sons, and sons become fathers. How blessed I was.

I spent a little over one year with Ger, this odd-looking man who didn't impress me when I first met him. Leaving him was as hard as leaving the couple who cared for me in Ravensburg, possibly harder. This warrior, this dangerous, lethal and wise man whom I had learned to love, respect and admire taught me not just self-defense, he mended my soul and taught me how to continue the process of healing and growth. After my time with him I was in peak shape, strong, limber, lean, trim, and flexible with a sense of confidence I had only seen reflected in the eyes of my son and his associates.

But more so, Ger gave me something that I treasured beyond all else, something no one can ever take from me. In his sapience he showed me a way inside, and through the inside, a way out. I was taught the end of all suffering.

In November 2009, I left Ger, and with my son's help I was able to board a merchant marine vessel in Hamburg that was sailing for Iceland. At Reykjavik I boarded another vessel that took me via Nuuk, Greenland, onto Canadian shores. I traveled under a German passport, courtesy of Ger's contacts who did work for the German SKS special forces. I had adopted the name Jonas Schatz. Because of my language skills, I could easily be mistaken for German, perhaps one who spent considerable time abroad and acquired somewhat of a slight accent.

I entered Canada through a small mining harbor town. I preferred a small port of entry, with its relaxed atmosphere and easy attitudes, above the screening and security measures one would expect in Quebec, the vessel's final destination.

We docked at Sept-Iles and one dark afternoon in late November 2009, I stepped off the vessel onto North American soil and just walked into town, without anybody paying any attention to me. Carrying a duffel bag and wearing a long, oiled-leather winter coat and woolen cap, I found a small hotel on the Laure Boulevard where I checked in, ate, and turned in for the night. The following day I took the ferry southwest to Rimouski, on the other side of the channel and from Rimouski the train through Quebec into Montreal.

I looked nothing like the banker I was eighteen months ago. Gone was the suit, expensive watch, shoes, and accessories. Gone too was the extra baggage around my waist. I must have lost close to forty pounds, and my stomach was flat. I had let my hair grow, and where I had a grey goatee previously, I had a clean-shaven face. I could blend in easily with the street population and just be one of those on the road, anonymous and constantly moving, finding greener pastures elsewhere.

During my training in Frankfurt I had come to the conclusion I wanted to move back to the United States. Although I grew up in Europe, it was the United States I considered my home. It's where I had my career, raised my son, made my friends and my home, and it's the country I have always wanted to live in for as long as I can remember.

Another decision I had made was to leave the information I had gathered at the Zurich conference alone for now, including the briefcase data and whatever was to be found on the digital drives. No wish to publicize or open Pandora's box. My only wish was to leave all that alone and learn a new life. I wanted to be at peace and blend back in. A different me at a different place and a different home, but home nonetheless somewhere in the United States.

The northern plains have always attracted me, and I invariably wanted to see the small towns. Perhaps I could find a quiet place to settle down, hang my hat, and call it a new beginning. Somewhere north, somewhere in the Dakotas, who knows?

Arriving in Montreal in the early evening I exchanged some of my euro currency at the train station into Canadian and American dollars to resupply my dwindling inventory. Out on the street, I found a motel catering to the lesser fortunate amongst us. Rooms were by the hour, day, or week, and I prepaid for two days in cash. Junkies, winos, hookers, and the lost and lonely were my neighbors. An easy place to blend in where nobody noticed me, and if anybody did, I would know it. My room had its own bathroom, which was a luxury I gladly paid extra for, not wishing to share one down the hall.

It was freezing out, single digits at night and not above twenty during the day. Snow hadn't fallen that winter season as of yet. It was dark when I checked in, and after eating in a small café around the corner I locked myself in my room and opened my computer. I emailed Anthony advising him of my safe arrival and the general location of where I found lodging. The date was Friday, November 27, 2009, and I recalled just two years earlier, traveling with Nicole the day after Thanksgiving to Paris. In Canada, Thanksgiving is celebrated the second Monday in October, even so, I had missed another American Thanksgiving Thursday. In just two years so much had changed.

My idea was to enter the United States through Vermont and from there make my way west, skirting the Canadian border and arriving on the other side of the Great Lakes. Once there I would decide where to go next, or what to do. Meanwhile, I had to find a way to get across without being seen by custom officials. My German passport would hold up, but I didn't want any record of entering the States and leaving a trail. I was hoping to find out how and where to sneak across during the next few days, using Google Earth and my GPS. I could rent a car and pass through an unattended crossing, or hire a cab to take me. I was not sure yet how to pull it off. The first priority was to find a route, and I spent the evening doing so.

Ger had trained me to spot the unusual by understanding and recognizing what unusual is under the circumstances. My hotel was not in the better part of town, but being close to the station meant a variety of people would travel and pass through on their way elsewhere. So when I saw somebody linger I wondered what he or she was really doing there. Did they fit in, did they belong, what was their reason for being there? I'd learned how to walk and stop and walk randomly again to observe behavior, using car windows and shop fronts as mirrors. How to spot being tracked by unexpectedly looking behind. Those following will instinctively turn his or her head away, in fear of being exposed. Or change course 180 degrees and see who else follows suit. Easy tricks that most tails know about, but it is surprising how even they can be fooled by an unexpected move, turn, or look. So I kept an eye open for those not fitting in and not moving on, or an overly nice vehicle hanging around too long. Occasionally, it might not be clear why something didn't fit, but I had learned to trust my intuition, and I paid attention to my internal alarm telling me to be careful.

It was during my second day in Montreal that I noticed the two men. I was having breakfast in a diner, and I could see down the street from where I sat. An American made car, black, with nondescript features, drove up slowly looking for a parking spot. Nothing unusual there. What caught my attention were tinted windows in a city where hardly anybody tints theirs. That, plus it being perhaps too clean and it was trying to park in a not-very-clean part of town. Again, not really so unusual, but enough for a small alarm bell alerting me to take notice and keep track, just in case. It was when the occupants exited the vehicle that the alarm went off for real.

In khaki pants, sweaters, and open grey trench coats, they dressed identical. Their pants were baggy and their coats wrinkled, but the shoes were too nice, too polished. Sunglasses on, they stood out. Each sported an army crew cut and were about six feet tall. One seemed older and heavier built, but certainly not overweight.

The street separating us had two lanes with additional parking space on either side, and they parked about forty feet up and across from me. From the distance I noticed the younger one's face was marked by a boxer's nose and the older of the two had a slight limp. They stayed put for a few moments next to their vehicle, looking up and down the street.

I stayed in my booth, being able to observe them without being seen myself, but feeling too close for comfort, exposed and vulnerable. They separated, went opposite ways, and started working the street. I watched them enter one lodging house, then another and reappear only to enter the next. They were looking for somebody. If they were looking for me, why here? How did they know I was in Montreal, and why were they searching in the correct location?

My hotel wasn't far, one street behind the one I was on, so I decided to make my way back to my room. Then, I would try contacting Anthony and learn if there was any news.

Waiting for me in my room was an encrypted email from Anthony. Confirming my intuition and fear, it was short and to the point. "You were spotted Montreal train station money exchange. Expect two ops looking for you. Suggest move on with haste. A."

No time to figure out how I was caught, I needed to get going immediately. I was packed and ready within five minutes, and made my way down the stairs from my second-floor room. I was halfway down when I heard a voice on the ground floor ask, "T'as vue ce mec ici?" The French was well spoken with a slight accent, the voice forceful, but with a pitch giving it an uneasy quality. Too high with a feigned sense of camaraderie, it forebode a promise of violence if not cooperated with.

"You seen this guy around here?" was the question. The answer was an inaudible mumble, but judging from the reaction it was clear the desk clerk had no intention to part with any news. Not because of any loyalty or wanting to protect his customers. He just didn't want to be bothered by some schmuck walking in and hustling him for information.

"Te donne une aut chance, tu l'as vue ou non?" Meaning, "A last chance, you seen him or not?" The voice was still pitched, but the words were more deliberate and clearly did not expect resistance.

"Salot, fout le camp, tête de con. Lesse moi tranquille."

This time I did hear the answer and I knew it was the wrong one. "Piece of shit get out of here and leave me alone" was a loose translation. It was followed by some commotion and a sudden scream emanating from the clerk. I couldn't tell what was done to him, but I did know it hurt. It must have been excruciating, judging from the continued cries coming up the stairs.

I made my way back to the second floor, and continuing up to the third I heard the high voice commanding loudly, "Ta gueule, ou est-t-il?," or, "shut up, where is he?" The resulting exchange didn't carry through the stairwell and I couldn't tell what was being said, even though I was sure I knew.

Then, hearing two men coming up to the second-floor landing told me the clerk had given them what they were looking for, and this time I was sure it was me.

I waited until they moved down the hall toward my room before I descended down again, quickly and quietly making my way to the ground floor. Once there I saw the desk clerk sprawled on the floor behind the counter, his back propped up against the wall. The side of his face, neck, throat, and shirt were drenched and copiously flowing in red. A puddle had formed on the floor around him. He looked stunned and moaned softly, staring with disbelief at his open hand. In his palm was the cause of the bloodshed. His left ear had been torn clear off the side of his head, ripping some of his cheek with it and then been given back to him to hold on to. His nose lay flattened sideways on his face, shattered by a well-placed blow, and a deep cut over his left eye in the brow added to the gore.

He was a mess, the victim of an easy and very intimidating measure to gain somebody's attention in a hurry. It apparently worked. As he noticed me, I made a single gesture, moving my index finger to my lips, telling him to stay quiet. I don't believe he was interested in another confrontation and complied with my demand as I exited the hotel and stepped out into the street.

They would notice my absence quickly enough and be back out within a few minutes. No time to waste. Making an effort not to run and attract attention, I walked to the nearest corner and turned down a side street. I continued moving on, removing myself from the location, randomly

183

turning corners, putting distance between myself and the two freelancers. They obviously meant business and were serious at getting the job done one way or another.

Mid-morning and the early sun had made place for an overcast sky with darker clouds rolling in, announcing a winter storm. First of the season, with promised gale-force winds and heavy snow in the afternoon and through the night. That would be my cover for getting into the United States and away from the two goons. I needed a cab and to get to a sporting goods store of some kind and then out of town.

I found a taxi a few blocks further down and asked if he had time to drive me out of town for a two or three hour drive. It was received without objection, and I inquired next where to find an outdoor store where I could locate camping gear. We spoke French, and having lived in France my accent was perfect, so all he would remember was a ride with some French guy out of town. Just in case somebody asked.

I bought extra batteries, wind- and waterproof down pants, a long fur-lined jacket with a hood, two pairs of gloves, special water-resistant boots that covered my feet with shoes on, extra socks, a large thermos, and a waterproof duffel bag able to convert into a rucksack. Finally, I bought a pair of ski goggles and some silk and cotton long underwear to keep me warm. The whole idea was to keep body heat in and not let it escape. It was going to be a cold night, and I was about to spend most of it outside. In an afterthought, I bought a large collapsible knife and a stun gun, just in case some animal interfered, two or four legged.

The cab had waited patiently while I was stocking up, and back inside I told the driver to drive southeast in the direction of Frelighsburg. The distance was no more than sixty miles or so, give or take, but the roads being primarily two lane county routes, it would take us about two hours to get there. I settled back in the rear seat of the vehicle and gave myself some time to figure out how I was spotted in the Montreal train station.

As Anthony indicated, it had occurred while exchanging funds. Then I thought of it and shook my head in disbelief. I'd been really careless. Surveillance cameras covered all public places, specifically travel spots, airports, bus depots, and obviously train stations. It hadn't occurred to me that today's technology and face-recognition software can pick out one face from within a crowd of thousands and match it to a profile in a database. Who knows under what heading a request for my profile was entered into the system, but obviously it had been done. Probably through the UN and its law-enforcement arm Interpol, who don't have to give any explanation or reason why they are looking for somebody, just the fact they are will give them access to the North American systems.[9]

So now they knew I was on the North American continent. Not really a development I had been hoping for. The whole idea of taking commercial sea transports was to elude prying eyes and stay one step ahead of those who might still be looking for me. After a year and a half of having been invisible and undetected, their system was triggered through a fleeting moment at an exchange counter on a foreign shore. Not only that, it had taken them less than a day and a half to track me down after the Montreal train station. I had to admire the efficiency of the system. One thing it did accomplish, was to put me on notice that the threat was very real, alive, and too close for comfort.

Frelighsburg is a small town, really just a village, less than three miles from the United States border. My plan was to check in at a small inn for the night and prepare for the trek ahead of me. All my belongings combined didn't weigh more than twenty-five pounds. With the extra supplies, I probably had close to thirty pounds altogether, but I'd be wearing a lot of it. Fitting it all in the new duffel bag wouldn't be a problem, and it being waterproof would keep extra clothes and electronics dry.

Using Google Earth and my GPS, I had marked and waypointed a route from Frelighsburg to the United States border on the old Chemin du Verger Modèle, where it dead ended without any inspection, fences, or check-points. The distance from the town to the dead end was slightly less than three miles. From there I would cross the border, enter a wooded area, and connect to a discontinued road, which in years past used to connect to the Chemin du Verger Modèle, the remnants of which should still be recognizable. This old road, the Boston Post Road, connected with Scott Road, from where I had to cover eight miles to Enosburg Falls, Vermont, where I already had a reservation at the Somerset Inn for a mid-morning arrival.

Altogether the distance I had to cover was close to twelve miles. Not far, but considering I didn't want to be seen, had to carry about twenty-five pounds, and would travel off road in the midst of night during a snowstorm, I couldn't underestimate either distance or risk. The forecast

---

[9] About two weeks later, on December 17, 2009 president Obama would grant Interpol unprecedented access to US law-enforcement systems by amending Executive Order 12425, designating Interpol as a Public International Organization.

called for extreme cold and snow, with blizzard conditions starting mid-afternoon. Judging the obstacles, I estimated my progress to be two miles per hour at best, which meant it would take six hours at least out in the open, possibly eight. It would be dark by four thirty or five o'clock, and the morning light would not be apparent until eight to eight thirty the following day. Enough time for me to make my move.

Looking out the cab window, the snow had already started, and it wasn't even noon yet. The storm was coming in quicker than anticipated, and the driver commented about potential problems in trying to make it home. I ignored the statement, filing it away as an attempt for an increased fare.

As we arrived at Frelighsburg, the weather deteriorated substantially. I tipped the driver extra to compensate for a difficult trip back home, and checked into the small establishment in the center of the village on the Rue de l'Église. The streets were empty, with no tourists this time of year, and the weather ordered everybody to stay home. A small grocery store two blocks down the road had a few essentials I needed for the night, and I stocked up on Snickers, beef jerky, bagels, three super-bright LED flashlights, and a handful of lighters in case I needed to make a fire. My thermos would be filled with hot coffee or soup, depending on what was available.

The afternoon was spent resting and preparing for the night. Not much more to do than securely pack my stuff and keep out what I would wear. It was done quickly. I connected with Anthony, thanked him for alerting me and told him how I had been able to get away unseen and unscathed. In turn, he wrote how the search for me had intensified after I had been spotted. Next he said as the result of the data obtained from the briefcase about the Haqqani organization, events would become public about its effectiveness.[10]

I could tell from his words that a sense of responsibility bothered him, and that he felt bad I was in this predicament. But even if he had chosen not to give me the intel, they would still be coming after me. So I reassured him none of this was his doing.

---

[10] Mohammed Haqqani was killed on February 18, 2010 as the result of a US airstrike in Danda Darpa Khel, North Waziristan, Pakistan, home of the Haqqani Madrassa.

FEDERAL

Evening came, the temperature dropped, and the wind blew until it snowed at nearly horizontal levels. Minus ten degrees Fahrenheit and falling, with winds in excess of forty-five miles per hour, it would be rough outside. At the same time, it supplied great cover, assuring no traffic and empty roads. My thermos filled with hot, strong coffee, my new weatherproof clothes on top of my regular apparel, I was ready to go at about ten o'clock. GPS with flashlight in my right front pocket, knife and stun gun in the other, food and coffee within easy reach, rucksack on my back, outer boots over my shoes, gloves, jacket, and pants secured against the cold and wind, I was set, and quietly left the small inn through the back door. Once outside, the frigid air immediately took my breath away, and I had to turn my head from the power of the wind in order to breathe. My fur-lined windproof jacket was velcroed shut and covered everything up to my nose. The hood covered my head so that only my eyes were exposed, protected by the goggles. I felt the power of the storm, but the cold didn't seep in, not to my feet, legs, or upper body and my hands stayed warm in the gloves. I was ready for the night.

A surge of excitement went through me, feeling the gale pushing and pulling at me as I stepped away from the protection of the hotel. Aside from attempting to cross the border unnoticed, I was embarking on a dangerous journey, but a journey back home, back into the United States. And I felt safe, being well prepared with the right protective outerwear, I was strong and in the best physical shape I had ever been before. This was an adventure, and I could feel my heart beat in anticipation.

As expected, there was nobody on the roads, no cars, no trucks, no police, and certainly no other pedestrians. I had been worried about being seen in the streetlights, but visibility was so bad that I was no longer concerned.

Within minutes I left the village lights behind and turned onto the dead-ending Chemin du Verger Modèle, moving south into a pitch-black night. The snowfall was thick and muted most of the sounds usually associated with raging wind. I heard trees groaning and creaking, at times the wind howling through branches, but it seemed as if a blanket had been pulled over all of it. Then through this muffled noise of the storm I heard, to my surprise, thunder. The accompanied lightning illuminated flashes of bizarre white and grey landscapes, awash in explosions of snow-driven waves, eerily lit up from above. Something I had never seen or heard happening during blizzards, but it occurred nonetheless.

Following the waypoints on my GPS, which I had spaced at one to two hundred feet intervals, I knew I would arrive at the dead end in about an hour and a half, perhaps longer if my pace was slowed. The dead end would not just be the end of the road. It would be the end of Canada and the beginning of the United States. Even though the Chemin du Verger Modèle was not a thoroughfare, it served as an access to the few farms and homes sparsely set alongside the country road. So I could expect traffic, notwithstanding the weather. The traffic, though, would not expect me, and it could creep up on me unnoticed.

Forty-five minutes into my walk, and I had trouble distinguishing the road from the berm. The snow obscured the shoulder, even though it was lower than the hardtop surface, the white powder filled the gap and the wind leveled it all. It was the trees and growth on the side that guided my moves, if and when they were visible. Mostly I trusted my feet sensing the hard road surface for confirmation.

I moved along until, without announcement, the snowy ground under my feet changed. I noticed the springiness of grass and dirt. My GPS told me I was at the border, but it was my flashlight that confirmed it. With a little searching I found a concrete marker, resembling a miniature obelisk, about three feet high, with "USA" on one and "CANADA" on the opposite side sunken into the stone. And after midnight, in the very early morning hours of November 30, 2009, I stepped across the border back into the United States.

Walking on, I entered the protection of a small forest. Once deeper into the woods, the wind was still forbidding, but the trees buffered the bite, and I was able to locate the remnants of what used to be the Boston Post Road. Still partly paved but overgrown, it was noticeable through the absence of taller vegetation. Knowing I was on the right path, I found a sturdy tree and positioned myself leeward against the trunk, sat down, drank hot coffee, and ate. Right there in the pitch-black freezing night, in the midst of a blizzard, in the middle of nowhere, I smiled and felt complete, safe, and finally home.

Chapter 17

After arriving in the United States, I stayed constantly on the move. Sleeping in homeless shelters, Salvation Army rescues, public bathrooms, under bridges, and a couple of times out in the open in freezing temperatures. Staying away from conventional sleeping quarters, randomly moving from city to city, sometimes spending a night, other times eating something and moving on once again.

I kept my behavior as unpredictable as possible, even to myself. I didn't touch my cell phone and only twice used my computer at a Starbuck's Wi-Fi. I sent Anthony a sign of life without disclosing my location, informing him I was safe and doing well. He in turn explained the thugs had lost track of me after getting close in Montreal, but they were very much on the warpath and I should expect them to continue their search. Be alert and don't stop moving. The message was not lost on me.

Truck stops were the best place for finding rides. My offer to help with the fuel expense always found a trucker willing to take me along without wanting to know too much. I remember passing through Colchester, Syracuse, Rochester, Buffalo, and Erie. Spent a night in Pittsburgh and then to Columbus, up to Cleveland and Akron. Went from Toledo to Fort Wayne to Indianapolis, up to Chicago. From there to Rockford, up to Milwaukee and then to Madison, and down again to Davenport.

I remember Cedar Rapids, Des Moines, and Omaha. From there I moved north through Sioux City to Sioux Falls. There I caught a long ride with a trucker up to Fargo. It was cold all the time.

From Fargo I connected with a local driver making the rounds within North Dakota. It was close to Christmas, but I lacked the spirit even though it screamed at me wherever I went. I was tired and wanted to rest, and North Dakota was as good a place as any. This was my first time in the state, and I decided to let my intuition take over and find a place to stay wherever I liked the feel.

Somewhere along ND 11, the truck made a stop in Hankinson at the local grain elevator. From the cabin I watched as the driver spoke with a burly, large man in overalls, cowboy boots, and a company cap drawn down on his forehead, which I assumed to be the elevator manager.

Mid-afternoon. In another hour dusk would set in with an icy night to follow. When the driver pulled himself back up into the truck, I thanked him, took my duffel bag, and walked down Main Avenue into town. It was quiet, snow on the ground, probably more to come soon, and people were indoors. A block from City Hall, in a single-dwelling building, I spotted a diner. Parking in front and on the side, and a sign indicated more in the back.

The place was clean, and well kept. Big windows to the front and side gave it an inviting atmosphere. Two stories with what appeared to be living quarters upstairs. Not big, but certainly not small, it could easily accommodate a crowd. "Open For Breakfast and Lunch—Homemade Pie." My kind of place. No hassle in the evenings, just a day crew. Even though the sign clearly stated "Closed," a woman inside was cleaning counters and the lights were on. I walked up and knocked on the door.

She opened the door halfway, protecting herself from the cold, not the stranger in front of her. "May I help you?" About five feet seven inches tall, short blond hair with a grey streak, it was the eyes that stood out. Blue eyes, very pretty blue eyes in a strong face with full lips. She was attractive without showing it off, in a very natural way. As she looked at me, I was taken aback. Akin to some type of recognition, I felt a sudden memory long since gone as when I first met Nicole. Not sure if she felt the same or even noticed, I stumbled over my words.

"I, ehh, hi there... I am, I mean my name is Jack. I have no idea if you need any help in your diner, but if you do I'm looking for a job, preferably inside. I'm not picky. I'll do what is needed, as long as I can work."

She took a few seconds before responding. Quizzically looking at me, I could see her think and then make up her mind. "Come on in Jack. Let's talk inside, it's too cold out." She opened the door and reached to shake my hand, "My name is Trish."

CHAPTER 18

Tuesday, February 09, 2010

Seven weeks passed in peace. Working at the diner, Trish and I became friends, then lovers, and suddenly life was an oasis. Unexpected but welcomed, I had not been prepared for the peace and emotional comfort I encountered in the midst of the remnants of my upturned, and disarrayed existence. At the same time, seductive as it was to open and tell all, I withheld the truth of my past. She knew me as Jack, and had the good notion there was more, but trusted she would learn when the time was right, and did not pry for which I was thankful.

Only once, in the dark of an early morning night with her, she touched my scars and asked what happened. Wanting to make her part of my life, but in fear of drawing her in too deep, and expose her to my past, I choked up, and remained quiet until I just told her I had been shot. She did not ask again.

But the peace did not last.

Two guys dressed in grey overcoats, walked up to the cash register at Trish's Diner at about three thirty this afternoon. It had been quiet and the lunch rush was over. I heard them ask Trish if she had seen anyone resembling me.

They showed her a picture.

"No," she lied while I stood stark still, holding my breath back in the kitchen.

Trish had bought the diner about ten years back after leaving an engagement run aground. She had never married and, as I, yearned for the quiet life in a small town on the big plains, with a wish to find some peace and a simple business to sustain her through the years.

It seemed she found it, whereas I'm still on the run, far from anything close to it.

Trish had a home on the other side of town. Hankinson being what it is, this meant just a few streets over. Even though I had my place upstairs at the diner, I'd spend the night at hers frequently. We enjoyed each other's company. But no expectations were expressed, both knowing my stay had a deadline. We just didn't know when.

I guess Trish must have been in her early forties, and she was used to dealing with life alone. Attractive and pretty, she had met customers who had hinted at romance, only to discover a determined and strong attitude with no place for courtship. Without damaging egos, she always managed to keep flirts at a distance and maintain a professional relationship with the men and their female companions alike.

I had told her enough to make her understand that I wanted to remain unknown, and that perhaps at some point somebody could come asking if she had seen a guy with my features. I savored the moments of relative peace until now, but I had assumed this moment of dread would ultimately arrive.

These two guys in overcoats asking Trish about me are bad news. When I ended up in Hankinson, as in any new spot, I had altered my name and looks just slightly, as I had in every new spot along the way. But they tracked me down somehow, so I had to pack and get out, immediately.

As soon as the overcoats were out of sight, I ran upstairs, opened my laptop and scanned my email. It had been several days since I checked. My routine was to look every day, but as time moved on at Trish's diner and no news came my way, I assumed I could afford to be less alert.

I learned otherwise. An email from Anthony awaited me dated a few days ago. The text simple. "Move on, you were seen, same crew after you."

"Damn it..." I hiss under my breath, pissed off at myself. I had become too complacent and let my vigilance slip. Now they are on top of me again.

No time to waste. I had to run. Being on the run had taught me to travel light and set up home so I could get up and go within fifteen minutes. The practice had saved my life before.

I placed my duffel bag on the bed and loaded it with my clothes and stuff. No more than twenty-five pounds max, should I have to walk any distance with it. I was packed in less than ten minutes and went downstairs looking for Trish.

She's waiting with a look in her eyes telling me she already knows what's coming.

"I have to go. I can't let them find out I'm here and make you part of this."

FEDERAL

The corner of her eyes well up, and it is a moment or two before she says anything.

"Look, Jack," touching my face, "I don't know what kind of trouble you're in and don't really care. But I hope this isn't the last I see of you."

She took my hand in hers and passed me the keys of her truck.

"Take these, and wherever you can find a ride leave it there with the keys in the tailpipe. Then call me and tell me you're OK and I will figure out how to get it back here. Please, please be safe." She cupped my face in both hands and kissed me on my mouth. I tasted the salt of her tears mingle between our lips and felt her body fold against mine, and knew I wanted to stay. Immersing myself in the feeling, I pulled her close, just for a moment.

"I have to leave."

The sudden emotion shook me. I look her in the eyes and tell her, "No matter what, you will see me again. I promise you will." I kiss her again and I don't want to leave. Finally, I let go of her and walk through the kitchen out the back where her truck is parked.

A dark-blue short-bed crew-cab GMC, about six years old. It had seen better days, but it was reliable and everything worked. I start the engine, and turning my head I lock eyes with Trish one last time. Then I drive away from her, heading down Main Avenue into the late afternoon sun.

Those weeks, the ease of being with her, the sense of home I had started to feel in her presence, all of it was unplanned and unexpected. Leaving made me realize the loss, and I had to let go of any dreams I had quietly fostered.

It was going to be a long night.

CHAPTER 19

Spotting the guys is easy. They were driving a rented car that was too clean for the hard scrabble small North Dakota town. Next to the dusty pickups and older models on Main Avenue, it stood out, new, clean, and shining.

Not speeding up so as not to attract attention, being one of only a few cars on the road, with my heart pounding in my chest, I noticed them ahead of me, walking in the same direction as I was going, the heavier one with a limp in his stride. If things were not so serious I would nearly regard it amusing how obviously they were out of character and how comic book kind of predictable they were dressed. Black shined shoes, khaki slacks visible under grey trench coats, and neatly cut short hair. Sunglasses.

But there was nothing funny going on here, I feared these men. I recognized their gait and demeanor and knew they were the ones who found me in Montreal a few months ago. I could tell they were heading for the grain elevator's office, perhaps a half a block down the road. Being the main business in this part of the county, the elevator was the biggest employer around and an obvious place to look for a guy in need of work and money.

The manager, a local guy in his late fifties known as Butch, always dressed in well-worn overalls, cowboy boots and a company cap which, once removed showed a white forehead against a wind and sun weathered face. He was a big man you wouldn't want to cross, or find yourself on the wrong side of his anger. He had lived here all his life and knew who I was, but never exchanged more than a "How a'ya" with me, demonstrating a natural homegrown tendency not to engage strangers who wandered into town.

Even after ten-plus years, Trish wasn't considered a local by his standards. But he liked her, and I suspect at some point he must have harbored more than just friendly feelings, which were never reciprocated. Liking her made him tolerate me, and I was told that the fact he acknowledged me at all was more than I could have expected for a long time to come without Trish's endorsement.

FEDERAL

I just hoped he'd treat these two goons as he would any outsider rambling through. By now, dusk had set in and I felt safe driving past the two of them. Cap over my eyes, I passed them and drove up to the only stop sign in town and observed them in the mirror. They minded me no business and continued walking to the grain elevator's office, speaking to each other only. Finding no traffic coming my way, I accelerated and started west on North Dakota Highway 11 out of town.

I was ill at ease for the next hour. I didn't appreciate the close call and keep checking my mirrors for lights that followed and didn't change. These guys were nothing to joke about. I had seen what they could do to a person who decided not to cooperate.

I was very clear about the fact that my future prospects for living would be greatly diminished if they apprehended me and took their sweet time convincing me to regurgitate all I knew. These poor prospects were not just for myself, but for anyone in my past. They'd be in danger as well. So it was vital to stay out of their hands.

That day was a close call, and I wasn't sure how they did it. Where did I go wrong? Where was the leak? How could they have possibly known where to look for me? I had to figure out where I'd made a mistake.

Two hours into the drive and I was sure nobody was following me. I stopped at a gas station and filled up the truck, bought a bag full of snacks, a gallon of water, one of those ultra-bright LED flash-lights and toilet paper. It wasn't the first time I would spend the night in a car. I had a good sleeping bag, and while it could very well freeze that night, I knew I'd be OK. After a toilet run I was back in the truck and drove into the night, following the road west.

After driving for about three hours or so and another refuel, I pulled off the road in a deserted area. It's too dark out, but the terrain is hilly and wooded. It was close to midnight when I parked the truck, making sure it wasn't visible from the road and position it so I can pull out immediately and be driving without having to turn, if necessary. I stretched out and dropped off to sleep.

A few hours later, something startled me. I didn't know if it was a dream or a noise outside the truck. Pitch black all around, inside and out, I held my breath and listened.

I heard it again, rustling leaves, something or someone was outside, moving around very close to the truck.

Flat on the seat bench covered by my sleeping bag, I stayed still. I heard it again, distinctly now very near the driver's door, only separated from me by inches. Very slowly, not making a noise, I moved my body from under the cover, and shifted myself behind the wheel, and reached for the keys in the ignition. Whatever was outside moved from the door to the front of the truck. I still couldn't make out any shapes. But I could feel the hairs on my arms rise in alarm as I started the engine.

The headlights sliced open the black night around the front of the truck, and relief washed over me like a shower. Caught in the headlights was a dog, medium sized, spotted black and grey with a stubbly, matted coat, obviously malnourished and cold. Shivering, tail between his legs, hunger overcoming fear, he didn't move and I felt a pang of compassion. I knew how he felt. Using my flashlight to scan around the truck, making sure no other visitors were around, I slowly opened the door and stepped out into the frigid night air, not wanting to frighten the poor thing.

"Come here, puppy, it's alright, come on."

I tried to sound calm and at ease, without urgency. I wanted him to make the move and come to me. But he just stood there in the bright light of the headlamps and didn't move. I lowered the beams to stop blinding him and repeated my words.

"Come on, puppy. It's alright, just come over. It's OK puppy."

I reached for a box of crackers from the dashboard and carefully lowered myself on one knee. As I placed a few of them on the cold damp ground, I kept quiet while just looking at him. He noticed the crackers right away and shifted his gaze from me to the spot in front of me.

"It's OK puppy, it's OK."

He inched slowly toward me, stopping just out of arm's reach, legs shivering, eyes fixed on the food. This poor little creature was hungry and cold. I moved back ever so slightly to give him space, and as I did, he moved forward and inhaled the crackers. Placing a few more crackers on the ground he surmounted his caution and crouched closer to get them.

"If you want more, you'll have to get it from my hand," I whispered gently.

Eyes on me, ears perched up, he approached and took one from my open hand ever so gently. I noticed the collar around his neck that wasn't visible in the dark. Worn and ragged, it told me this dog was once cared for, but had been in the wild for some time. Just as me, lost, trying to find his way home. No tag on the collar, so whatever name he had was gone, again just as me. I offered him a few crackers at a time, and he let me touch the top of his head. His coat was dirty, matted, and wet. God knows how long he had been out there alone, trying to fend for himself.

He let me scratch behind his ears and pet his shoulders. He sat down and just looked at me. Sweet eyes, long ears, strong legs and hips, with a full tail. Perhaps thirty-five pounds. Elongated snout resembling a retriever, he reminded me of Sparky, whom I had to leave back in 2008 when things turned ugly and my life changed. Too skinny and not cared for, this dog used to be good looking, and I guessed his age at about three to five years.

If he was hungry, then he must have been thirsty as well, so I reached for the jug of water from inside the truck. Pouring a small trickle into my open cupped hand, I let him drink. I was right, he drank from my hand and the feel of his tongue against my palm lapping up the liquid was gratifying.

The night air was cold and it felt like either rain or snow moving in, perhaps both. I wanted to get back in the truck, and looked at my new friend, gently prodding him and I knew one way or another, he was coming with me.

"Let's go puppy. Get in the truck, it's OK." But he didn't move. Legs still shivering either from fear, but more likely the chill, he looked up at me. Ears up told me he was not afraid, just not sure what to do.

Then in an unexpected move, I knelt down next to him and before he could protest, I put my arms around him, lifted him up onto the driver's seat, and closed the door, locking him in. Then I walked around, opened the passenger door, and spread out my sleeping bag.

"Come on puppy, lay down, it's OK, you're safe here."

He moved his body from the driver side over to the right on top of the sleeping bag. When I climbed back in the truck he had laid down, curled his body with his snout on one of his paws, and had his eyes open looking up at me.

"Good boy, you are a good boy."

I petted his head and neck and the curve of his spine. He was so skinny and I felt grateful to have found him, or he me. The heat on, it was comfortable in the cabin and I noticed it was four fifteen in the morning.

I sat in the truck, let the engine idle, and peered through the windshield into the dark. I knew I had to start driving again but didn't want to. I wanted to think.

Trish was still on my mind. My time with her had been an island, a safe spot, unexpected and welcome. Savoring her lips and feeling her body rise against mine left its mark. I had tasted the sting of hope. Hope for a new life. I hadn't felt any for so long that when it slipped quietly into my consciousness, I didn't want to let go of it.

I knew, though, whatever was there, now was not the time. I had to let it pass. But I could feel the emotion bite inside of me, a hunger and yearning that wanted me to turn around and go back and believe all would be well.

But that was a bad idea. Impossible. I had already invited evil into her diner. This was too narrow an escape. Nor could I allow anything to interfere with staying ahead of those men. I had to stay out of their hands and somehow at some point reach an understanding with them or their organization so they would let me be.

Leaving Trish also made me miss Nicole, whom I hadn't spoken to for two years. My last discussion with her had not been pleasant, where she was angry because of a female nightly caller who had asked for me. Many were the moments I had wished our final conversation would have been more enjoyable. But there is nothing I can do about it anymore, she thought me dead, killed back in Zurich. It seemed impossible to dispel Nicole and Trish out of my memory or my future. But I had to do it, for their safety. I had to disappear and stay disappeared. In fact, I had succeeded in vanishing from the lives of all my old friends and relatives, except my son.

I looked over at my new companion. This lonely, cold and wet dog reminded me of Sparky. I had left him with my neighbor Carol, but I never came back and he had no idea where I was, or what happened. It was the innocence of his unwavering and loyal trust that cut my insides. I had found him at a shelter on death row, underfed, emaciated, abandoned, and sick. It took time, patience, gentleness and care, but I watched him come back to life and attach himself to me and I to him. It was cruel how our life together had turned around and I seemingly abandoned him. I know he's still waiting and perhaps in time the memory will fade and he will not feel as if I forgot about him. It is the kind of sorrow that knows little remedy.

With those somber thoughts I eased the truck into gear and started driving. Whenever I glanced his way, my new friend on the seat next to me returned my gaze.

At around five o'clock in the morning, we reached the junction where North Dakota Highway 11 ends, and I turned right onto Highway 83, continuing the drive north to north west.

CHAPTER 20

Several hours later, I checked my GPS for potential towns down the road and found I wasn't too far from Linton, North Dakota.

Once there, I paid cash for a room at a small motel on the edge of town. I parked the truck and took my stuff, including my friend, whom I guided by the collar inside. Taking inventory, I counted about thirty-four hundred dollars in cash, a large collapsible knife, the new flashlight, my laptop, the GPS, an extra pair of all-weather boots, a handful of lighters, and cold weather clothes. This would last me some time without having to work, and I would still have plenty left to keep moving on.

I needed to go into town, get supplies for myself and my new companion, take a shower, and call Trish later. Calling anyone was tricky, since there were so many ways to track somebody's moves and locations. I had a little baggie with SIM cards of various phone companies, each with its own number, and made it a practice to change SIMs every other day. I never called a number twice in a row with the same card. I hoped my precautions would keep me safe.

An hour later I was back with toiletries for myself and the dog, including a leash I found at the gas station convenience store. The rest of the morning was spent showering both of us and untangling and brushing Dakota's coat. I decided to call him Dakota, since that was where he found me, suppressing the impulse of calling him Sparky. Not changing the names of their pets is how people who want to disappear are located. So Dakota it was and I decided further that from now on, the sleeping bag was his.

He was one sweet dog. He sat in the shower, allowing me to scrub and wash and comb and push and shove and do all that was necessary to clean him. With big eyes looking at me, he licked the shampoo and let the water run over his head. After, he ate and drank and lay down in front of the queen bed that dominated the room. Head on his paw, he kept an eye on me. His clean coat was brindle grey with some black. Long hair, he looked fine, if not a little skinny.

Mid-morning and I felt as if I'd had a full day behind me already. I lay down on the bed and turned on the television looking for a mind-numbing movie to fall asleep with. Before I drifted off, I called Dakota to join me on the bed, and this time he didn't hesitate. Curled up in the hollow of my knees we both fell asleep.

It was late afternoon when I woke up. I was hungry and disoriented, and for a moment, didn't know where I was. Then, realizing where we were I knew we had to get up and leave. I couldn't afford to stay here any longer. They were on my trail yesterday, and any methodical search would guide them in this direction.

Dakota looked at me while I packed my stuff and jumped off the bed as I zip the duffle bag closed. I snapped on his leash and before exiting the room, checked through the blinds to see if all was clear. Feeling good about it, I opened the door, walked the few yards to the truck, and threw the bag behind the passenger seat.

After letting him pee in peace, I said, "Come on Dakota, get in boy," and he jumped in the cabin without pause. With him next to me, I gunned the engine, and slowly exited the small parking lot to continue north on Highway 83.

I planned to stop and get food and water for the night at the next convenience store I passed. We'd be spending more nights on the road, I was sure, so another sleeping bag would come in handy as well.

While driving, I went over anything I could have done over the past weeks that could have brought the overcoats to Trish's diner. I hadn't used my cell phone for months. I didn't send letters, nor did I receive any. The only communications I had were with Anthony. But the contact with him was sporadic at best and transacted through email only.

I didn't frequent bars, restaurants, or any public places. While working for Trish, I was either in the back washing dishes and prepping the food, with her, or in my room upstairs. The only time I ventured into a public place was about five days ago, when Trish had no time to go to the local bank and asked me to make a deposit for her.

Then it came to me.

I had noticed the cameras behind the teller. The bank's policy was for each patron to remove any headwear and sunglasses, which I reluctantly complied with after having been prompted twice to do so by the teller behind the counter. I do remember trying not to make eye contact with the camera and leaving the bank's premises as soon as I could.

There are no coincidences. I had been in a bank with cameras, and within a week two men showed up from nowhere looking for me. The fact was I had been spotted. And that bank deposit would be linked to Trish, which meant her blue GMC would show up missing, and with little effort they would know where I fueled up. Which meant I was no longer safe. Nor was Trish.

Fumbling through my bag behind the seat and trying to keep the truck on the road, I located my cell phone. I hadn't used it recently, so no worries about which SIM card to use as I pushed the battery into place. A minute later I heard the ringing of Trish's phone. By now they had probably figured out I worked for her and that a connection between the two of us existed. Very likely they were monitoring her calls and activities, and if so, calling her would reveal my cell phone number and a general location from where the call was placed. I knew I was taking a big risk. The urge to warn her, though, was stronger than any self-protection, so I stayed on the line.

"Hello." It was her.

"Trish, it's Jack."

"Call Butch."

Her answer was immediate and final and followed by the instantaneous disconnection of the line.

"Fuck."

I stopped the truck and dismantled my cell phone, took out the battery and SIM card. I broke the tiny card into pieces and discarded the remains out the window. From the little plastic bag I took another card at random, noticing it was a T-Mobile issue, and installed it. I didn't want to waste signal time calling 411, so I decided to drive on and hit the next gas station to refuel and use their phone book to locate Butch's business number. All this while Dakota looked up only once when I expressed the profanity, and for the rest he slept at my side on his sleeping bag.

The amount of traffic on the road had increased considerably, and a scan on my GPS showed I was getting close to a larger town. Services and stores lining the road began to multiply, and I spotted a large gas station connected to a country feed, liquor, and convenience store all in one, where I found a new sleeping bag. I stocked up on water and food items that wouldn't perish easily and decided to buy a ten-gallon plastic tank. Not a bad idea to have an extra supply of gasoline just in case. An idea jumped in my mind when I spotted a large can of black truck-bed liner paint, and I purchased it on a whim along with a wide industrial paint brush.

The phone booth actually had a phone book, and I tore out the page with Butch's company number and folded it in my pocket. Then after I filled up the truck and the extra tank, I was back on the road. The whole thing didn't take more than twenty minutes.

It had started to rain and it was cold out. The country was flat, the asphalt hardtop cutting through it like an endless ribbon, promising only more empty land ahead. Dirt roads leading to small farm communities branched off every so often, adding to the forlorn feature of the expanse. A few trees randomly dispersed through the boundless plains offered little protection against the low temperatures and blowing rain.

The time was about five thirty in the afternoon, and I realized Butch wouldn't be in his office after six o'clock, so I decided on calling him when I could find a quiet spot. With more traffic on the road it was harder to figure out if somebody was following me. I drove on for a couple of miles and turned right onto a small country road. Five minutes later I felt fairly confident that no one was following me. I turned the truck around and parked on the side. Engine off and lights dimmed, I found my phone and unfolded the directory page.

"Butch here," is all he said answering the ring.

"It's Jack," I responded, not sure where to go from here.

He didn't waste time.

"Look Son, I don't know what you're involved in, but I sure didn't care for them two thugs who asked me about you. I seen plenty of guys like them before when I did my tours in Nam, and I didn't care for them there either. Too glib and smooth acting they know everything, telling me what not to do and giving me orders. I don't think so. I don't give a damn who they work for. They ain't impressing me none."

He waited a second, and before I could say anything he continued.

"Trish got herself in a bit of a jam with them goons, so I had to convince them with a few buddies of mine that this was no place for them to hang around. They got the message alright and even if they choose to come back, I think they understood there's more trouble here for them than they want to deal with."

The topic closed, he changed the subject. "Trish wants you to keep the truck as long as you need it and not to worry and it's better to stay in touch through this number. Don't use hers, just to be sure." I know it was the most words he ever uttered to me before.

"Is she OK?" I asked. I refrained from inquiring how he persuaded the guys to leave Trish alone. I was grateful, though, and told him so.

"Thank you, Butch, for watching over her."

"You're welcome Son, and she's OK. I guess you understand you're important to her, so you be careful and watch your back," was his answer.

With that he hung up. I felt a mixture of relief and concern, but mostly I was reassured that Butch was there. He seemed genuine and in control. For him to indicate what I mean to Trish said a lot about the man.

An hour later, in the dark and rain, I arrived in Bismarck, North Dakota. Driving toward the center of town, looking for a place to park, I found a four-story public parking garage and entered unnoticed. No attendant present, nor any cameras. I parked on the third floor in a far corner, shut off the engine and lights, sat back and waited for everyone that had worked late to go home.

Dakota and I ate some beef jerky and smoked sausage and drank some water. A few hours later, when the already low activity in the garage ceased altogether, I exited the cabin and inspected the outside of the vehicle. It seemed dry enough for me to do what I had in mind, and I let Dakota out while keeping him on his leash wrapped around the front bumper. The neon lighting of the garage was adequate, and I pried the top of the truck-bed liner paint can open with a screwdriver I found in the glove compartment. It was a nasty thick, flat black type of polymer that sticks to everything, mixed with coarse pieces of silica and stuff to create a nonskid surface. It was perfect for giving the truck a quick but lasting new look. I dipped the wide paint brush in the goo and start at the back.

It went on quickly and easily and I made good progress. The back and right side done, I opened both cabin doors to reach the roof and hood, and I began working on the driver side of the truck. With my back to the garage ramp, trying to finish the job quickly and move on, I didn't notice the black Lincoln Navigator slip into position, blocking the exit.

"Mr. Vinson, you are a difficult man to find." The male voice behind me was smooth and soothing, but with a pitch slightly too high to be masculine. I recognized it as the same high voice I'd heard interrogate the Montreal hotel desk clerk a few months back. He didn't fare well in the exchange. A cold adrenaline chill washing through me. Big trouble just showed up.

As I turned, can in one hand, brush in the other, I saw the same two men who were walking down Main Street to Butch's office the day before. They had left their Navigator with the engine still running and were about four feet away, too close for comfort. The one who spoke was smiling, his partner was not.

Sensing the danger, Dakota growled.

Khaki pants and grey unbuttoned overcoats. For the first time I was able to have a good look at them. They stood in front of me about two feet apart, the one on my right, the heavier of the two, favoring his left leg. They made no move and neither did I.

The heavier one addresses me again.

"Well, Stephen, do you have some time for us?"

Smiling and his voice still a pitch too high. A round face with dark hair and thick eyebrows, he could be perceived as a nice guy until you saw his eyes—cold, without a trace of the phony smile. He was the heavier and older of the two.

His non smiling partner was as tall, but younger with a more lithe physique, his face revealing the result of previous physical encounters. Eyes too close together gave him an odd, uncomfortable look, as if there was something wrong with this guy, not too smart and a bit crazy. A faded scar ran from below his left eye to the top of his lip, and a crooked nose resulting from an earlier fracture gave him the menacing look he probably used as an intimidation factor. Lips slightly parted sported a black hole where a front upper tooth should have been, and his eyes fixed on me through squinting lids.

It worked, he intimidated me.

With a nonchalant move, Smiley pulled aside the left lapel of his unbuttoned trench, exposing a holstered handgun. Just a display, not in hand, which tells me they want to get me in one piece and "talk" to me. Had they wanted to kill me, they would have done so already. No mistake about their intentions. No good would come from this.

I moved slowly sideways with my back to the truck, trying to find some protection and saying nothing.

"If you work with us, it will be a lot easier for all, especially you." Again the high voice, absent the smile.

A short move with his head activated Scarface, who with one quick step slid forward on his left foot and effortlessly executed a right sidekick, hitting me with the outside edge of his wingtip just above my left hip under my ribs. An immediate and intense sharp pain shot from my spleen to my shoulder, and I stumbled back inside the open door against the truck seat, which broke my fall. My attacker stepped forward readying himself for the next assault, and in a reflex I used the only weapon at hand and threw the bucket with the bed-liner goo at him. The rim hit him just below the chin on the chest bone and a large amount of the black gunk sloshed in his open eyes and mouth, stopping him dead in his tracks.

Ignoring my pain, training took over. In rapid succession I delivered a forward kick to his groin immediately followed by a right sidekick. As instructed by Ger and practiced thousands of times with him, the impact was maximized by aligning my breath with the physical explosion. My reaction was instinctual and immediate. The result was devastating.

The first blow to the groin made Scarface's upper body move up and forward, the second connected with his throat for instant immobilization. It hit home with a sickening crack. Without a sound he fell back and sideways.

Not expecting the turn of events, Smiley stepped forward in an attempt to arrest my motion, but when his partner fell, he froze and looked sideways. Dakota had come around the front and jumped at him, but was restricted by his leash and now threatened the man with only a deep guttural growl. Enough to create a split-second distraction, I yanked the truck door open, hitting Smiley in the face with the freshly painted doorpost, leaving a black streak from eyebrow to chin, blood spurting from a broken nose. He staggered back, grabbing for his sidearm, as I reached out with my left arm and took a hold of his trench collar. Jerking him forcefully toward me, I simultaneously turned my upper body left and with all the power I could muster from my midsection, connected my right elbow into his face, as I simultaneously expelled the air from my longs with a loud hissing sound through my pursed lips. This time opening the length of his nose up into his forehead. His knees buckled and he slowly went down, not before I administered another door/face impact, which hit him across the forehead with the lower door panel.

No words were spoken, hardly any noise was made and in less than ten seconds, the two men were on the ground motionless, with a pool of blood forming around them. Wide eyed, adrenaline rushing, I looked around and found we were still alone, Dakota still growling, their Navigator still running.

I approached Scarface carefully. I could tell his neck was broken, so he posed no further danger. The impact of realizing I just killed the man escaped me for the moment, being too wired and pumped up dealing with the situation.

Exposed through his open coat was a gun tucked under the shoulder and cuffs on his belt. I pulled out the weapon, a Colt .45 ACP, and the cuffs. Pistol in hand I approached Smiley who had stopped smiling. His eyes open, he tried to lift his head, blood running freely down both sides of his face. He opened his mouth in an attempt to say something.

Not wasting time, I turned him over and positioned my feet on either side of his head and dropped all my weight on one knee between his shoulder blades, immobilizing and pressing the air out of him. I cuffed his hands behind his back, tightening the metal constraints into his flesh, making him groan. Then turning him halfway again, I reached inside his jacket and removed his firearm and wallet. Just a driver's license issued in Virginia and a wad of cash, both of which I put in my pocket. In the overcoat's inside pocket, a heavy, elongated object caught my attention. It was a suppressor that could be screwed onto the extended barrel of his gun. I placed both firearms and silencer inside my truck and continued my search, confiscating another wallet from Scarface, but nothing else of consequence.

I walked to the Lincoln Navigator, then parked it next to my truck so the two bodies on the ground were out of view. A quick scan of the SUV delivered four boxes of fifty .45-caliber rounds each, two cell phones, a laptop, two carry-on suit cases, and some paper work. I wanted to get out of there quick, so I took the rounds, cell phones, paperwork, and laptop to my truck. The carry-ons held only personal clothes and toiletries, and I left them alone. Then with plenty of effort and revulsion, I placed the dead assailant behind the Navigator wheel and turned to deal with Smiley.

Dakota, still tied to the GMC's front fender, suddenly barked and a movement surprised me. The next moment I was in a daze, not understanding what just happened, and stumbled with my back up against the Lincoln. Another loud thud, my head cracked back on the sheet metal, and I could taste blood in my mouth. And as if through a fog, I saw Smiley's bloodied head coming in for a third head butt. Dakota continued barking.

Lifting my right forearm to deflect the move, I blocked him at the throat. The momentum of the interrupted forward motion made his head snap, and I could feel his blood splatter on my face. My forearm on his throat, he pressed his full body up against me, pinning my back against the Lincoln. Using his knees to hit me in my groin, waist and thighs, he attempted to overpower me, while trying to shove his shoulder under my chin and immobilize me.

Arms restrained behind his back, this guy was hurting me and under different circumstances I would have admired his tenacity and drive. But I had to stop him right now, before he gained more of an upper hand.

I turned my body sideways, trying to minimize the impact of the barrage of knee kicks coming at me, and raised both my hands up to his neck. Using a choke grip, I applied full pressure with both thumbs on the cartilage in his throat and almost immediately felt the tissue give and then break altogether with a nauseating popping and gurgling noise. The kicking ceased immediately and Dakota stopped barking.

FEDERAL

Smiley's eyes fixed on me, turning wide and bulging out. No sound at all, aside from my breath slowly exhaling under pressure in keeping my hands on his throat. He shuddered in a vain attempt to loosen my hands, and for what seemed an eternity we kept eye contact. But then his glazed over and rolled up and back into his head. Still I didn't release my grip. Nor when Smiley's knees buckled and in an instinctual flight reflex vacated his bladder and bowels of the extra weight. Even then, smelling the waste, I didn't remove my hands and followed the movement of his torso to the ground.

Not until his head fell back and muscles ceased to spasm, did I know Smiley would not smile again, and I let go. I stepped away, the thought of what I just did, with the stench of urine and excrement, made me gag. Sick to my stomach, hurting all over, I retched over and over, heaving until I tasted bile coming up. My eyes welled up, I was on all fours trying to regain my composure. I wanted to cry.

Looking around, I realized we were still alone. Dakota next to me, nuzzling and licking my neck and face, wagging his tail anxious for me to be OK again. I stayed there with him, out of breath, shaking and covered with blood, not sure which was mine. After I caught my breath and poise somewhat, I stood up and cleaned my mouth with water and then my hands and face as best I could. A look in the mirror told me the cut over my left eyebrow was open, but not bleeding. I knew it would soon enough though. A huge welt was forming in the middle of my forehead just under the hairline, red at the edges and white in the middle. The whole thing would start to look bad in a hurry.

I needed to get away from there, but first I had to clean up the scene. I opened the Navigator passenger door and jostled with the lifeless proximity of Smiley's mass all over me as I pushed and shoved the dead weight into the seat, unsuccessfully trying for him not to rub off on me in the process. I turned off the SUV's engine, closed the doors, and left the keys in the ignition. Then I wiped it down in as little time as possible, hoping to erase my prints.

Back in the cab of my truck with Dakota next to me, I sat and leaned with my arms on the wheel, head down. I smelled bad, looked worse and felt miserable. I had killed two men. My muscles were still trembling, but it was over.

Turning to inspect the area left behind, I saw a puddle of blood, the stain of urine, vomit and black paint. That was all that remained of the activity that took place. I started the truck, slowly exited the parking garage, and drove away not really understanding how I made it out of there alive.

Dakota sat next to me as only a dog can do, looking at the road ahead as if nothing unusual occurred. After a short while he lay down, stretched his legs and made himself comfortable. Snout on his paws, he looked up and wagged his tail.

"What are you happy about?" I asked and stroked his head. The wagging didn't stop. I thought about it for a while and realized he may very well have saved my life, and we came out of the confrontation unscathed. Shaken, yes, but intact nonetheless and that was something to wag your tail about.

CHAPTER 21

I killed two men and was still in combat-survival mode, hyped by the adrenaline running through me. As much as I wanted to feel victorious, I just couldn't. It was one thing to train for battle and practice lethal techniques. It was entirely another to put it into motion and see the effects in front of you, two eyes staring into mine with a mixture of surprise and anger. To see the expression change to pain and fear, then just fear. Then terror. Then death....

I couldn't get Smiley's face out of my mind as his eyes finally gave in and rolled up, eyelids trembling, muscles slumping. Violence up close of this nature carries a strange intimacy, and even though he wished me harm, I said a prayer in my mind for him, and for his partner. But strange as it sounds, I felt connected to Smiley and I wished him safe passage and asked we both be forgiven.

Meanwhile, I was hurt, dirty and bloody, and I had to get away as far as possible from the scene where I had left the Lincoln Navigator. Before anything else though, I had to tend to my injuries without attracting undue attention. Within ten minutes I found a convenience store not far from a Salvation Army and homeless shelter. A crowd of ragged men were huddled around an open fifty-five gallon drum with a fire blazing. It was late and freezing cold. I parked the truck out of the way and left Dakota in the cabin as a deterrent.

I bought bandages, dressings, super-glue, a bottle of peroxide to disinfect, and a black woolen cap that would keep me warm and hide the huge welt forming on my forehead. Then I stocked up on aspirin and other pain killers, a bottle of No Doze™ to keep me awake, more water, and I returned to the truck.

Beat up, nobody even looked at me twice, not wanting to be part of whatever trouble my injuries represented. Walking towards the truck, a few of the winos tried to get my attention in a conditioned reflex to hustle some booze money, but backed off when they saw me.

Judging from the cold hood, which I felt with a quick touch of my palm, I decided that the car next to my GMC had been parked there for considerable time. I put my stuff away, retrieved the screwdriver and within a minute had the plates removed from my neighbor and placed on my truck. Still hurt and increasingly exhausted, I sat in the cab with Dakota watching my every move while I used all the supplies I'd bought to clean up and bandage my wounds.

Peroxide, or oxygenated water, is basically water with an extra oxygen molecule, the chemical formula being H_2O_2. It is this extra oxygen molecule that acts as the disinfectant and cleaner and in fact oxidizes, or burns the area clean it is exposed to.

After washing my hands, I dabbed a generous amount on the bandage, and with my head held back, soaked it into the cut, being careful not to let it drip into my eye. It hurt like a son of a bitch and the foaming action let me know the stuff was working. I squeezed the cloth, wet it again with the H_2O_2, and repeated the activity. Once I was sure the open wound was clean enough, I dried the cut as best I could and opened the tiny tube of super-glue. This would have to be done delicately, and it had to be done right the first time. I squeezed the little tube until a small glistening drop appeared at the cone-shaped end. While looking into the rearview mirror, I position the exposed drop over my cut and gently applied more pressure to the tube and moved the tapered end with the glue through and into the cut.

If the peroxide hurt, this was killing me, but I repeated the action once more and then physically closed the wound by applying pressure on each side with two fingers. I was careful not to get my fingers stuck to the wound and I didn't. After about thirty seconds of pressure, I let go and was pleased to note the glue held and closed the gaping cut. Then I placed a butterfly bandage over my handiwork to keep everything in position. Next, I turned off the dome light, removed my soiled and blood-soaked shirt, cleaned my upper body as best as I could, changed into clean clothes and when done I actually felt and smelled much better.

I wanted and needed to sleep, but I had to get away from the area. Very possibly the Lincoln would not be noticed until the coming morning, perhaps even later in the day, but it was a risk I could not take. As tides have a way of turning and events have a way of spinning around, the odd chance the two dead men would be discovered early, causing a search for a freshly painted truck in black bed-liner, wasn't worth the risk, however small it may be.

So I drank water, ate Excedrin™ and No Doze™ to stay awake, and left town. To push myself I kept the windows open, letting the cold air blow in to keep me alert. My head hurt, the cut was throbbing and my eyes were falling shut, but I had to make distance.

FEDERAL

After driving north for about an hour, I pulled into a large truck stop where a wall of them were parked spending the night. Unobtrusively, I backed my GMC between two, shut the engine and the lights. Finally, I could rest.

I say another prayer and roll out my new sleeping bag and stretch out on the bench, Dakota adjusting himself to my pose. Sleep comes immediately.

Some of the trucks around us were pulling out, and the large diesels woke Dakota. His stirring woke me, and all I saw were Smiley's eyes looking into me. With effort, I dispelled the vision and realized my mood was dark and angry, not helped by the lack of sleep and numbing headache. Initially, the anger was displaced by the events in the garage, but now it was crystalizing clearly.

The Montreal experience, although not physically affecting me, warned me about the nonchalant violence these men were capable of. Where I had been wanting to slip back into the United States and perhaps quietly find a new life somewhere, I was forced to be on the defensive and made to run.

I had already paid a price higher than I would have thought possible as penance for infiltrating the meeting. I had lost literally everything, including my identity, and had it not been for my son, I would not have survived the ordeal. Having to start over again, in the shadows and on the fringes of society, was hard enough. Add to this the threat of being caught while fearing for my life, and it made it virtually impossible.

Aside from an illegitimate attendance at the Zurich meeting, I had not provoked anybody, nor attempted to publish, blackmail, or otherwise make use of any of the information I had been exposed to. Even so, a crew had been sent after me, well equipped to extract information from unwilling subjects. And they meant me harm. There was no reason to go after me, other than to prevent me from divulging my knowledge. And that being the case, it meant they would not stop until they were successful.

The garage incident had given me an advantage, small as it might be. Even so, I was realistic enough to understand that the tally would not remain in my favor. But while it was, I could potentially make use of it. Somehow I had to come up with a plan that would stop their chase and let me live my life.

Both Dakota and I had to pee. The ground was covered with frost and steam rose like smoke where our urine hit the ground. It was about five o'clock in the morning, very cold and dark. Four hours wasn't much sleep, but it did the job for me, and I was ready enough to move on. I fed Dakota and let him prowl around on the leash for some time, after which he and I were happy to get back into the cabin. My head was killing me and as I inspected my doctoring of the cut, I was pleased it looked good. Though still puffy and swollen, the cut had remained closed and didn't bleed overnight. The bruise on my forehead was starting to discolor, and I would need the wool cap to cover it up, just as much to stay warm. I started the engine and let the cabin heat up as I ate a generous amount of Excedrin™ extra strength and drank some water.

In a past life, before I stopped drinking, I used to carry Excedrin™ with me all the time. The first drink of every day, usually mid-morning, sometimes earlier, would be followed by an excruciating headache in my left frontal lobe, going into my left ear and blood-shotting my left eye. It would hang on for a few hours and then be gone. It never was reason enough to stop drinking, though. I learned that if I ate ten to twelve Excedrin™ prior to the first drink, the headache would only last half an hour or so. Believing the effect of the painkiller would be hastened, I developed the habit to chew the pills and acquired a somewhat perverse enjoyment in the pasty, bitter taste knowing it would be followed soon by the anesthetizing effect of whatever liquor came next. To this day I chew Excedrin™, and each time it reminds me with gratitude that I have chosen not to drink any more.

The streets were empty in the cold, early morning. One of only a few cars on the road, I drove the speed limit, making sure no cop would look at me twice. It wouldn't be long before the Navigator and its lifeless occupants would be spotted, if it hadn't been already.

Heading back south, I wanted to connect with Interstate 94, go west, find a greasy spoon somewhere to eat, and make up my mind where to go next. Perhaps the anonymity of a larger town would make it easier to hide, so I crossed the Missouri River and continued west on I-94.

It was quiet, still dark, and daylight wouldn't arrive for at least another couple of hours. Dakota next to me on the passenger seat, seemingly asleep, but I knew he was awake keeping an eye on me and making sure all was well. All *was* well... for now. But I would have liked to have some contact with my son, hoping the act of telling him about what happened would somehow alleviate my emotional distress. And maybe, if possible, I could even hear Trish's voice. The thought of her quickened my breath. I wanted to hold and kiss her again. Only a few days ago, it seemed a lifetime removed.

The TV at the café where we stopped was tuned to the news. No mention was made of the Lincoln, or its dead occupants. The weather, on the other hand would not get much better they reported, with more snow and potential freezing rain in the coming days.

I found a small hotel that afternoon in Billings, Montana. The rooms were a step up from the usual down-and-out places I had frequented when I stayed close to the street. After the events of the previous night, I longed for a shower and clean clothes, and my body ached for a bed with fresh cool linen. I ordered room service, and Dakota and I spent the rest of the day in the room, tallying my inventory and getting myself back into some semblance of order.

After lunch and a shower, and feeling much better, I laid out all the goods I recovered from the Lincoln. Two wallets and two cell phones, two firearms, both Colt .45 ACPs with extended barrels, one Impuls silencer that fit either handgun using a counter-clock thread, a couple of boxes of ammo, one laptop, and some loose papers. The wallets produced a combined $6,432, which added to my cash, giving me close to ten grand. Clearly, they too preferred paying cash and leaving no trace.

No credit cards or any other credentials were present, except for two driver's licenses, both with identical addresses in Washington, D.C. I was certain the names weren't the ones these guys were given at birth. Stuck in the back of one of the wallets I found a small piece of paper, folded very neatly in quarters. It had an international phone number and a quick scribble in pencil, a single word, "herder."

At first the word made no sense, so I read it again. Then slowly, a cold sense of doom slipped into my stomach and I could feel a knot form as if I had swallowed a stone.

I knew that name.

"It can't be the same." I muttered. It was unthinkable that this scrap of paper actually contained what I thought it did. And if it was what I feared, then my son and I were both in immediate danger.

Before I called Anthony, before anything else, I needed to find out more about the two dead men I left behind. Whom were they in touch with, where did their orders come from, what could I learn from their laptop and who was their handler? Mostly though, I wanted to know about Herder.

The paperwork I took out of the Lincoln Navigator consisted of four pages, three of which were pictures. One was a blow up of my passport photo, taken a few years back. The other a close-up of me at the money-exchange counter in the Montreal train station about three months earlier, and the third when I was at the bank making the deposit for Trish. Just as I feared. The only written page listed my physical description. A final note caught my attention. It read, "Treat with extreme caution—avoid local law enforcement, apprehend for debriefing—do not liquidate, repeat, DO NOT LIQUIDATE. H"

I assumed the "H" signature corresponded with the "herder" I'd found in the wallet. I had to remain clear-headed now. If Herder was the handler of the two thugs, than he might not know they were dead yet, and might not for some time, as I left their bodies without any identification.

Studying the phone number, I saw the country code thirty-three for France and city code four, which I knew was Lyon. The headquarters of Interpol was in Lyon. There are no coincidences. I fought an impulse to call the number, knowing it would be the wrong course of action at this point.

I needed to speak with my son and tell him about my encounter and the information I intercepted. Before doing so, however, I had to have as much certainty as possible about who "H" really was, and how I had been so well tracked. So I opened the laptop I retrieved from the Lincoln and turned it on.

As the computer booted up, I noticed no special user accounts were set up, and the default "Admin" account had no password. It was clear the machine hadn't been used extensively, and aside from the usual array of programs that come preinstalled, no other software seemed to be present. The document file was empty, and when I opened the MS Word program, it was for the first time, and wanted to register itself.

The system-restore feature would tell me what activity had altered the registry and was quick verification to find out if anything was modified or installed that may have been hiding in the background. Only one Windows update and one additional change a few weeks ago appeared. The entry reads "Outlook block cipher modified." which told me that the content of the Outlook mail client more than likely was encrypted. I opened the Outlook file, and a dialogue box opened which simply asked for an ID. As I suspected, it was the encryption software interrupting access to the email file. But to my surprise, I watched six asterisks appear in the pop-up box.

The password populated itself and the email opened.

Apparently, the users of this computer only worried about somebody intercepting the transmission of the emails, and they encrypted the content, but the encryption program itself was left enabled without a password and thus granted me full access.

The Deleted Items folder was empty, but the Inbox and Sent Items were not. Not much history was there to be found, only three communications coming in and one going out were visible. The transmissions were short and to the point without signatures in any of them, just the signed initial 'H'.

The earliest incoming was dated the morning after I arrived in Montreal last November 2009 with an attachment of two pictures of me. I realized the paperwork I took from the Lincoln was a printout of this first communication. The one outgoing message was a short report explaining that they located the hotel where I stayed in Montreal and subsequently lost track of the target, which was me. The third incoming message was received about ten days ago and detailed my appearance at the bank and its location, with the picture. A similar note with this reiterated to bring me in for debriefing only and not removal. Again signed, "H."

Continuing my inventory, I checked the two cell phones and noticed one was locked. I knew the SIM card would self-destruct if I entered a wrong code three times in a row, so I just removed the card, marked it "LinNav1" and stored it with my stash of other SIM cards. The other phone was unprotected, and I found numerous international calls to and from the number in Lyon that was scribbled on the piece of paper. The voicemail contained two messages, either saved on purpose or just not deleted.

The earliest originated from a number characterized as 0000100299800. This not being a standardized telephone number, I knew it meant the message was transmitted electronically through a VOIP line. The caller, a male voice identifying himself as Anton working in the Genève UN IT department, addressed the owner of this cell phone as Mr. Bruce. He explained how to download and install a specific encryption software that was used throughout the system by all participants. He then clarified how the installed default password would not lock the system, but would encrypt messages. If the user wanted to lock the system, a self-generated unique password had to be installed, but this wasn't necessary for the program to function. Evidently, the users of the confiscated laptop did not exercise this last option. Anton ended the call by leaving his direct number at his office and invited a call if any help was needed.

I wasn't surprised to learn the UN IT department was involved. Jean-François was a high ranking UN official, and using his death as an excuse to bring me in would provide a logical impetus behind the search for me.

The second voicemail was more ominous. It was a short call, no more than ten seconds in length at most. The date of the incoming call was the day before, February 10, 2010. In a raspy voice the caller said, "Your target in the GMC was spotted on North Third Street between Broadway and Main in Bismarck, entering a multi-level parking garage. We'll leave him alone as requested. Call if you need assistance."

The two dead men had help finding me. This was very bad news. It meant one thing, the GMC was compromised, no matter what color I painted it. Obviously they had figured out I took Trish's truck, with or without her approval and employed others to be on the lookout for it. The fact it was painted black may just have saved me for the moment, but I had to dispose of it and find some other transport. Now. Immediately.

I dressed suitably against the cold, placed everything in the room's safe, and left with Dakota.

It was around six o'clock in the afternoon when I returned to the hotel. I left the GMC in an empty field east of town, close to the river. The extra gasoline container I had purchased a few days earlier came in handy. I doused the inside and the bed of the truck and lit a cigarette, which I had bought just for this occasion, and I stuck in the match-book, such that it would delay igniting the whole thing. I then walked back with Dakota on the leash. When we were a couple of hundred feet away the first flames caught fire, and when we were much farther, thick, black smoke started to rise.

I did my best not to stand out, just a guy walking his dog in the afternoon. After about half an hour and far enough away from the burning vehicle to be associated with it, I hailed a cab, which took us to First Avenue North, where there were plenty of used-car lots.

After some haggling and without having to provide identification, I bought a nine-year-old white Ford Explorer with plenty of miles on it for just under five grand cash. Everything worked, including the heater, and when I entered the parking lot of my hotel, I replaced the dealer temp plates with the ones I took from the car the previous night.

It was time to get in touch with Anthony. I knew he had always kept a professional distance from Herder, but I wondered how surprised he'd be when I tell him that the two men hunting me were working for his old friend and colleague.

Calling Anthony directly was somewhat of a risk, so I did not call before I had made sure via email he was alone. I wanted to hear his voice when I explained the events of the last few days.

Anthony answered after two rings. He listened quietly as I started at the beginning and told him about the two men's first visit at Trish's diner and how I slipped out of town. How I moved west and decided to change the truck's color and about my final encounter in the parking garage. I'm sure he understood the implication of my words when I told him the two tough guys wouldn't be bothering me any longer and that I recovered their firearms, cell phones and laptop. I didn't mention ditching my truck and buying the Explorer. Not out of distrust, but because it seemed immaterial, and I felt more secure keeping the specifics to myself.

When I told him about the piece of paper with the phone number and Herder's name on it, Anthony interrupted me for the first time with just one word, "Interpol."

And when I explained the email and pictures, he asked, "What was the signature on the incoming email?"

"H."

"What's the sender's email address?"

"guia01010@gmail.com," I replied and went on. "I must have been spotted by surveillance cameras in the bank last week, making that deposit for Trish, just as in Montreal. But at the time in Montreal nobody knew about my stay there, let alone a hotel close to the train station. You were the only one I told."

My tone wasn't accusatory and there was no blame in the sentence. I just wanted to make the point of where a possible leak could have occurred.

"Your cover was blown when the cameras caught you at the exchange counter in Montreal," Anthony replied. Then his voice trailed away as if in thought, "It was my contacts in Interpol who informed me you were spotted and about the two ops coming after you. Their routine is first check hotels and boarding houses close by to see if they can find out more. That is why I sent you the email to move on. Why didn't you move when I told you?"

"I got comfortable and hadn't checked my email for a few days, instead of doing it daily. So I missed your message at first, and only read it when it was nearly too late. You think it is Herder acting as the handler for the two guys who were after me?"

"Guia is Spanish for guide and herder is akin to guide, so the email address makes sense, and I know Herder has worked for Interpol in the past, so that fits as well." Anthony next asked, "Repeat the phone number and don't call it."

My son could read my mind. He knew I was itching to call and confirm who and what was on the other side. I intended to heed his order.

"You know, I never told Herder where you were after Zurich, but he knew you were alive. My contacts in the UN and Interpol have kept me current, and until Montreal there was nothing going on. Nobody had a clue where you were. I know it was even rumored that you actually did die, perhaps not during the Zurich affair, but sometime later. Then from nowhere you were spotted in Montreal, and things moved quickly into action. For the US authorities this wasn't an issue, because FINRA and the SEC closed their files on you. So I know this is UN initiated, but I actually believe it may not be a fully UN authorized activity."

"What do you mean not fully authorized?"

"The whole motivation behind the investigation into the accident, the way it was hush-hush and how the findings were withheld from the authorities, doesn't sit right with me. It all smells of a personal involvement of somebody who doesn't want you to discredit or embarrass them, but at the same time has enough clout to make things happen from within the UN. I can't prove it, but I suspect this may ultimately point to Austin van Buren."

Again I was reminded of Johan's words during my last day in Zurich warning me about Austin van Buren.

"But if my followers' handler and Herder are one and the same, how does that work? That would be a big problem for us."

Anthony was silent for a moment before he spoke again.

"I'm going to assume they're one and the same and will try to find out what's going on. My contacts are mine alone and they do not deal with Herder, I am absolutely positive about that. Somehow we will figure it out. Meanwhile, stay low and don't do anything without contacting me first."

"Son, this is not going to go away, is it?" I phrased the question as a matter of fact.

"You are a liability. You know too much to be left walking around unchecked. Johan warned you about this. So, yes, I agree, it will not go away, unless we make it go away somehow." Anthony responded.

I had a final question before we disconnected.

"Son, I can't get his eyes out my mind. I keep seeing him look at me just before he died, he continues to look at me. How do I get rid of it?"

Anthony had never spoken to me about his tours and missions, but I knew he had seen enough action to understand what I was asking.

"Dad, remember what Ger taught you? Violence without emotion, but with personal intent? Sometimes it is impossible not to feel the aftermath. That's why you were taught to sit. Go inside, use the technique, stop your thoughts, become still, and let surface what may. The answer will come."

"He taught you too?" I shouldn't have been surprised, since I knew Anthony was trained for many, many years in the art I was exposed to for just one year with Ger.

"Not by Ger, but somebody just like him. It's the only antidote against the type of work we sometimes have to do." And then a moment later, he said, "I love you, Dad."

"I love you too, Son."

We spoke a bit more and after I assured him I was OK, he told me to be safe and wait for him to contact me with news.

CHAPTER 22

I was drained and my head hurt something awful. The lack of sleep dulled my thinking, and my brow had started throbbing again. A trickle of colorless liquid was slowly seeping from the cut and had loosened the butterfly Band-Aid I had applied the night before. After cleaning and redressing the cut, I picked up my phone, changed SIM cards, and called Butch's number.

It took two attempts to connect with Trish. I was overcome with emotion and relief listening to her. I told her I was OK, not troubling her with the details of the previous days, and assured her that she wouldn't have to worry about those two guys in overcoats ever again.

I suggested she report her truck as stolen and thus disassociate herself from me, just in case. We engaged in some small talk, both experiencing the underlying emotion and excitement of knowing our interest was mutual. I kept it short even though I wanted to feel close to her, remembering her lips on mine, the way she smelled. I said that I would call again in two days.

"I miss you around the place," Trish said.

"I miss you too," I returned and ended the call.

Following my son's advice and true to what I was taught, I put a pillow on the floor, free from walls and bed and sat down. I crossed my legs, straightened my back, folded my hands and closed my eyes. Checking my breath helped fight my weariness, and I could feel my body and mind anticipate the meditation. Narrowing the focal point until no thought was present, I stayed still and expected nothing.

I was gone, and then I was back. From next to me on the floor Dakota found a spot on the bed and was asleep. It seemed not a moment passed from checking my breath to where I returned from the trance, but judging from the clock on the TV, forty-three minutes had passed. I didn't remember time moving, or thoughts flowing. Just an endless void, a nourishing emptiness and the pervasion of peace.

I took off my clothes, slipped between the cool sheets, and fell asleep immediately.

FEDERAL

It woke me with a jolt. A thought came to me in a dead sleep that made so much sense in its simplicity that I was surprised it had not occurred to me earlier. Still night and the clock read 1:45 a.m., I climbed out of bed, with Dakota surveying the sudden activity. I peed, brushed my teeth and went looking for my duffel bag.

Buried deep in a corner, tucked away in an inside zippered compartment, was Jean-François' thumbdrive next to his disk. I had stopped trying to retrieve their contents, not getting past the encryption lock. But what if it worked on the laptop I retrieved from the Lincoln Navigator? As I learned from the cell phone message, they installed encryption software issued by an IT guy from the United Nations. Jean-François was associated with the United Nations, so it made sense I'd be able to get into the device using their laptop and encryption.

The computer booted, I inserted the CD into the drive compartment and navigated using explorer to the D drive. Clicking in it had no effect, other than being prompted for the usual password. The box did not populate itself and I was disappointed realizing the installed software had no effect on the CD. Next I slipped the thumb drive into a USB port. I double clicked on the email icon and the password box popped up, populated itself and I was in Outlook. But in the left margin where the folders were located I find no new information.

Then in the bottom of the left margin I open the "More Options" folder and a single new item showed up under the existing Personal Files option. "JF" was the header with subfolders for Inbox, Sent Items and Deleted Items. I held my breath realizing the initials corresponded to Jean-François and I placed the curser on the Inbox.

I was wide awake now and felt the rush of anticipation. The Inbox under the JF Outlook folder was full with received communications. The Sent Items was less populated, but still several pages of messages, while the Deleted Items was empty.

The email messages conveyed discussions between Jean-François and Austin van Buren, with the latest entry dated May 15, 2008. A few of the discussions involved further communications between Austin and the Haqqani brothers, including one from the old man Jalaluddin himself, supplying absolute proof of a direct link between van Buren and the Haqqani Network. The communications exposed requests for the financing of arms purchases, to which Austin agreed and then forwarded the dialogue to Jean-François with instructions to set up the invisible infrastructure necessary for the flow of funds.

Another email caught my attention after I reread the text. The initial communication was not directed to Jean-François, but he and Austin van Buren were copied in. The email was between an IMF official and the CEO of the British division of a large United States arms manufacturer. The subject dealt with currency exchange rates on the North African continent, which I thought was odd, as I could not understand what a munitions and weapons factory had to do with the topic. The IMF person intimated that certain currencies in the region bordering the South Mediterranean would experience drastic changes in the near future. "A certainty" were the words he used, as currency expert Austin van Buren orchestrated it himself. The time horizon was set at three to five years, within which to expect the irregularities.

As I was reading this, I realized the text was written in 2007, making the projected timeline between 2010 and 2012.

The irregularities were to instigate popular uprisings against "repressive" regimes. According to the email, the seeds to create this civil unrest were already being sown by the Secret Teams of the United States and United Kingdom in Tunisia and Egypt. The manufacturer was put on notice to substantially increase its production of air-to-land and sea-to-land missiles and develop specific incendiary and explosive devices that could be delivered through the use of unmanned drones. A zero-interest rate credit facility to the manufacturer was already put in place by the IMF and Federal Reserve to aid in the immediate startup of the program.

That was when I understood why the arms-factory owner was part of the discussion. In the subsequent messages the conversations were primarily between Jean-François and the IMF, discussing strategies on how to target specific goals they had in mind.

The first goal of the uprisings was to disrupt and then destroy certain nation's currency operations. Specifically, those countries that worked outside of the United States dollar reserve currency system. The uprisings would create a public groundswell and spill over to other neighboring countries. Ultimately, the movement was targeted to reach Libya, which was the final goal of the exercise.

If at first I wondered why Libya was targeted, it became clear when Jean-François elaborated about the need to overtake its central bank. The emails stated that Libya's Central Bank worked autonomously and was nationally owned. This meant that when anybody wished to do business in the nation, for example buy crude oil, it could only do so by first exchanging funds into local currency, the Libyan Dinar. To subsequently transfer money out of the country, the funds transaction had to be reversed from Libyan Dinar back to the currency of choice. Thus, Libya had no need for a reserve currency to conduct its business with international markets. The net effect of this was that the country was financially outside the reach and influence of the Federal Reserve and its associated financial systems.

When Jean-François made note of the fact that Libya had the richest oil and gas resources in North Africa (NW Europe being its largest customer with 32% destined for Italy and at least 10% to France) and that the vaults of the Libyan central bank stored a daunting 145 metric tons of gold, I understood the evil extent of the operation. Mention was made as well of substantial Libyan assets and reserves deposited and invested on foreign soils, approaching many hundreds of billions of dollars which would be ripe for confiscation when appropriate.

This was a country worth targeting, rich in assets and gold, a large oil producer with vast reserves, politically and militarily vulnerable. Obviously, the time had come to place it under the auspices and control of the Federal Reserve and IMF systems. This would not only create an inroad into the African continent, it would protect the United States dollar as the currency that oil is traded in.

Jean-François made an interesting observation when he wrote that is was "imperative for Libya to discontinue selling its oil and other exports in either Euros or Gold Dinars." Iraq's greatest sin was not their Weapons of Mass Destruction, which they used against their own population, the Kurds in the northern part of the country and it is immaterial whether any were ever found, after they had over three years to get rid of them before Hans Blix went in to look for them. No, their real sin was to sell crude oil in Euros starting in November 2000. The United States invaded the nation in 2003 and Iraq is selling its oil in dollars again.

This was why Libya was of interest. It was of vital importance to enforce the United States dollar as the reserve currency and thus the oil currency. Doing so protected the Parent behind the Federal Reserve, behind the UN, the IMF, and even NATO, which were all those present at the Zurich meeting, against a dollar value erosion. This would hurt Big Oil and the military/industrial complex, and decrease financial control. Maintaining the US Dollar as the world's reserve currency means that any nation who wants to trade dollar denominated commodities (crude oil, gasoline, diesel, gold, platinum, silver, corn, wheat, soybeans, cattle and on and on) has to borrow dollars to do so. It secures the strength of the dollar and positions the banks in firm control and thus the Parent.

The final communications dealt with differing media strategies of how to paint Colonel Gadhafi as a villain and murderer who killed and maimed his own people. This would motivate United Nations resolutions, and with NATO support, an attack on Libya could be orchestrated. Of course, the freezing and confiscation of Libyan assets would pay for the reconstruction of the country in the aftermath of the attacks.

Next would be control of the oil industry, the central bank and its gold contents, followed by a "humanitarian" effort to rebuild the infrastructure of a freshly destroyed country. Then install a puppet government, make the local coin dependent on the United States dollar as reserve currency, and establish a new central bank under the patronages of the IMF (and Federal Reserve) and export oil in United States dollars only.

Here I was privy to the inner workings of how and why new international targets were located and cultivated in order to gain public support under false pretenses. What's more, Austin, Jean-François, and all those working with them would get away with it. They conspired social meltdowns and currency manipulations with the intent to overthrow established governments, then using the Responsibility to Protect (R2P) Doctrine they mobilized NATO, attacked a nation, supported rebels (whomever they were), and divert and steal the resources. The world would watch and nobody would even question it, believing Colonel Gadhafi deserved what he had coming. Not a word was mentioned about casualties, property destruction, or even the legality of it all. These guys were so incredibly confident their machine would shape public opinion their way, that success was a foregone conclusion.

"Absolutely fucking scary," I heard myself mumble.

Many of the other emails dealt with loan provisions for differing groups and entities the world over. The diversity of factions that benefited from the Federal Reserve's willingness to part with funds belonging to the people of the United States was astonishing.

The discussions I read dealt with how much, at what interest rate, through which banks, foundations, or charitable groups the funds were to be disbursed and how to disguise the origin (being the Federal Reserve) of the outlay. There were financial arrangements for the Kurdistan Workers' Party (Parti Karkerani Kurdistan, PKK); Hamas; Hezbollah; Tamil Eelam in Sri Lanka; the Haqqani Network; the Lashkar I Jhangvi group responsible for the Daniel Pearl kidnapping and beheading in Pakistan, and the Al-Qanoon network of which it is a part; the Pakistani Intelligence group ISI; the Egyptian Al-Gama's al-Islamiya with longstanding Taliban contacts; the

Egyptian Islamic Jihadist group Al-Jihad who assassinated president Anwar Sadat in 1981; the Al-Aqsa Martyrs Brigade through the Fatah-Tanzim military wing of the Fatah, which was fighting against any peace effort with Israel; Mujahedeen Al-Khalq who fight the Iranian Islamic Regime; the Partisan group Asbat al-Ansar in South Lebanon; the Sudan government and through them the Janjaweed; the GIA Armed Islamic Group in Algeria; the Columbian FARC; personal financing provisions for Venezuela's Hugo Chavez; the Kashmir group Harakat ul-Mujahedeen; and the list goes on and on.

In one email dated February 2008, Austin addressed both Yuri and Jean-François, instructing them to use the funds wired from the Mitha Investment Company in Pakistan to Belarus Central Bank for organizing Mohammed Haqqani's visit to Zurich in May the same year. Special note was made to use prearranged vehicles, which stood ready with drivers at key locations along the long trip from Waziristan to the West.

All the financing was intended and specifically structured to keep conflicts alive, instead of aiming for peace. Notwithstanding their individual differences, what most of these groups had in common was their hatred of Israel and desire to see the country and its Jewish population destroyed. Israel, being one of the largest benefactors of United States weapons and military financing, clearly symbolized the prevailing principle of arming both sides of the conflict. The common denominator in all dealings was that the funding facilities were all tied to weapons transactions. I recall Johan's remark that there exists a near perverse relationship between the military/industrial complex and the Federal Reserve.

Where they supported governments, they secretively supported their opposition as well, perpetuating a state of turmoil and crisis. You never want a serious crisis to go to waste, and when you control the crisis, you control the solution. The discussions actually weighed how much opponents received in order not to supply one side with a decisive advantage. Keeping opposing forces alive, kept the conflict and the need for more financing alive. And this is what runs economies, banking, and weapons, and airplanes, and ammunitions, and transportation, and on and on.

I'd been reading for two hours when I finally took a break. It was four o'clock in the morning, so I decided to check out and move on early. Even though I didn't appear to be in immediate danger, I was weary about the help the two thugs received and not sure if it was local law enforcement or similar free-lancers. Either way, I felt more secure physically removing myself from Trish's truck, which I had been recognized in a few days earlier.

The truck would be, or already had been reported stolen, and I didn't want to be anywhere close when the burned out shell was recovered.

After feeding Dakota I packed up and left.

Passing the large double-pane hotel entrance and we were outside. It had started to snow. No wind, just a steady continuous fall of thick, dry flakes. It transformed the scene into a silent and tranquil panorama. The entrance and streetlights glowed in the dark, their aura mottled by the heavy snow falling in absolute silence through the illuminated patches. My gaze was transfixed for a few moments in its quiet beauty. It struck me how different the world can look from what goes on in our lives, contrasting my previous days with the stillness in my sight. "One day," I murmured to myself, suggesting that one day I will have peace, one day.

It was cold, but unaffected by it, Dakota pranced around in the white powder, and each time a flake drifted close by he set about trying to catch it while producing audible snapping noises. I let him run around a bit, but when the cold set in, I opened the car door and he immediately jumped in. Once in, I let the engine run for a good five minutes. The roads should be fine according to a news flash and we left the parking lot, carefully making our way to I-90 to travel farther west.

Driving has always been a great way to sort out thoughts and gain some clarity. 'Wind shield therapy' a friend of mine once called it and the term described exactly that.

So while traveling through the snow laden landscape with my little friend Dakota next to me on the front seat, trusting I would watch over him and be his higher power, I knew my problem would not go away. Others would follow, better equipped, more prepared, and more determined. And ultimately I would cease to be successful in holding them off. I knew that for a fact. "Unless we make it go away somehow" rang through my head. Anthony's last remark on the topic. But how to make it go away evaded me at the moment. The only leverage I have was my knowledge and what may lay hidden in the USB and CD drives in my possession.

Forty-five minutes into the drive, I pulled into a large all night truck stop. Aside from the featured food items they advertise free Wi-Fi. The place was big and catered to truck drivers, with shower facilities and anything a traveler on the road might need. The weather and time of day made the brightly lit place seem even larger with the absence of customers. There were only a few of us, and I found a booth in a corner with relative privacy.

FEDERAL

With Dakota at my feet, I opened the laptop with the encryption loaded. I pulled out the cell phone scavenged from the Lincoln Navigator and found the phone number that the UN IT guy named Anton left for Mr. Bruce. It was about six o'clock in the morning for me, so given the time zones, it was around two o'clock in the afternoon for Anton in Genève, Switzerland.

After three rings, a male voice said in perfect French that I was connected to the United Nations IT department. I was making the call with what I believed to be Bruce's phone, and since Anton left the message in English, I said, "Is this Anton?"

"Un moment, si-y-il vous plait," followed by, "Anton here, can I help you?"

"This is Bruce. Remember you left me your phone number in case I needed help?" I made a mental note to keep track of what name I was using, there was Stephen, Jonas on my passport, Jack to Trish and now Bruce. So, being Bruce, I acted I knew nothing of computers and explained how I installed the encryption, assigned a password, and then forgot it and couldn't get back into the system again.

"Happens all the time," he assured me laughingly. He informed me he would gladly help remedy the situation and walked me through the process finding a hidden file in the system which contains the serial number of the software. Using this he assigned a new password and said this is a one-time fix which only works on my computer, based on the serial I just gave him. With this I could unlock the cipher and assign a new permanent password.

"Try it out while you're on the phone with me," he said.

I put the disk in the drive and the now familiar password box popped up. I entered the one Anton gave me. The screen blanks for a second and then filled in with a new box with three lines.

"It's asking for my old password. Is that the one you just gave me?" I asked Anton.

"Yes, enter it and under it type your new key, twice to be sure. Don't forget it this time" he added smiling.

I knew I wouldn't forget the first three letters of my real first and last name combined as the new key. Entering it twice, the screen disappeared and I was looking at a directory listing of the D drive, which was the CD.

I was in. Unbelievably and easier than I could ever have imagined, I was looking at the contents of something that my son had given to me close to a year and a half ago, and that used to belong to Jean-François.

"Did it work?"

"Yes. Thanks a lot."

"OK, one more thing. Exit the system, boot down to flush the cache and then boot up again. I want to be sure all is working as it should."

But before I followed his advice, I highlighted the four directories with my mouse, right clicked and copied it all to the desktop. Just in case.

After we closed down and rebooted with no problems, I thanked Anton again, and asked if I could call him in the event I needed more help. Who knew what might turn up, and to have a guy on the inside unknowingly working for me could be invaluable. Anton agreed to my staying in touch if needed and with that we bid each other farewell.

I then turned my attention to the new information available to me.

The four directories on the CD were named PDF, Excel, Word and Pics without any other files present in the root directory.

The Pics directory was filled with photos of Jean-François with different people at various functions. In a few I recognized Yuri, Margaretha, Nigel and others I met in Zurich, but for the most part it was filled with people who were strangers to me, although some of the faces were familiar.

In one, I saw Austin van Buren in the company of what must have been a motley crew of Mujahedeen fighters somewhere in a mountainous location. In another he was flanked by heavily armed turbaned men posing in front of a container full of wooden boxes in some harbor on the docks. The pictures had no names, but were numbered with the .jpg extension, with no apparent sequential reason.

Not taking time to study it further, I looked into the other folders and found each filled with files, except for the Excel directory which only contained a few. Too much to look at for now, but I recognized names of public figures, politicians, companies, and foundations, not just American, but European and Middle Eastern. File after file with detailed data, seemingly without end. Whatever Jean-François was involved in, he liked having tabs on those he dealt with and he was thorough as far as I could tell.

This was incredible. I realized I may have struck a vein of information the size of which required more time to mine before it could be of use to me. First, I had to move on and find a safe place to stay the night. I didn't want to remain in the same location where I made the call. For all I knew, Bruce's cell phone was loaded with tracking software.

CHAPTER 23

After about a seven-hour drive with various stops along Interstate 90, we arrived in Missoula, Montana. I decided to stay here, find out what exactly was on the CD, and put into play an idea I dreamed up during the drive. It would be tricky, and it would involve me contacting those whom have been after me. But as long as I stayed in control and had a backup plan, perhaps I could pull it off. I want to live a life with some relative degree of freedom.

Missoula being the county seat and a college town, catered to a diverse public. Gone are the days of the mid-nineteenth century when the first settlement was named Hellgate Trading Post, referencing the fierce continual conflicts between settlers and natives. In contrast, the small downtown area was hospitable with plenty of restaurants and bars and places to find lodging and I found a small motel where both Dakota and I were welcome.

Settled in the room, I sent an email to Anthony to say I was able to access the thumb drive and CD. Refraining from specifics, I told him my findings were valuable and could provide us with leverage and hopefully offer a solution to my situation. I assumed he was working to verify what the situation with Herder was and would let me know when he found out more.

Meanwhile, I kept reading. The CD contained two distinct types of records. One was a full documentation of the meeting topics held during the Zurich conference that I participated in. It contained all discussions and topics, with more in-depth material on sources and references to events, speakers, participants (myself included), earlier meetings, and future expectations.

The other records were file after file dealing with personal data of some very well-known personalities, politicians, philanthropists, CEOs, and so on. There were background checks, personal bank accounts, ownerships in various enterprises, and connections to other companies and foundations. The lists specified stock holdings, debts outstanding, personal guarantees, ownership of buildings and properties through blind trusts, and other ways of attempting to disguise holdings and possessions.

Tired from the drive and reading, I laid down and dozed off to sleep.

My cell phone rang and I recognized Anthony's number.

"Hi Dad, how are you doing?" His voice was concerned and I could hear the worry come through the line.

I sat up too quickly, making the cut in my brow throb and my head hurt, but it felt dry to the touch.

"I'll be fine Son, thank you," I said, feeling comfort in his care.

"What did you find out?" He came right to the point reacting to my earlier email. "You said it was important."

I told him how I was able to get into the CD and give him a general idea of the data.

"Very impressive intel. I like how you cracked the CD. That was pretty cool." I could hear the smile in his voice, and the compliment made me feel good. "We have copies of this in the bank vault, but having backups of the unencrypted data wouldn't be a bad idea."

I knew he was right, and I planned to copy the CD on my own computer and make a few backup copies for later use.

"Sorry to wake you," he said. "But after getting your email I wanted to give you an update on what I found out here, even though it's not much as yet."

I was all ears.

"I have to be careful with this," he explained. "I can't just go out and start asking questions. There are a few guys I thought would be able to find out what is going on in the background, but I decided not to involve them. Even though I trust them, I trusted Herder as well and now it seems there may be a crack in that veneer."

"Understood, go on."

"What I did learn is that Herder has worked for Interpol in the past. They sent him out on several covert ops, sometimes alone and a few times with others. His close association with me makes him ideal for keeping track of you. So I'm assuming he and the handler of your pursuers are one and the same, and I was a fool for not having suspected it. I can't believe I missed this."

I could feel Anthony's anger and disappointment with himself.

"At least we know now and have the upper hand for the moment," I said. "You did tell me Herder doesn't know about either the CD or USB drive, correct?" I wanted to be sure nothing had changed since he first told me this over a year ago, when I was leaving Ravensburg for Frankfurt.

"That's right, he doesn't know about them." Anthony reaffirmed. "But when he learns what happened to his two guys, he may guess, or at least assume his cover is blown. We have to be careful. People act unpredictably when they get caught."

"Others will be coming after me," I observed.

"Not only that, I think it is fair to expect they will have a more aggressive approach," he confirmed my prognosis.

"Then perhaps we should think of a different plan" and I laid out the idea I contemplated while driving to Missoula. We talked back and forth for a few minutes mulling over the pros and cons.

"It's very risky," he ultimately said. "You'll have to reveal yourself, and that means you lose your advantage. You don't know what you will be up against and what their plans are. But considering the options, it may be worth it."

I could hear Anthony think, then he concurred, "You contact Herder, set the bait, and arrange a meet. Do not even discuss me. He has to think you are doing this on your own." And we disconnect.

Thinking about the phone call, I realized there was something my son mentioned that triggered a thought. He said that Herder had previously worked for Interpol on various assignments and I had noticed some of the files on the CD referencing Interpol. I went back to the computer, opened the CD drive again and performed a search for Interpol related events.

What I discovered was more than I could ever have expected. I found concrete information I could use. I uncovered an event that allowed me to gain leverage over Herder and Austin van Buren individually and combined. It linked the both of them to an international political incident.

I uncovered what really occurred on February 14, 2005, in Beirut, Lebanon, when the former Lebanese Prime Minister Rafic al-Hariri and twenty-one others were publicly assassinated by a nanotech explosive device. And I learned that the event had everything to do with Austin van Buren and with Herder and the Parent they represent. But just to be sure, I read the information over and over to be absolutely clear about the facts.

I felt excited once done. What I gained from the CD was the ammunition with which I could use against those after me and convince them to leave me alone. All I had to do was decide whom to deliver the news to, and package it so that the impact would be felt hard and give me the bargaining power I was looking for.

Then I went downstairs, got some breakfast and much-needed coffee and took Dakota out into the snow. The morning was spent locating a few CD-RWs, backing-up the drive on my own computer and the new additional CDs. I then isolated a few choice discussions between Austin and Jean-François and stored them in a file which I forward by email to guia01010@gmail.com. I wrote one small message in the email, "Bassel Fleihan, Beirut, February 14, 2005."

That done, I was making progress. I changed SIM cards and called Anthony back. I explained what I had uncovered and my intent to contact Herder and press for a confrontation where he would receive the data and in turn promise to leave me alone as long as I would not publish any of it. Anthony made the point that Herder would insist on seeing me, forcing me to come out of hiding and that he'd not be alone. I said, "The fact is, I can't hope to evade these guys continuously. At some point they will succeed. So, even though I may not want to meet Herder in person, I believe I have no other option if he insists."

"I agree, " Anthony said, "Just make him feel it's his plan and that you're going along with him."

With that we hung up.

The cut over my eye was healing, though still throbbing at times, and the discoloration of the bruise on my forehead was starting to travel south. I looked as if I just came out of a car wreck and was better suited to stay in my room, which is what I did. TV on, Dakota taken care of, protected from the cold outside, I felt a sense of safety for the first time in a long, long time. Not so much because danger had dissipated, since it hadn't, but because I had a plan and could see a potential end to my run.

Tomorrow I would call Herder. I wanted to give him a chance to fully appreciate what was in my email.

"Numero de contrôle, si-'l-vous plait?" "Control number, please," was all the female French voice offered when I called the number scribbled on the piece of paper with Herder's name next to it.

"Herder," I responded. No answer was given other than the line going mute without being disconnected. A very long ten seconds later, I heard it ring twice and then was picked up.

"Oui." Just that one word "Yes," and I knew who was on the other side. Even though it was phrased in French, I recognized Herder's voice as if it had been only yesterday.

The silence between us was palpable. The absence of my reaction was answered in similar fashion. I couldn't shake the feeling he knew who was on the line, and finally I again let out his name, "Herder."

"Ahhh, Stephen. So long since we have spoken and so pleased to hear from you." His reaction was immediate, confirming my suspicion he somehow suspected the origin of the call. Followed by a casual, "How have you been?" Not a trace of concern or surprise in the voice, just as I knew him, in full control of any situation he found himself in.

"Say, how did you get this number?" he asked ignoring my silence.

"Who gives a fuck?" is all I said, cutting short the small talk.

A slight hesitation and a pause and then with a voice full of concern, he said, "That was a difficult situation there in Bismarck in that parking garage. I did make it very clear no harm was to come to you. Actually, I believe they were instructed to leave you be once located. As it is, it kinda backfired on them."

"I don't care what you told them, they attacked me." Herder's attempt to smooth over the event, and make himself look better, irritated me. "But they won't be doing me or anyone else any harm now."

Letting my words speak for themselves and not expecting an answer, I came to the point, "Why are you after me?"

"Stephen, once it was understood what transpired in the Zurich car wreck and that you were not amongst them, somebody was going to be sent after you. Who better than me? This way you'd be safe. I told Anthony of any actions taken and gave you time and opportunity to get away before harm was done. Anybody else, and no news would get to Anthony and thus none to you either. That's why I am the obvious choice. It's all for your safety." Herder's tone was convincing and the message was one of understanding, trying to sooth me into believing him.

But I had guessed that would be one of his arguments.

"It was you who tipped them off that I was not in that car," I said. The thought just occurred to me during Herder's last words, and it made sense as it would make him a logical choice heading the initiative to bring me back in. Not allowing for a rebuttal I said, "Why didn't Anthony know about your arrangements, and what was the attack in the garage all about? Your concern about my safety suffers from a lack of credibility." I could feel my temper rising and made an internal check not to let it take over.

"Anthony has no need to know about my assignments, just like I don't know about his." The answer was curt with an edge of irritation shining through. I decide to cut to the chase and make my point.

"I have a proposal. There is something I believe you will be interested in and I'm willing to trade for it."

"What may that be?" Herder inquired dryly.

"I emailed you some communications between Austin van Buren and Jean-François. There is a lot more where that came from and much more specific. You leave me alone, and I will leave the information alone. Simple as that."

"What do I care about their correspondence?" he snapped back.

"There is more. Did you see the note I included?" I knew this was going to be the point where I could gain the upper hand, and I waited for his answer.

"I saw it. What about it?" Herder sounded nonchalant, as if he did not care.

"I know what happened there," is all I parry.

Annoyed with the line of questioning he responded, "Why don't you tell me all about it." But still no sign of worry or concern about the topic.

"You executed a contract hit on Bassel Fleihan on February 14, 2005, in Beirut. It was disguised to resemble a hit on Rafic al-Hariri, thereby deflecting attention away from you and your employers and shifting blame to Hezbollah or Syria, or perhaps even Israel."

Apparently still not impressed with the topic, he asked, "Why would anybody want to kill Fleihan?"

No denial in that statement. If he had been absolutely innocent he would have categorically denied the allegation. Instead he was fishing to find out what I knew.

"Fleihan resisted installing the US dollar as the reserve currency and allowing Western banking consortiums to set the political tone in Lebanon. He wanted peace with Israel, knowing that was the only road to reconstruction. There is no profit in peace with Israel. But there is in the long-term continuation of the Israeli/Arab conflict."

I knew I had Herder's interest, but all he responded was, "Really..."

"Yes, really," I confirm. "What's more, I have Interpol internal investigative reports and communications explaining the trouble Fleihan caused and what to do about it. A request was made to make use of the Secret Teams and your name came up as a solution. The money flow and chain of command was to go through Austin van Buren to disguise the true origin of the order. It becomes even more interesting reading your reply and proposal to stage a diversion and make it seem the attack targeted Rafic al-

Hariri and shift the blame to Syria, Hezbollah, or Israel. It didn't really matter who, according to you."

It was quiet on the line, which meant I had hit my mark. His voice came back, much lower with the veil of a threat behind it.

"What do you want?"

"I want you to tell Austin that I have details of two wire transfers for $143,500 each from Karachi, through Mitha Investments to an account in Belgium, specifically stating for further credit your attention. The first dated mid-January 2005 and the second on February 16, two days after the attack. Just the circumstances of these payments, your designation to take care of the Fleihan problem, your response and proposal how to stage it, and the actual attack, should be enough to create serious troubles for all of you. Fleihan wanted peace with Israel, and Austin hates Israel. But more importantly, peace is not profitable for your employers, for the Parent."[11]

"Now what?" Herder asks.

"Now nothing. I keep the details private, and you leave me alone."

"There was a CD, wasn't there? I was told so, but it was never recovered." Phrased as a statement, as a matter of fact, revealing that he suspected there had been more data in the suitcase.

---

[11] the CD contains documentation compiled by Interpol on Bassel Fleihan. He worked for the IMF in the early 90's. There he uncovered money trails of funds destined for the reconstruction of Lebanon, instead went to Hamas, Hezbollah and Syria for weapons transactions. He then left the IMF and became active in Lebanese politics, believing that was the best way to apply his knowledge and stop the theft and corruption. He became the Lebanese minister of Economy and Commerce and a confidant of prime minister Rafic al-Hariri. He attracted his first real enemies when he started pointing fingers at the IMF as to whom was responsible for the embezzlement and corruption. His interest was in a new and stable Lebanon and he realized conflicts with Israel were counterproductive. He then rebuffed attempts at installing the US dollar as the reserve currency and fought against IMF mandated government bail-outs and interventions. Peace with Israel and a monetary policy outside of the control of IMF and United Nations and thus the Federal Reserve was not in the long-term interest of the banking community, so it was decided he was expendable. To disguise the attack as a public execution of then ex-Prime Minister Rafic al-Hariri was fiendishly smart. Still many years later, people are guessing who may have killed Rafic Baha El Deen al-Hariri, while nobody realizes or even suspects what really occurred.

I didn't answer him. Let the silence speak for me again. What I wanted to hear was his agreement, nothing else.

"There is no deal unless we meet personally," he finally said. "And I get the data."

The words were spoken carefully and slowly. He wanted me to expose myself, to come out of hiding. He wanted me vulnerable so he could control the outcome.

"There was no CD," I replied. "Only a thumbdrive." I wanted to keep the bulk of that data to myself and only give him a token with the least information. It would be easy to transfer the relevant material from the CD onto the drive. It felt safer this way. I kept a trump card, known only to my son and me, just in case I might need it in the future.

Then I gave him my condition. "I will not meet you personally. There is no need. I will get the information to you. Just tell me where."

Herder's voice came back devoid of any emotion, spoken deliberately as if to add importance. "This is not negotiable. If you don't want to meet, I will find you, it's just a matter of time. And when I do, all bets are off. This is my demand. We exchange the data personally. *You* just tell me where." He emphasized "you," making sure the ball is back in my court.

I let him wait before responding, and the silence was near physical. Anthony and I had anticipated his argument and so, seemingly reluctant I agreed and told him my decision. "It will be at a location of my choosing. You come alone, or there will be no agreement and the drive will be publicized. That is final."

"How do I know you will keep your word?" Herder asked and I knew he had agreed.

"So far, it is your credibility that is in question, not mine. I have everything to gain in keeping my word, and I'm sure your employers agree they'll benefit by keeping their part of the deal."

This time it was Herder who waited until I heard, "I will have to bring them the thumbdrive."

"I'll give it to you, but obviously it is not the only copy." I replied.

"Fine. Where and when do we meet?"

"Next week Wednesday, the seventeenth. Check into the Edgewater Hotel in Seattle. I'll call you there at 6 p.m. local time," and we disconnect.

In as few words as possible I constructed a stega message to Anthony, informing him of the discussion with Herder, and told him I'd be in Seattle a few days early, scouting the area for a good meeting spot.

FEDERAL

Even though I placed the call to Herder through the internet, using VOIP, and connected via a proxy server to disguise my location, I knew with all the possible digital tracking tools at his disposal, he would very likely figure out my whereabouts. So I decided to leave that evening and packed my clothes and computers. One of the handguns I stored in my duffel, the other, complete with silencer, in my overcoat front pocket, which was large enough to mask its outline.

At about five o'clock that evening, Dakota and I left the hotel and were back on the road. We should be in Seattle sometime early Sunday morning.

Herder knew too much and had been at this game much longer than I. Whatever clever schemes ran through my head in trying to create an encounter where I could maintain the upper hand, I couldn't help but worry that he had already planned for it and had the ultimate advantage. I knew he would not be alone, and that meant I had to prepare for an altercation. But first I had to arrange for my information to be released in the event our encounter went sideways.

Assuming Anthony's identity and using the agreed upon passwords when we transferred control over my trusts and companies, I emailed the two attorneys in Luxemburg. I told each to forward the packages they would receive to various news outlets in the event they did not hear from me (Anthony) via email or telephone by Thursday, February 18, 2010, at 6 pm (GMT). I then mailed them both copies of all the data transferred to the new CD's without encryption, a third and fourth package were kept for Anthony and myself.

Next I called Anthony and informed him of my conversation with Herder. He agreed with my assessment that no matter what was promised, Herder would not come alone. "Son, I have a feeling this thing will get ugly, and I'm afraid I won't be able to hack it on my own. I need you to be there with me"

"First, I agree with you. We have to assume Herder to be aggressive. The fact he insists on seeing you, and considering the two goons he sent after you, tells me he is very serious, and that is not good news. Second, of course I'll be there." His answer is stated as a matter of fact.

I felt a wave of relief, "Thank you Son, this makes me feel much, much better." I knew I would at least stand a chance against the formidable foe Herder represented.

Then I laid out how I saw the situation. "This is how I perceive Herder's attitude. He has two options, either bring me in, or silence me. Anything else means that whoever employs him will be subject to whatever I may do and that is a liability they will not accept. So I think they may risk the data to be published, but they'll just deal with it. It may hurt, but at least they will know the extent of the damage and handle it."

Anthony agreed, "I know how they think. They cut their losses and do not want loose ends dictating their future. That's why Herder is dangerous and we should be ready to deal with him likewise."

"So what do you suggest?" I asked.

"I am suggesting we should be ready for anything. And with that I mean we should be armed and willing to use weapons."

The reality of what I had set in motion overwhelmed me. It was nothing less than a confrontation with only one of two outcomes. Either Herder or I would be eliminated. I could not have Herder chase and ultimately catch up with me, nor could he or his employers afford to keep me walking around. I broke into a cold sweat.

CHAPTER 24

It's a beautiful morning driving into Seattle. Steel-blue sky, no clouds. Mount Rainier clearly visible in the south and in the west the snowy peaks of the Olympic Mountains anchor the view over the Puget Sound and Bainbridge Island. It's windy, and there's a chill in the air, but nothing compared to the cold we just came from. This climate is a temperate sea climate, with mild winters and mild summers, similar to Northwestern Europe where I grew up, just more beautiful.

I found a Travelodge close to the Space Needle. Cheap, efficient, and the perfect spot where no one looks twice at you. I intend to use this as my home base for the next couple of days while I scout the area. On the advice of Anthony, I have to get comfortable with the layout of downtown in case I need to know how to disappear quickly and with ease.

It's Sunday and I spend most of the afternoon driving around, figuring out how to get off and on the interstates and the quickest way to and from home base, until I find my way easily.

Seattle has an eclectic mix of residents. From the extremely affluent to street people at the waterfront, either pan handling or playing an instrument, trying to separate pedestrians from their loose change. The two common complaints about the constant rain and the highest suicide rate are flatly wrong. On an annual basis both Louisiana and Florida have more rainfall than Seattle and according to the CDC National Center for Health Statistics, Washington state doesn't even make the top ten on the list of highest suicide rates per state.

The following day, Monday, I receive an email from Anthony through our usual encrypted method informing me he's on his way and will arrive sometime tomorrow afternoon.

I call Trish, through Butch. Talking to her feels different now that there's a chance that my running may be over. I don't disclose details, but tell her I may see her soon and promise to call her later in the week.

"I'll be glad to see you," she says.

By the time we hang up, I feel content and excitement at the prospect of being with her soon. Whatever is to pass, I made up my mind that I would see her again, no matter what.

Wednesday, February 17. I'm looking forward to seeing Anthony again for the first time since leaving Frankfurt, over three months ago. He arrived the day before through Vancouver airport, rented a car, and made his way south to Seattle, but he didn't contact me until later in the day. Hours were spent driving around randomly, parking, walking, then driving again to be sure no tail was on him that could lead to me. He found a room in the Seattle Pacific Hotel, only a few blocks from where I am staying, and finally, late in the afternoon, he texted me, and we met up at the original Starbucks on Pike Place.

We agree on the Westlake Mall as the location to meet Herder. It's a public place with plenty of people around, which will give us some cover. Then Anthony confides in me about some additional safety measures he had put in place.

"Remember my two Swiss associates from Zurich?"

"The one that got shot and his partner," I offer.

"Correct. They are here as well and even though they may not be visible, they will be around, just in case the situation escalates. But in the background only. In case we can't control what's going on. I have instructed them to keep a visual on us, but only interfere if and when Herder gets the upper hand and forcefully tries to either harm you or bring you in. And that will only happen over my dead body. So let's just hope they will not be needed, but it's good to have them here."

I am starting to get the feeling that perhaps the odds could be stacked in our favor.

"Something else, Dad." Anthony gets my attention. "We have to discuss what to do if any of us gets hurt, or worse. If either of us is killed, the other has to leave, that is imperative. In that case, there is nothing else to do and it will protect the survivor and the information we have. If you get hurt, I and my Swiss partners will get you out of here. On the other hand, if I get hurt, you have to promise that no matter what occurs, you leave. You'll have to keep your cover and maintain your anonymity. If somehow you're taken you into custody by local law enforcement you will become a target without being able to get away, and knowing Herder, or whomever he works for, they will take advantage of it. Police custody means nothing to them, they can and will get to you no matter where you are. So promise me you'll get the hell out if it's needed."

He isn't pleading, nor asking, just making absolute sense. And then, against my protests he makes me promise I will do as he asks. But he isn't finished.

"One final thing you should know. Once I understood Herder's role, I took it upon myself to contact Johan."

"Why?" I ask. I had not expected this and was intrigued about my son's motivation.

"He'd been your friend for a long time and took the risk of tipping you off in Zurich about the trouble coming your way. Even though he was involved with Jean-François and may even be part of the Parent, he demonstrated a loyalty to you. But it is his knowledge of the inner circle of the UN, those they refer to as the Parent, I am interested in."

"I think you may be correct as far as the Parent is concerned." I say to my son. "I suspected as much after his appearance at the Zurich meeting and how confident he was of how to deal with Jean-François."

"When I called him, I just wanted to feel him out and understand the level of his involvement. Without mentioning anything about you, he brought up the subject himself. He just asked, 'How is your father?' And when I responded that he knew what had happened in the car crash he was quiet for a moment. Then he said 'Yes, I do know what happened in the crash, and your father was not in it.' That's when I knew he is very much involved with the Parent. Very, very few people are aware of the true events that day."

"Go on." I prompt him, very much intrigued by the development.

"Since he knows your status, I assumed he knows who is after you and that he himself may be one of them. No matter what he did for you back in Zurich, we have to consider that his interest may not be yours."

That option had crossed my mind, much as I did not like the idea. "OK, let's assume he's one of them. What good will contacting him do us?"

"I wanted him to know, or at best relay the idea that we have credible information that will hurt if it were to be released. So far we have only dealt with Herder, and we aren't even certain if he involved those who employ him. He may just be acting on his own trying to get rid of a problem. This way we are sure all are informed and aware of what's at stake."

"I like it. That makes sense." I say. "What did you tell him and how did he react?"

As Anthony relays the conversation—informing Johan about the actual events of the Beirut assassination—and says how Johan just listened and with few words agreed to have the message reach those it was intended for, I keep wondering about him. I could not imagine him to be an adversary of mine, even though his last words to me were, "After all these years I am quite certain you don't truly realize who I am." In that same conversation he had made it abundantly clear we were in different camps, and that intruders were dealt with in no uncertain terms. For him to agree to forward Anthony's message, without even trying to feign ignorance, told me he was deeply involved and knew very well what was going on, and most likely he was aware of the fact they were after me. So after all the years of friendship I had to reconsider and ask whom he really was.

The Westlake Mall on Fourth and Pine is a lively place. There are shops, restaurants, vendors with carts, areas in which to sit and drink coffee, and many hundreds of people milling around. From the third level a monorail connects the center with the Space Needle, so the place buzzes not just with shoppers, but sightseers, which makes it a good location to meet. The plan was simple, Anthony would be close but only make an appearance if needed. The Swiss associates would be around, but not available for immediate interference. They were there as a backup, to stop Herder attempting to extricate me forcibly.

That morning we all meet for breakfast in my room. We go over the plan with the Swiss operators and confirm where they will be in relation to Anthony and myself. Far enough not to be associated with either of us, and close enough to step in if needed. If all works to plan, we will reassemble again at my room later in the evening.

When we are clear about all the details they leave, and my son and I spend the rest of the morning together. In a mutual need to reconnect we talk about the past, when we were living in Florida, about school and friends and memories we shared. Just as a calm before the storm, the sense of being close dissipates the nervous anticipation I feel about the upcoming confrontation.

Before noon we pack our gear and load everything in our cars. We park downtown near the designated meeting place, Dakota staying in the Explorer with the windows cracked for fresh air. If everything works out, both of us should be able to get away and disappear on short notice.

In the front pocket of my weatherproof hoodie I carry a .45 with the suppressor attached, a fully loaded clip with one in the chamber, and an extra clip as backup. The pocket acts as a marsupial's pouch, the whole front of the garment, accessible from both left and right with Velcro closures and large enough to hide the weapon with its extension. Anthony took the other .45 without suppressor.

FEDERAL

To remain unseen I wore the full hood to sidestep surveillance cameras that are present everywhere. No fear of standing out as the weather justifies its use.

After parking my Explorer and Anthony's rented car, we walk the few blocks to the Westlake Mall where we arrive midafternoon. In the mall, we scout for secure spots, observation areas, getaway routes, layout of the stairs, and get a general feeling of the area. We agree on positions from where to observe Herder's arrival and how to keep him in our sights when we tell him to move. Anthony finds a spot where he can see me and the entrance below, while still keeping an eye on the Monorail's gates. The place is packed with tourists and locals buzzing with activity.

At six o'clock I phoned Herder at the Edgewater Hotel and told him where to meet me.

"I'll be there," was all he said in reply.

At precisely six thirty, I see Herder arriving at the main entrance to the Mall. It is early evening and dark out. People are shopping, visiting for an after work drink, children running around while others are drifting in to escape the evening chill.

I text Anthony that our target has arrived and watch Herder carefully. I want to see if he talks or calls anybody, where his eyes are looking, and what his body language says. But he does nothing. He stands with his back to the entrance, hands clasped behind his back, feet apart shoulder wide, eyes hidden from view by a Stetson. He is facing straight ahead, he does not move and seemingly is not aware of the people passing around him.

"Call him," is the text message I receive from Anthony.

The phone rings only once and a single word comes through the line.

"Herder."

"Take the escalators and go to the second floor. Wait there at the top."

I hang up and make my way to the side of the building, where I descend to the second floor using the stairs. As I enter, I can see the top of the escalator and Herder isn't there yet. Five seconds later he is.

Standing off to the side so as not to block any traffic, Herder assumes the same pose as he did when entering the mall. I make my way around and approach him from his left. I didn't see anyone with him, but then again they're pros and know how to blend in and remain invisible. Nor have I seen Anthony, but I know he's close by and can see me.

If I surprise Herder, it is not apparent. When I'm a few feet away I say in a normal tone, "Just move ahead of me, past the ice cream kiosk at your left and make your way to the wall behind it."

I want to be away from the open escalator so we can't be seen or targeted by anybody from the floors above or below. He walks ahead of me, hands still clasped behind him and stops five feet from the wall. Behind him, I follow, the .45 in my left hand in my pouch.

"Do you have the thumb drive?" is all Herder asks as he turns to me. I see his eyes, and am confronted with their palling chill. I remember those eyes from Zurich, when they conveyed such supreme confidence. Now there is disdain and arrogance and they're not on my side any longer. He would kill me without a moment's hesitation.

"I do," I answer.

He unclasps his hands for the first time and brings them to his front.

"You will do as I say and leave with me," and he displays a small-frame automatic with a silencer attached in the palm of his right hand. It must have been there all this time, with the extended suppressor hidden up his coat sleeve. He'd been palming the gun with both hands behind his back.

I'd anticipated something similar happening, but being confronted with the reality was entirely different. I backed up instinctively and prepared to answer as I felt a sharp nudge in the bottom of my back.

"Not so fast." A low voice behind me. "Do as he says. You will get hurt if you don't."

Perspiration and a lack of deodorant. Body odor reeks from the man behind me. It's too cold to be sweating, this guy is nervous. A nervous man with a gun. Not a good combination.

I've made a mistake. When walking to the side of the building with Herder leading the way, I had allowed him to turn to me where he could observe what was behind me, while all I could see was the wall behind him. So I never saw his partner make his way through the stalls and crowds until he was right behind me. I now have two firearms pointed at me and the advantage I thought was mine is gone.

Addressing the man at my back, Herder says, "I have him. Keep your eyes open. I'm sure he's not alone."

After the words are spoken I hear Anthony's voice, unseen but sounding as if he's right next to us.

"Dad, step away to your left," followed by, "Herder, you're in my sights. Let him go."

"You're interfering with an Interpol-sanctioned extraction," Herder replies immediately. "Continue and you will do so at your own risk. I was promised the drive. Where is it?"

"And I was promised you'd be alone, so no drive," I say and move left as instructed by my son.

Anthony appears from between racks of overcoats. Pointing his gun from the hip at Herder, he approaches him from the rear, intending to defuse the situation and allow me time to get away.

What happens next is over in seconds, as without warning an arm forcibly comes around my neck, pulling me back in a chokehold and three muted puffs come from my attacker. I see Anthony stagger back and drop to his knees. His coat shows where he is hit, three clean holes evenly spaced from his sternum down to the middle of his abdomen in a perfect line, and in an emotional dissociative moment my mind flashes, 'Just like buttonholes...'

Then my training takes over and in one fluid motion I grab the hand on my throat, anchor it on my body and turn 180 degrees. Rotating with me, the pinned-down wrist locks, turns with me and I feel it break. My opponent's face in view, I see his eyes widen in pain and surprise at my unexpected move. His smell is overpowering.

My other hand, still in my pouch, has a firm grip on the .45 and with my thumb I pull back the hammer. Fully facing him, I fire four shots in rapid succession from my pocket into his body. Any sound from my gun is muffled by the suppressor and the cloth of my jacket. My target never made a noise as the rounds entered him.

Another shot rings out. This one clearly not suppressed, and so loud it shatters my eardrums. The explosion reverberates and resonates off the walls and ceiling and back into me. Shoppers look in our direction, wide-eyed with terror and alarm, screaming, ducking and running in all directions.

I let go of my attacker as he drops lifeless to the ground.

I check if I'm hurt but feel nothing and realize it's not me. Herder stands frozen, eyes bulging and fixed into the distance, mouth open but no sound and his automatic drops to the ground. The Stetson he wore is gone. He falls forward, face first bouncing on the cement and I see the back of his head is missing. Bone and brain tissue are splattered as a red spray everywhere, the open gaping hole not bleeding, crushed strawberry-like filling speckled with white slowly dribbling out.

Then I see Anthony on the floor, the .45 with which he shot Herder and saved my life slowly slipping from his hand. The three buttonholes converging into one large, dark spot and growing.

"Dad? Dad... Dad..." I hear his voice when he was four and hurt his hand. I hear him calling me from camp when he was twelve and missing me, I hear him departing home for the Navy. And I hear my son saying good bye, leaving me.

CHAPTER 25

I am next to him on the floor, cradling his head on my thighs, taking his hands. He looks up and I know he sees me. His beautiful face grey, lips thin and stiff, the skin around his nose drawn and pale. He is dying and we both know it.

"Dad," he manages. "G.....ot shot...., I'...m sorry..... I ... I screwed up."

His voice weak and hoarse, I see the effort to form words. "Son, don't speak. I'm here." Helplessly I don't know what to do but be close and hold on to him, as if I can prevent him from slipping away. My tears fall on his face.

His eyes fixed on mine, wide open, glistening pupils large and dilated, his face an ashen-grey, he calls me closer. Whatever he tries to say does not come out. The only sound is the rasp of his breath, a rosy-colored froth forming on his lips. All I see are my son's eyes, whose shine is fading, his hand in mine slacking its hold and falling to his chest.

At that moment I am firmly grabbed by my shoulders and gently but resolutely moved aside. And in a flash I recognize the Swiss colleague who was wounded in Zurich. His partner, same as from then, kneels opposite him, and with one swift move of his blade he slices open Anthony's coat, sweater and shirt, exposing the bullet wounds.

"Missed the aorta and esophagus," he diagnoses on the spot. "Heart is clear, lung punctured." He places cotton compressions on the profusely bleeding openings to stem the blood flow, and produces a syringe. "Ephedrine to keep blood pressure up," he explains as he administers the injection.

"It's bad." He looks straight at me.

As if waking from a dream, my surroundings come into view. Pandemonium around us, children screaming, people running, cries for 911, onlookers pushing in, and others in shock from the blood and gore but unable to look away. My eyes on Anthony, I keep hold of his hand while both guys are working on him.

"How you doing, Son?" I ask.

No answer, just his eyes on me.

In a final effort, his eyes focus and beckon, "Dad...., you ..promised... leave. My friends here......, you... go..... please..., please."

I can't do this. Even though we discussed it, I never imagined it would become reality. As Sophie's Choice, this is an impossible one. "I won't leave you. You're all I have, all that's left. I can't leave..." An ostensible vice grip tightens my throat, and everything inside me screams to stay with my son. Anthony too weak to answer, just stares at me, begging me to do as we agreed.

It is one of the Swiss who speaks. "Stephen, we are here and we will do all we can. Leave it to us. Staying will not change the outcome, but it will compromise you, and you know it."

I do and hate knowing it and realize I have to leave before I can't do so any longer.

Gently, ever so gently, I place Anthony's head on the floor, kiss his lips, his eyes, his forehead and his lips again and I think, 'Farewell, farewell my Son, farewell ....'

"I love you, Son," is all I can mutter. "I love you." I kiss his face, look in his eyes, see his good-bye and let go of him.

I stand up and as if in a dream, walk. The most difficult and hardest steps of my life, leaving all I have behind. Hood pulled far over my face, I merge into the panicked crowd. Mall security trying to gain control, sirens outside announcing massive police and ambulance arrivals, the chaos is total while I slip away down the stairs, out into the dark evening. Nobody stopping me, nobody even looks at me. As if invisible I walk the few blocks to my car, through the commotion, unseen and untouched. Away with the thumb-drive still in my pocket, away from my son.

In the Explorer my little friend Dakota licks my hand and smells my son's blood on me. He lays down on the seat quietly, as if he knows what occurred. At Anthony's rented vehicle parked three spots from mine, I slow down for a final look, then move on.

Driving away from him, leaving my son and finding the road out of town, into the dark, going east. My world has turned all black.

CHAPTER 26

Overlooking Central Park from behind his desk on the 33rd floor of one of the buildings he owns, Austin van Buren answers the phone himself, he already knows who it is, and expects the call.

The nerve center of his financial empire, the New York office is cautious and averse to publicity. Investments and strategies are only fit for public consumption after they have been put in place, and even then, the full extent of the positions will only be hinted at for the rest of the financial world to guess. Austin plays his cards very close to the vest, and does not tolerate uninvited intrusions into his secret and complex world.

"You screwed up," were the first words spoken on the line.

Clenching his teeth, jaw muscles visibly standing out, a slight tremble appears.

"Excuse me?" Austin demands.

Not in the habit of being spoken to in this manner, Austin conveys a spurt of anger and surprise at the unexpected affront.

"You screwed up." Impervious to Austin's tone, the words are repeated, just louder. "Not only that, because you thought you knew better and ignored our instructions, you placed all of us in an untenable position."

"What are you talking about?" The words are uttered in anger. Very few people raise their voice to him, and most who do live to regret it.

"I remember telling you that after my discussion with Anthony, the better approach would be to exchange the data and take care of the Stephen issue at a later date, when everything has calmed down. Instead, you went ahead, and now four of our best assets, including Herder, are dead."

"None of us can afford having a loose cannon out in the open." Austin argued. "Who knows what this Stephen is capable of? We are not even sure what intel he's holding. So elimination was an appropriate solution, and Herder assured all of us he was more than capable of taking care of that. I trusted his expertise, as we all have so many times. This time it backfired. The real question is, why did it? Tell me, Johan, why?" Turning the argument around and reversing blame is always a good tactic.

A moment's pause, followed by, "We don't know where or how Stephen acquired his skills, but he clearly is not who he used to be. For him to kill the first two operators and then somehow eliminate the next two, including Herder, means he has become one himself. We never even considered that option. Obviously we have to change tactics."

"What about his son? Where is he?" Austin asks.

"In a naval hospital under heavy security. It will be some time before he recovers. Either way, he is not our guy. He will never lead us to his father, and as for him, Stephen has gone back underground, and we have no idea where he is."

"Then why this call? How did I screw up, according to you?" he hissed.

"Stephen just called me. He emailed the details on the Beirut Hariri-/-Fleihan affair. The same Herder told us about. The truth is I was not prepared for how detailed and minute his data is. He has Interpol intercepts directly implicating you and Herder, and indirectly, the whole financial system behind us, including the Federal Reserve, IMF, and United Nations. He said he will publish it all."

"*Baszd meg*." Reverting back to his native Hungarian, Austin swears. "How did you find out about this before I did?" The question is as much a compliment as it is an inquiry.

"Because of our past relationship, and because I warned him in Zurich of the shit storm about to be unleashed on him. But I ask him too, why not publish it and get it over with? Why warn us?" Johan explained.

Austin, feeling the pressure mounting, tries not to sound too hurried and impatient, but the urgency with which he articulated the next words betray his fears. "What'd he say?"

Confident about being one up, Johan delays his response. It isn't often he gets the better of Austin van Buren, and he relishes the moment.

"Stephen indicated he holds all of Jean-François' dossier, including financial details on your Karachi Mitha Investment Company, disclosing origin and recipients of funds, going back decades. He has pictures of all of us with people we should not be associated with, and according to him, much more that will make the Hariri-/-Fleihan assassination look like a walk in the park. It will incriminate not just us, but our network of contacts, the financial institutions we represent and expose the origins of the Secret Teams we use."

This is not just bad news. This touches the core of the business, potentially endangering all. Austin knows very well what the reaction would be. Ostracized from banks, funding, politics, and politicians, he would have to fight it alone. But exposing the Team's origins could prove to be lethal. They work in the dark, in absolute secrecy and exercise zero tolerance to those threatening it. In the end there would not be enough money to battle the world. This could become either a financial or personal death blow.

"So why has he not done what he wants to do?"

"Because of my past with him, he gave us a warning. It's up to us to heed it." Then in a lower tone Johan states, "And you owe me. If it were not for me, all this would be public." His voice had become cold and detached, accentuating the veiled ultimatum he just relayed.

Astute enough to understand the underpinnings, Austin comes to the point. "What is it you want?"

"All decisions concerning Stephen and Anthony, all without exception, are mine. Nothing will be done, undertaken, discussed, or even thought about without my understanding and approval." Johan demands.

"No problem, the *faszfej* is yours. I want the data he sent you, that's all, just so I know the extent of it," he says, confident he got off easy.

But there was more. "I will forward the email, and you should remember, it is not just Stephen who has the knowledge, I now have it as well. One last thing, I will assume Jean-François' position. The meetings, invites, programs, coordination of assets, transfer of funds, and allocation of resources will go through me, just as they did with Jean-François."

Both men remain quiet for a long time.

"Very well." Austin finally agrees. "That's settled then. What about Stephen. What are his demands?"

"Stephen made it clear he holds some powerful cards, which he is willing to leave alone as long as he and his son are untouched. He left it at that, no need to confirm anything." Then after a second, Johan adds, "I do know him well and if he says he will not publish it, then he won't. I don't believe we have to fear any unpleasant surprises from him in that respect."

"Understood," is Austin's reply. "It will give us time to regroup and figure out what's next." And he ends the call.

Austin looks around his domain, the incredible view, the huge office dominated by his desk, a large array of monitors silently bringing in the world in numbers, five very large flat screen TVs, each muted and tuned to different news stations, art on the walls acting as trophies of success. All the result of deals past and present. A good trader knows when to give and when to take. 'Today I gave some,' he thinks. 'There will always be others when the roles are reversed, and then I'll take whatever I want.' He gets up, tells his secretary to have the car brought up front and leaves his office.

At the building's entrance, the doorman holds the door open and wishes Mr. van Buren a good evening. One bodyguard, shielding him from paparazzi and the like, escorts him to the waiting Maybach 62S and readies the vehicle for Austin to enter.

Out of nowhere a figure emerges from the pedestrians and places himself between Austin and the car's entrance. The bodyguard, trained for these events, steps in, shielding his boss from an expected attack. But the only attack is aimed at the guard, who is immediately and totally incapacitated by a devastating jab of an open hand to his throat. Gasping for air, he staggers back exposing Austin to the stranger in front of him.

If there is fear in Austin, it is not apparent. Had this person wanted to harm him, he would have done so already. Whomever he is, he is very good, and in an exciting kind of way it impresses Austin. The two men see eye to eye, and for a second they recognize strength, determination and power in each other. The stranger, though, is not in any way impressed with the other. He lifts his hand and with his right index finger lightly touches Austin's neck on the jugular vein and speaks.

"Perhaps you remember we met in Zurich. My name is Stephen and this shows I can touch you anywhere, anytime, whenever I choose."

Taken back by the unexpected physical intrusion, intimate and lethal in equal measures, Austin sneers and searches for an appropriate answer.

Not giving him any time, Stephen says, "You placed four men in front of me and they all died. Look at your bodyguard and know you will never be safe."

For an instant Austin moves to see his guard on one knee reeling to regain his breath and turns back again. By then, Stephen is gone. Invisible, as if the event had not taken place.

CHAPTER 27

Friday, February 26, 2010.

Traveling north on North Dakota Highway 29 in my white Ford Explorer, I slow down and exit onto Highway 11. Waiting for a few cars to pass, I turn left, follow the sway of the road and with a sense of anticipation I enter the small town of Hankinson. It is close to sundown, the workday not over, yet the streets are quiet. The intense cold of the previous weeks brought snow, making walking difficult and driving uneasy through the narrow paths cleared by the ploughs.

My world has changed since I left from here only two and a half weeks earlier, a lifetime ago. I have woken from the illusion that I will be granted a quiet life and realize a war is waged against me, perhaps at an awkward armistice, but ready to erupt anytime without notice. Even so, this small town was the one place I experienced a moment of peace and I wished for more of the same.

The diner looks unchanged flanked by an empty parking lot. In the dusk, the lights inside emit an inviting atmosphere, even though the "Closed" sign is on. I park my car, get out followed by Dakota and walk up to the entrance. A lone figure is cleaning tables, preparing for an early and well-attended breakfast. I knock on the door. Trish looks around and her eyes light up. I know for now I am safe.